Study Guide

to accompany

Krugman/Obstfeld
INTERNATIONAL ECONOMICS:
THEORY AND POLICY
Third Edition

Study Guide

to accompany

Krugman/Obstfeld
INTERNATIONAL ECONOMICS:
THEORY AND POLICY
Third Edition

Linda S. Goldberg
New York University

Michael W. Klein
Tufts University, The Fletcher School of Law and Diplomacy

HarperCollinsCollegePublishers

Study Guide to accompany Krugman/Obstfeld, INTERNATIONAL ECONOMICS: THEORY AND
POLICY, Third Edition

Copyright © 1994 HarperCollins College Publishers

ISBN: 0-673-52307-1

95 96 97 9 8 7 6 5 4 3

Contents

How to Use the *Study Guide* For *International Economics: Theory and Policy*

This *Study Guide* is designed to enhance your understanding of important ideas in international economics. As a supplement to the text, it provides you with an opportunity for independent and self-directed review of the key concepts of each chapter. Each chapter of the text is represented by a corresponding chapter in the *Study Guide*. The individual chapter entries include an overview of the key themes of the chapter, a section on defining important terms, a set of multi-part review questions, and answers to the odd-numbered problems from the textbook. Answers to all *Study Guide* Review Questions are provided at the back of the *Study Guide*.

The Key Themes section of each *Study Guide* chapter reviews the important points stressed in the text. These points are placed in the context of the materials from other chapters of the text. To underscore the practical significance of some of the theory presented in the text, the theory is related to real world scenarios.

The next section of each *Study Guide* chapter asks you to define key terms. This exercise serves as a check on your comprehension of the chapter. You may want to reread those parts of the chapter which contains those terms that you find hard to define.

The Review Questions section of each *Study Guide* chapter requires you to work through a series of problems designed to enhance your ability to work with important mathematical tools. Real world data and examples often are provided. In addition to working with these tools, you are asked to interpret your results. After you complete these exercises on your own, you can check that you have grasped the material by going over the solutions to the questions presented in the back of the *Study Guide*.

CHAPTER 1

Introduction

CHAPTER ORGANIZATION

What is International Economics About?
    The Gains from Trade
    The Pattern of Trade
    Protectionism
    The Balance of Payments
    Exchange-Rate Determination
    International Policy Coordination
    The International Capital Market
International Economics: Trade and Money

KEY THEMES

The intent of this chapter is to provide both an overview of the subject matter of international economics and to provide a guide to the organization of the text. The study of the theory of international economics generates an understanding of many key events that shape our domestic and international environment. These include the causes and consequences of: the large current account deficits of the United States; the dramatic appreciation of the dollar during the first half of the 1980s followed by its rapid depreciation in the second half of the 1980s; the Latin American debt crisis of the 1980s; and the increased pressures for industry protection against foreign competition broadly voiced in the late 1980s and early 1990s. The text presents material which will enable you to understand the economic context in which these events occur.

Chapter 1 of the text presents data demonstrating the interdependence of the U.S. and the rest of the world. This interdependence arises in the context of: 1) international trade in merchandise and goods, including manufactured products such as clothing, textiles, and chemicals, or raw materials, such as diamonds and copper; and 2) trade in financial assets, such as securities, stocks, bonds, and even ownership of plants and equipment in other countries.

This chapter also highlights and briefly discusses seven themes which arise throughout the book. These themes include the gains from trade, the pattern of trade, protectionism, the balance of payments, exchange rate determination, international policy coordination and the international capital market.

So many of the issues hotly debated in the press, on the streets, and in Washington boardrooms come under the rubric of one of these themes. Indeed, next time you pick up a newspaper, think about the number of articles that are concerned with our trade and economic interactions with other countries. The scope of international economics is enormous. Below, a brief overview is provided of the themes presented in the first section of the text. Other section overviews are provided within the *Study Guide*. While you will probably not understand all of the terms and concepts which are introduced briefly in these sections, they will give you a good idea of the emphasis of the text and the scope of the knowledge which you will have when you complete this course in international economics.

OVERVIEW OF SECTION I: INTERNATIONAL TRADE THEORY

The first part of the text, Section I, is comprised of six chapters:

Chapter 2   Labor Productivity and Comparative Advantage: The Ricardian Model
Chapter 3   Specific Factors and Income Distribution
Chapter 4   Resources and Trade: The Heckscher-Ohlin Model
Chapter 5   The Standard Trade Model
Chapter 6   Economies of Scale, Imperfect Competition, and International Trade
Chapter 7   International Factor Movements
Chapter 8   Regional Economic Issues

Section I Overview: Section I of the text introduces you to the theory of international trade. The intent of this section is to explore the motives for and implications of patterns of trade between countries. The presentation in the text proceeds by introducing different models of international trade. Each one of these models of trade is a more general model than the one in the chapter before it and each model is used to illustrate a different concept. Usually, the models evolve by either increasing the number of factors used in production, by increasing the mobility of factors of production across sectors of the economy, or by introducing more general technologies applied to production. Throughout Section I of the textbook, policy concerns and current issues are used to help you comprehend the relevance of the theory of international trade for understanding the world around you.

Chapter 2 introduces you to international trade theory through a framework known as the Ricardian model of trade. This model helps you to understand the issue of why two countries would want to trade with each other. This model shows how trade arises when there are two countries, each with one factor of production which can be applied toward producing each of two goods. Key concepts are introduced, such as the production possibilities frontier, comparative advantage versus absolute advantage, gains from trade, relative prices and relative wages across countries.

Chapter 3 builds upon the insights from Chapter 2 by introducing a slightly more complicated model of trade between countries. In this framework, countries can produce a group of goods using a production technology that requires more than the single factor of production that was the basis of the Ricardian model. One important reason for this addition to the model is that this more general framework highlights the effects of trade on income distribution.

The first model presented in Chapter 3 includes factors of production which are specific to the production of each of two goods. Then, a more general model is introduced, with this latter model allowing for factors of production which are specific to the good being produced and other factors which can be reallocated across production sectors within an economy. This extension provides an even richer analysis of the income distribution effects of trade. These models set the stage for an initial discussion of the political economy of trade and for justifying economist's support of the principles of free trade among nations.

Chapter 4 introduces what is known as the classic Heckscher-Ohlin model of international trade. Using this framework, you can work through the effects of trade on wages, prices and output. Many important and intuitive results are derived in this chapter including: the Rybczynski Theorem, the Stolper-Samuelson Theorem, and the Factor Price Equalization Theorem. Implications of the Heckscher-Ohlin model for the pattern of trade among countries are discussed, as are the failures of empirical evidence to confirm the predictions of the theory.

Chapter 5 presents a general model of international trade which subsumes the models of the previous chapters as special cases. This "standard trade model" uses relative demand and relative supply curves of countries to analyze a variety of policy issues, such as the effects of economic growth, the transfer problem, and the effects of trade tariffs and production subsidies.

While an extremely useful tool, the standard model of trade fails to account for some important aspects of international trade. Specifically, while the factor proportions / Heckscher-Ohlin theories explain some of the motives for trade flows between countries, it's bottom line idea is that the differences between countries provide some incentive for countries to gain from increased specialization. However, alot of trade occurs between countries that are quite similar. To explain this latter type of trade, models are introduced that place much more emphasis on economies of scale in production and imperfect competition among firms than they do on different initial endowments of factors of production such as labor and capital.

Chapter 6 presents models of international trade that reflect these developments. The chapter begins by reviewing the concept of monopolistic competition among firms, and then proceeds by showing the gains from trade which arise when such imperfectly competitive markets exist across countries. Next, economies of scale in production and comparative advantage are discussed. The chapter continues with a discussion of the importance of intra-industry trade, dumping, and external economies of production. As mentioned, the subject matter of this chapter is important, since it shows how gains from trade arise in ways that are not suggested by the standard more traditional models of international trade.

Chapter 7 focuses on international factor mobility. This emphasis departs from that of the previous chapters in which it was assumed that the factors of production available for production within a country could not exit a country's borders. Reasons for and the effects of this kind of international factor mobility are discussed in the context of a one-factor (labor) production and trade model. After the discussion of the effects of internationally mobile labor, similar arguments are applied to the international mobility of capital. International mobility of capital takes the form of international borrowing and lending. This leads you into a discussion of decisions to produce in the future rather than the present. There are strong implications of such inter-temporal decisions for observed international lending and foreign direct investment behavior.

Chapter 8 concentrates on regional patterns of specialization and development and associated issues. This material is important, since patterns of economic specialization may not be closely linked to the boundaries of countries. The considerations that arise include the specialization of regions, the clustering of industries in a few areas, and the problems of uneven development. The analysis highlights the role of economies of scale, which tend to make industries concentrate in a region, and transport costs, which increase the incentives for industries to set up production near their markets and thus reduce the tendency of an industry to concentrate in only one region. The chapter also emphasizes that regional specialization, once begun, may be self-reinforcing, a phenomenon called cumulative causation, so that the effects of initial small advantages are magnified to the point where there is a high degree of specialization. This, in turn, raises the possibility of uneven development where there are large discrepancies across regions.

CHAPTER 2

Labor Productivity and Comparative Advantage: The Ricardian Model

CHAPTER ORGANIZATION

KEY THEMES

This chapter in the text begins to address the question of why countries trade with each other. Answering this question requires an understanding of the differences among countries and the implications of these differences on the potential for benefits to all countries that trade. As you work your way through the Section I of the text, Chapters 2 through 7, you will learn about the motives for trade when countries differ in a number of specific ways. If you can master the fundamental concepts introduced in this chapter, you will be off to a good start in learning international trade theory.

The first way in which countries can differ from each other is in the productivity of workers in producing different goods. This is a key point emphasized by the Ricardian model of trade. The Ricardian model provides an introduction to international trade theory. The basic model involves two countries, two goods, and one factor of production, labor. Differences in relative labor productivity across countries give rise to international trade. This Ricardian model, simple as it is, generates important insights concerning comparative advantage and the gains from trade. These insights are necessary foundations for the more complicated models that you will learn in later chapters.

One important principle to understand is that of *comparative advantage*. The Ricardian model demonstrates that the comparative advantage, or relative strength, of one country over another in producing a particular product depends on international differences in the productivity of labor. In the Ricardian model, only one input into production is used, workers, and the differences in output per worker in different industries in different countries will determine the pattern of trade.

The *production possibility frontier* (PPF) depicts the limits on what a country can produce, given available inputs into production. It also shows the tradeoffs in production that arise: when an economy has full employment and an additional unit of one of the goods is produced, there must be a reduction in the production of some other good. The shape of the PPF shows the opportunity cost of increasing production of a good.

The unit labor requirements for producing different goods are important for determining the relative prices of goods in countries before they begin to trade with each other, and for determining the comparative advantage of a country in production. This information can also be used in determining the benefits from opening up an economy to trade.

Following the notation presented in the textbook, suppose a_{lw} and a_{lc} are the unit labor requirements in wine production and cheese production in the home country, and the economy is endowed with L workers. Suppose that the corresponding unit labor requirements and labor force for the foreign country are $a_{lw}*$, $a_{lc}*$, and $L*$.

This means that the home country's production possibility frontier is defined by the line a_{lc} C $+ a_{lw}$ W = L ,so that the maximum amount of cheese that can be produced domestically is: $C=L/a_{lc}$ (this happens when no wine is produced at home); and the maximum amount of wine produced at home is: L/a_{lw}. An analogous description can be provided for the foreign economy. The production possibility frontier is linear because of the assumption of constant returns to scale for labor, the sole factor of production. The opportunity cost of one good in terms of the other equals the price ratio since prices equal costs, costs equal unit labor requirements times wages, and wages are equal in each industry.

If the country is not involved in international trade, the production and consumption mix of a country will occur at the point of tangency of an indifference curve and the production possibilities frontier. As shown in Figures 2-1 and 2-2, since the PPF is a straight line in our example, the pre-trade price of cheese in terms of wine will always be the slope of the PPF. $P_c/P_w = a_{lc}/a_{lw}$ $P_c*/P_w* = a_{lc}*/a_{lw}*$

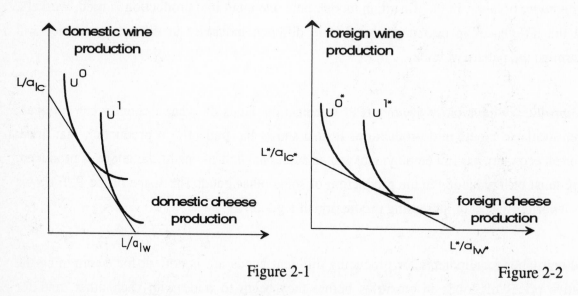

Figure 2-1   Figure 2-2

The pattern of trade that will arise between these countries is determined by the difference in these relative prices. If a higher relative price of cheese is offered than the foreign producers originally received, the foreign producers will shift out of production of wine, and earn more by producing just cheese. Similarly, the domestic producers would tend to specialize in wine.

If trade possibilities increase the relative price of cheese above the pre-trade level, the home country will specialize in cheese production. If trade possibilities reduce the relative price of cheese below the pre-trade level, the foreign country will specialize in wine. Each of the *RD* (relative demand) curves shows that the total world demand for cheese relative to wine is a decreasing function of the price of cheese relative to the price of wine. The *RS* curve shows the world supply of cheese relative to wine. This supply is an increasing function of the relative price. You can show that trade benefits each of these countries in one of two ways emphasized in the text. First, you can demonstrate this benefit by thinking of trade as an indirect method of production. Alternatively, you can show that trade enlarges a country's consumption possibilities.

The Ricardian model of trade has illustrated that countries whose relative labor productivities differ across industries will tend to specialize in the good in which they have a comparative advantage. Ultimately, the patterns of production and trade also depend on world demand patterns. When countries are permitted to trade with each other, they will export goods that their labor produces relatively efficiently and import those goods that their labor produces relatively inefficiently. In the text, this theme is also emphasized in the context of production with many goods.

KEY TERMS

Define the following key terms:

1. Opportunity Cost_____

_____

_____

_____.

2. Relative Demand Curve_____

_____

_____

_____.

3. Relative Supply Curve_____

_____

_____

_____.

4. Gains From Trade_____

_____

_____

_____.

5. Sweatshop Labor Argument_____

_____

_____

_____.

REVIEW QUESTIONS

1. Answer parts a through c using the information on unit labor requirements provided in the following table.

	Home	Foreign
Butter (lbs/labor-hour)	5	1
Cloth (yards/labor-hour)	1	3

   a. In which commodity does Home have an absolute advantage? In which commodity does Foreign have an absolute advantage? Why?

   _____

   _____

   _____.

b. How much will Home gain if it trades 5 units of butter for 3 units of cloth? How much would Foreign gain from the same trade? Why?

_____

_____

_____.

c. How much will Home gain if it trades 5 units of butter for 6 units of cloth? How much would Foreign gain from the same trade?

_____

_____

_____.

2.   Assume that the Home country has a total supply of labor hours of 1000 which the Foreign country has a total supply of labor hours of 1200. Each country can produce two goods: bicycles and skateboards. The unit labor requirements in Home production are 5 hours per bicycle and 2 hours per skateboard. Foreign requirements for both bicycles and skateboards are 3 hours per unit.

a. Graph the production possibilities frontiers for the Home and Foreign economies.

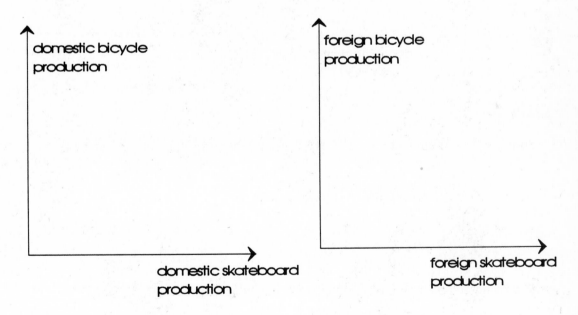

b. In the absence of trade, what is the relative price of bicycles in terms of skateboards in each country?

_____

_____

_____.

c. Trade is said to make each country better off by enlarging the range of consumption choices available to residents. Compare the consumption possibilities available to Home and Foreign consumers in the closed economy and open/trading economy cases. Graph the expanded consumption opportunities .

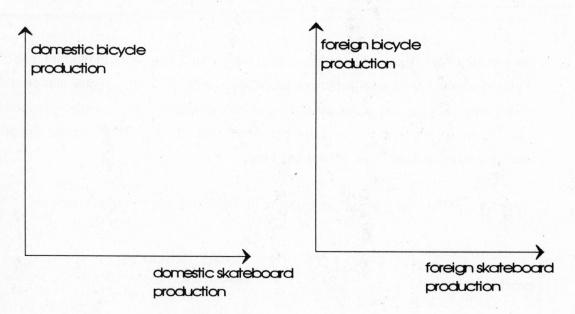

3.   Suppose that Home and Foreign have the unit labor requirements shown below.

	Baseball Bats	Tennis Rackets
Home	$a_{LB} = 6$	$a_{LR} = 2$
Foreign	$a_{LB}^* = 1$	$a_{LR}^* = 4$

a. In which good does Home have the relative productivity advantage? Why?

_____

_____

_____.

b. What is the opportunity cost of rackets in terms of bats for the Home country? for the Foreign country?

_____

_____

_____.

c. At world equilibrium *with trade*, what do you know about the relative price of tennis rackets?

_____

_____

_____.

d. Assume that a tennis racket trades for a bat on world markets at an equilibrium price of $P_r/P_B=2$. Why will each country will specialize? (Home will specialize in rackets and Foreign in bats).

_____

_____

_____.

e. Demonstrate that there will be gains from trade reaped by the Foreign country when it specializes in bat production.

_____

_____

_____.

4. Assume that Home and Foreign are both able to produce and consume the following four goods in autarky according the unit labor requirements provided below.

Good	Home Unit Labor Requirement	Foreign Unit Labor Requirement
A	1	12
B	2	18
C	4	24
D	15	30

a. In which good does Home have the greatest relative productivity advantage? In which good does Home have the lowest productivity advantage?

_____

_____

_____.

b. If the Home wage rate is 8 times the Foreign wage rate, what goods will be produced by Home? What goods will be produced by Foreign?

_____

_____

_____.

c. Show how this pattern of specialization, and hence trade, is beneficial to each country.

_____

_____

_____.

d. Would this pattern of specialization and trade change if the relative wage were $w/w^* = 6$? What would be the new pattern?

_____

_____

_____.

e. Discuss the reasons why, in practice, specialization is not as extreme as suggested by your response to part b.

_____

_____

_____

_____

_____

_____.

5. Assume that labor is the only factor used in production, and that the costs of producing butter and cloth are given by the table below.

	Home	Foreign
Cost in labor-hours to produce 1 unit of butter	1/8	1
Cost in labor-hours to produce 1 unit of cloth	1/4	1/2

a. Express the (cost or) price of butter relative to the price of cloth in terms of labor content for Home and Foreign in the absence of trade.

_____

_____

b. What do these relative prices reveal about each country's comparative advantage?

_____

_____

_____.

c. What do these relative prices suggest about the world price of butter relative to cloth that will exist once these countries trade with each other?

_____

_____

_____.

d. If the world price $(p_b/p_c)^w$ stabilizes at 1 with trade, what are the gains by the Home country achieved through trade with the Foreign country?

_____

_____

_____.

ANSWERS TO TEXTBOOK PROBLEMS

1. a. The production possibility curve is a straight line that intercepts the apple axis at 400 (1200/3) and the banana axis at 600 (1200/2).

   b. The opportunity cost of apples in terms of bananas is 3/2. It takes three units of labor to harvest an apple but only two units of labor to harvest a banana. If one foregoes harvesting an apple, this frees up three units of labor. These 3 units of labor could then be used to harvest 1.5 bananas.

   c. Labor mobility ensures a common wage in each sector and competition ensures the price of goods equals their cost of production. Thus the relative price equals the relative costs, which equals the wage times the unit labor requirement for apples divided by the wage times the unit labor requirement for bananas. Since wages are equal across sectors, the price ratio equals the ratio of the unit labor requirement, which is 3 apples per 2 bananas.

3. a. The relative demand curve includes the points (1/5, 5), (1/2, 2), (1,1), (2,1/2).

   b. The equilibrium relative price of apples is found at the intersection of the relative demand and relative supply curves. This is the point (1/2, 2), where the relative demand curve intersects the vertical section of the relative supply curve. Thus the equilibrium relative price is 2.

   c. Home produces only apples, Foreign produces only bananas, and each country trades some of its product for the product of the other country.

   d. In the absence of trade, Home could gain three bananas by foregoing two apples, and Foreign could gain by one apple foregoing five bananas. Trade allows each country to trade two bananas for one apple. Home could then gain four bananas by foregoing two apples while Foreign could gain one apple by foregoing only two bananas. Each country is better off with trade.

5. The answer here is identical to that in 3. The amount of "effective labor" has not changed since the doubling of the labor force is accompanied by a halving of the productivity of labor.

7. The problem with this argument is that it does not use all the information needed for determining comparative advantage in production: this calculation involves the four unit labor requirements (for both the industry and service sectors, not just the two for

the service sector). It is not enough to compare only service's unit labor requirements. If $a_{ls} < a_{ls}^*$, Home labor is more efficient than foreign labor in services. While this demonstrates that the United States has an absolute advantage in services, this is neither a necessary or sufficient condition for determining comparative advantage: for this determination the industry ratios are also required. The competitive advantage of any industry depends on both the relative productivities of the industries and the relative wages across industries.

9. Gains from trade still exist in the presence of nontraded goods. The gains from trade decline as the share of nontraded goods increases. In other words, the higher the portion of goods which do not enter international marketplace, the lower the potential gains from trade. If transport costs were so high enough so that no goods were traded then, obviously, there would be no gains from trade.

CHAPTER 3

Specific Factors and Income Distribution

CHAPTER ORGANIZATION

The Specific Factors Model
    Assumptions of the Model
    Production Possibilities
    Prices, Wages and Labor Allocation
    Relative Prices and the Distribution of Income
International Trade in the Specific Factors Model
    Resources and Relative Supply
    Trade and Relative Prices
    The Pattern of Trade
Income Distribution and the Gains From Trade
The Political Economy of Trade: A Preliminary View
    Optimal Trade Policy
    Income Distribution and Trade Policies
Appendix to Chapter 3
    Further Details on Specific Factors
    Marginal and Total Product
    Relative Prices and the Distribution of Income

KEY THEMES

The Ricardian model presented in Chapter 2 suggests that all countries gain from trade with each other, and because the single input into production can move to the sector where wage payments are highest, individuals also benefit from trade. This result may not seem fully plausible to you: in the real world trade has substantial effects on the distribution of income within a nation. The fact that there are some winners from trade and also some losers is amply demonstrated by frequent attempts by some producers to limit imports of steel, automobiles and textiles. This observation motivates the importance of the specific factors model presented in Chapter 3. International trade is observed to have strong effects on the distribution of

18

income because: 1) resources cannot move immediately or costlessly from one industry to another; and 2) industries differ in their needs for different factors of production. Trade increases the demand for some of these factors and reduces the demand for other factors. To examine the distributional effects of trade, the chapter introduces models which have factors of production that are used exclusively in the production of a single good.

The first model includes factors of production which are inexorably tied to producing one and only one good. The particular example presented in the text involves winemakers and cheesemakers. The immobility of labor prevents equalization of wages. An equilibrium relative price can be determined when the relative demand curve is specified.

Now, consider the effect of introducing another country which can produce the same bundle of goods. The second economy shares the same production technology, but has different relative amounts of each type of labor. Trade between these two economies benefits each in the aggregate since the possible consumption set of each country expands. However, distributional issues arise when trade is permitted since workers in particular sectors may not gain from trade. There will be no gain for the labor in each economy which was relatively scarce prior to trade as compared to after trade. The type of labor relatively abundant in a country will gain from trade. The source of this effect is the movement in relative prices which favors the good which was relatively abundant in each country before trade. The general conclusion is that trade benefits workers in the export sector of each country and hurts workers in the import-competing sector.

Next, a more general model is presented to investigate the distributional effects of trade. The significance of this specific factors model is that it allows you to trace the distributional effects of trade on factors inexorably tied to the production of a specific good as well as on those factors that can be used to produce either good. The three factors in this model include two specific factors, land and capital, as well as one intersectorally mobile factor, labor. The fixed amount of each specific factor results in diminishing returns to labor. The mobility of labor ensures an equal wage in the production of either good and perfect competition ensures that the wage equals the value marginal product of labor in the production of each good.

It is worth considering the specific factors model in greater depth. It describes an economy where labor can move between sectors however other factors are specific to particular sectors. For example, an economy might produce corn using labor and land, while it produces manufactured goods, such as machine tools, using labor and capital. The land and the capital are considered specific factors. Note that labor exhibits decreasing returns to production in these sectors: when a unit of labor is added to the production of corn, his productivity is limited by the fixed amount of land that now must be used by yet another worker. The additional output of this worker is smaller than the added output of the previous worker.

Labor will move across sectors until the value of its marginal product (MPL) is the same across all sectors. In equilibrium the wage rate (or cost of labor) is equal to the value of the worker's marginal revenue product. If food (f) and manufactures (m) are the two goods being produced, in equilibrium $MPL_f \times p_f = w = MPL_m \times p_m$. Rearranging this expression yields $-MPL_f/MPL_m = -p_m/p_f$, so that at the equilibrium production point the production possibilities frontier is tangent to a line whose slope is minus the price of manufactures divided by the price of food.

Changes in the relative price of the goods produced in an economy have clear distributional effects. Consider what happens when you increase the price of manufactures in the economy described above. Since more workers are demanded, the wage rate of workers increases. Are these workers better off? Clearly their wages will increase, however, at the same time the price of manufactures has also increased. The increase in wages is less than the increase in the price of manufactures, so that the real wage in terms of manufactured goods has declined. However, the real wage measured in terms of food (whose price has not changed) has risen. The overall impact on the welfare of the workers depends on the importance of manufactured goods and food in their consumption bundles.

Other distributional effects are experienced by the owners of labor and capital. Capital owners now pay lower real wages in terms of manufactures, implying that their income rises by more than their expenses and their spending power rises. Landowners, on the other hand, are made worse off since the price of food is unchanged while wage costs have increased. This squeezes their profits and lowers their income in terms of both goods.

Differences in the endowments of resources can affect the relative supplies of goods produced in different countries. In the absence of trade, this is reflected in differences in relative prices of the goods produced. When two countries are permitted to trade, the relative prices of the goods are equalized across markets and an aggregate supply of goods meets aggregated world demand. If, for example, Japan is better endowed with capital relative to its endowment of labor, and is not well-endowed with land, food will be expensive compared to manufactures. The opposite would be true in the relatively land rich United States. It is straightforward to show that Japan will export the good which is initially relatively cheaper, manufactures, while the United States exports food. Both countries are made better off through trade. You should spend some time going over Figure 3-13 in the text. Make certain that you understand which production and consumption points will arise with trade.

There are still the distributional effects of trade to consider. Trade benefits the factor of production that is specific to the export sector of each country but hurts the factor specific to the import-competing sector. As mentioned above, the effects of trade on the mobile factor of production will be ambiguous. You should make sure that you understand these arguments about who benefits and who loses from trade. Only with such insights can you begin to understand why some groups fights so hard for protectionism. Despite this distributional argument. it is quite clear that the losses to these individuals are far outweighed by the gains from trade to the rest of the population. This will be illustrated more vividly in later chapters.

It can be discouraging to realize that economic arguments do not have the final say in the formation of economic policy. When some groups that stand to lose from trade lobby their governments to protect their earning by restricting trade, their voices are often louder, and pockets deeper, than the groups that stand to gain from trade. The political economy of trade theory is introduced at the end of Chapter 3 and discusses the motives of these groups and the way in which they interact with the political process. The text returns to these ideas in Chapter 10.

KEY TERMS

Define the following terms:

1. The Specific Factors Model_____

_____

_____

_____

2. Mobile Factor_____

_____

_____

_____.

3. Marginal Product of Labor_____

_____

_____

_____.

4. Diminishing Returns_____

_____

_____

_____.

5. Budget Constraint_____

_____

_____

_____.

REVIEW QUESTIONS

1.   Assume that the United States has two sectors: the food sector has land as a specific input factor and the manufacturing sector uses capital as a specific factor. Labor is mobile across sectors. Suppose that exceptionally good weather enables several states to enjoy "bumper" crops which lead to an 8 percent decline in the price of food.

    a. In the figure below, graphically illustrate the effect on the labor demand curves for food and manufactured goods.

    b. What is the impact on wages?

_____

_____

_____.

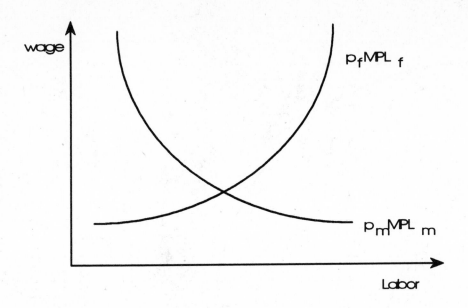

c. How does the distribution of labor across sectors change? How does the output of each sector change?

_____

_____

_____.

d. How does the change in relative prices affect the economy's production mix? Demonstrate this impact graphically in the figure on the next page.

e. How does the decline in p_f relative to p_m affect the income distribution across capitalists (capital owners) and landowners?

_____

_____

_____.

f. What can be said about the impact on the earnings of workers? Could you provide a more definite response if you were told that food was by far the most important item in a worker's consumption basket?

_____

_____

_____.

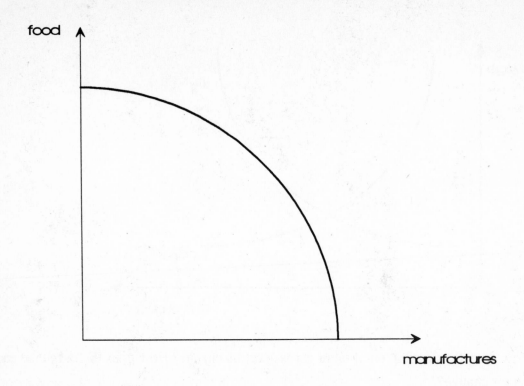

food

manufactures

2. Assume that inflation increases prices disproportionately in manufactured goods and food. Manufacturing prices rise by 10 percent while the price of food increases by 5 percent.

a. How does this change in relative prices affect the labor demand curves in each sector? How does the distribution of labor across sectors change? Show this shift in the diagram below.

_____

_____

_____.

b. What are the implications for wages paid to labor? What are the implications of this differential inflation for the owners of capital and the owners of land?

_____

_____

_____.

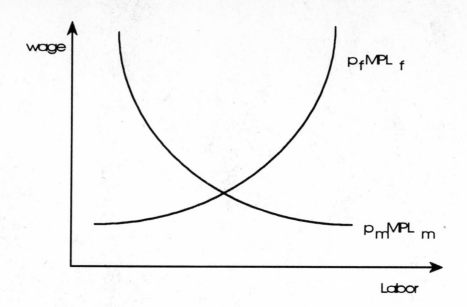

c. How does the output mix of the country change?

_____

_____

_____.

3.   Suppose that a hurricane destroys may acres of arable land in Jamaica. This temporarily reduces the country's endowment of land, an important specific factor in the production of food. Jamaica's output of food and of manufactured goods will be affected by this change.

a. All else equal, what are the implications of this change in resources for the marginal productivity of labor in each sector? What will happen to the demand for labor in each sector? Use graphical analysis to illustrate your response.

_____

_____

_____.

b. What is the impact on wages paid to workers in food and manufacturing production? How will the distribution of workers across sectors of the economy change?

_____

_____

_____.

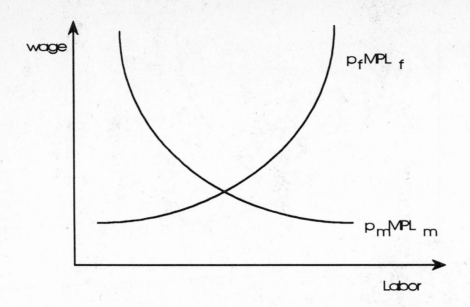

c. What is the affect on the output of each sector? Discuss the intuition behind this result.

_____

_____

_____.

4.   When an economy is prohibited from trading, the consumption possibilities of its' citizens are constrained by the amount of domestic production. When trade is permitted, a fundamental gain which occurs is the expansion of the consumption choices available to a nation. Now, assume that a nation is land scarce and capital abundant (and cannot borrow resources from other countries!) . It produces 100 units of food and 300 units of manufactured goods. Regardless of the price of manufactured goods, demand for manufactures is inelastic at 150 units.

a. Using the open economy budget constraint, determine the amount of food which is imported at a relative price of manufactured goods (p_m/p_f) equal to 2.

_____

_____

_____.

b. Using graphical analysis, show the country's budget constraint, output and consumption choices when the equilibrium price is equal to $p_m/p_f=2$.

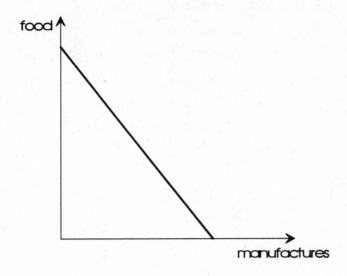

c. How are the results of part b are altered when the equilibrium relative price shifts to $p_m/p_f=4$. Discuss the intuition behind these results.

_____

_____

_____.

d. How are the results of part b are altered when the equilibrium relative price shifts to 1? Compare the intuition with that of part c.

_____

_____

_____.

ANSWERS TO CHAPTER 3 TEXT PROBLEMS

1.   Texas and Louisiana are states with large oil-producing sectors. The real wage of oil-producing factors of production in terms of other goods falls when the price of oil falls relative to the price of other goods. This was the source of economic decline in these states in 1986.

3. a. To solve this problem, one can graph the demand curve for labor in sector 1 , represented by ($w=MPL_1$=demand for L_1) and the demand curve for labor in sector 2,

represented by ($w=MPL_2$=demand for L_2) . Since the total supply of labor is given by the horizontal axis, the labor allocation between the sectors is approximately $L_1=27$ and $L_2=73$. The wage rate is approximately \$0.98.

b. Use the same type of graph as in problem 2b to show that sectoral output is $Q_1=44$ and $Q_2=90$. (This involves combining the production function diagrams with the economy's allocation of labor in a four quadrant diagram. The economy's PPF is in the upper right hand corner, as illustrated in the text.)

c. Use a graph of labor demands, as in part a, to show that the intersection of the demand curves for labor occurs at a wage rate approximately equal to \$0.74. The relative decline in the price of good 2 caused labor to be reallocated: labor is drawn out of production of good 2 and enters production of good 1 ($L_1=62$, $L_2=38$). This also leads to an output adjustment, whereby production of good to falls to 68 units and production of good 1 rises to 76 units.

d. With the relative price change from $p_2/p_1=2$ to $p_2/p_1=1$, the price of good 2 has fallen by 50 percent. while the price of good 1 has stayed the same. Wages have fallen, but by less than the fall in p_2 (wages fell approximately 25 percent). Thus the real wage relative to p_2 actually rises while to real wage relative to p_1 falls. Hence, to determine the welfare consequences for workers, information is needed about their consumption shares of good 1 and good 2.

CHAPTER 4

Resources and Trade: The Heckscher-Ohlin Model

CHAPTER ORGANIZATION

A Model of a Two-Factor Economy
      Assumptions of the Model
      Production Possibilities
      Goods Prices and Factor Prices
      Allowing Substitution Between Inputs
Effects of International Trade Between Two-Factor Economies
      Relative Prices and the Pattern of Trade
      Trade and the Distribution of Income
      Factor Price Equalization
Empirical Evidence on the Heckscher-Ohlin Model
      Testing the Heckscher-Ohlin Model
      Implications of the Tests
Appendix to Chapter 4: The Heckscher-Ohlin Model with Variable Coefficients
      Choice of Technique
      Goods Prices and Factor Prices
      Allocation of Resources

KEY THEMES

In Chapter 2 trade between nations was motivated by differences internationally in the relative productivity of workers when producing a range of products. In Chapter 3 labor was no longer the only factor used in production. Specific though immobile factors of production were introduced and some distributional effects of alterations in sector specific factors and prices were discussed.

In Chapter 4 the Heckscher-Ohlin theory goes a step further by considering the pattern of production and trade which will arise when countries have different endowments of factors of production, such as labor, capital and land. The basic point is that countries tend to export goods that are intensive in the factors with which they are abundantly supplied. Trade has strong effects on the relative earnings of resources, and tends to lead to equalization across countries of prices of the factors of production. These theoretical results and related empirical findings are presented in this chapter.

The chapter begins by developing a model of an economy with two goods which are each produced using two factors according to fixed coefficient production functions. The assumption of fixed coefficient production functions provides an unambiguous ranking of goods in terms of factor intensities. Two important results are derived using this model. The first is known as the *Rybczynski effect*: increasing the relative supply of one factor, holding relative goods prices constant, leads to a biased expansion of production possibilities favoring the relative supply of the good which uses that factor intensively. The second key result is known as the *Stolper-Samuelson effect*: increasing the relative price of a good, holding factor supplies constant, increases the return to the factor used intensively in the production of that good by more than the price increase, while lowering the return to the other factor. This result has important implications for the distribution of income across different groups of agents in the economy.

The central message of the Heckscher-Ohlin theory is that countries tend to export goods whose production is intensive in factors with which they are relatively abundantly endowed. This is demonstrated by showing that, using the relative supply and relative demand analysis introduced in chapter 2, the country relatively abundantly endowed with a certain factor will produce that factor more cheaply than the other country. International trade leads to a convergence of goods prices. Thus, the results from the *Stolper-Samuelson theory* demonstrate that owners of a country's abundant factors gain from trade but owners of a country's scarce factors lose. The extension of this result is the important *Factor Price Equalization Theorem*, which states that trade in (and thus price equalization of) goods leads to an equalization in the rewards to factors across countries.

Some of these points should be developed in greater depth. Recall that an important theme of this chapter is the pattern of trade that will arise between nations which differ in their relative endowments of factors of production. The Heckscher-Ohlin or factor-proportions theory is developed using two countries, each of whom can produce two goods using the same technologies and using two inputs into production. This two country, two good, two factor set-up is the simplest way of illustrating some important points. If land and labor are the

30

inputs into production, the theory illustrates that an economy with a high ratio of land to labor will be relatively better suited for producing a good which requires a relatively high intensity of land (such as the production of food) than will a country with a relatively low endowment of land relative to its endowment of labor.

Factor prices, wages paid to workers and the rent paid on land use, all change when goods prices change. The Stolper-Samuelson effect is that changes in relative goods prices have a magnified effect on factor prices. For example, if you increase the price of manufactured goods, then the wage paid to workers (production of manufactured goods uses workers intensively) will increase proportionately more than the price of manufactures. This is an important result: you should make sure that you understand how wages move in each sector, and how the size of the increase or decrease in factor prices compares with the proportionate increase or decrease in the prices of the goods which will eventually be consumed by the workers, the land-owners and the capital owners.

Consider the effect of allowing two countries to trade with each other. Suppose that the only difference between these countries is that Home has a higher ratio of labor to land than does Foreign. Thus, Home is described as *labor abundant* and Foreign is described as *land abundant*. Both produce a labor intensive product, cloth, and a land intensive product, food. Before trade occurs between these countries, food is relatively cheaper in Foreign, the land intensive country, and cloth is relatively cheaper at Home. When trade is permitted, each country will export the good in which it has a comparative advantage in production. This comparative advantage arises because of relative endowments of factors of production which are more favorable to the production of some goods than they are to others. This is a key theme of the factor-proportions theory.

Next, you can ask the same type of questions about the effects of trade on the distribution of income when the world is like the world in the Heckscher-Ohlin model of trade. (Recall that you asked similar questions for the Ricardian and specific factors models). Analogous to the results for the specific factors model, you should be convinced that the owners of a country's abundant factors will gain from trade, while the owners of a country's relatively scarce factors will be made worse off from trade. In the example provided above, at Home the land owners are made worse off and labor benefits as production shifts towards cloth, the more labor intensive product. In the Foreign country, workers are made worse off and landowners are made better off as production shifts toward the land intensive good, food.

Another interesting outcome of permitting trade is that as the relative prices of goods converge across countries, the relative prices of factors of production will also tend to converge across countries. This point is related to a more abstract idea about what is actually occurring when two countries trade: since the trade arises because countries differ in endowments of factors of production, the goods trade really is a way of trading factors of production. Since the factors of production can't move across a country's borders, the goods which move across borders act as an alternative to trade in factors. The theory predicts that goods trade serves to equal the prices of goods across countries, and therefore, the prices of factors of production.

In the real world, factor price equalization does not really occur. This tells you that there are some shortcomings of the model-- or at least that some of the assumptions of the model are inconsistent with what we observe in the world. These assumptions of the model that are not true are that both countries 1) produce the same goods, 2) using the same technology, and that 3) trade equalizes the relative prices of goods across markets.

In terms of the real world, you should also understand that the Heckscher-Ohlin model provides predictions about the world that are not supported by many empirical studies. Empirical results concerning the Heckscher-Ohlin theory, beginning with the Leontief paradox and extending to current research, do not support its predictions concerning resource endowments explaining patterns of trade. This observation has motivated many economists to consider motives for trade between nations that are not exclusively based on differences across countries. In fact, whereas the factor proportions theory predicts that trade between countries is motivated by differences in relative factor endowments, in reality, it is observed that trade between countries instead is motivated by differences in production technologies. This brings you back to the main point of the Ricardian model. So, the simple Ricardian model provides useful information about trade patterns, while the Heckscher-Ohlin framework provides useful insights into the distributional effects of trade.

KEY TERMS

Define the following key terms:

1. Factor Intensity_____

_____

_____

_____.

2. Biased Expansion of Production Possibilities_____

_____

_____

_____.

3. Magnified Effect of Goods Prices on Factor Prices_____

_____

_____

_____.

4. Equalization of Factor Prices_____

_____

_____

_____.

5. Leontief Paradox_____

_____

_____

_____.

REVIEW QUESTIONS

1. Suppose that a country produces wine (W) and cheese (C) using its supply of 400 units of labor (man-hours) (L) and 600 units of land (acres) (T). To produce a gallon of wine requires 10 units of labor and 5 units of land. A pound of cheese requires 4 units of labor and 8 units of land.

a. Which inputs are used intensively in the production of cheese? Which inputs are used intensively in the production of wine?

_____

_____

_____ .

b. Is it possible for this country to produce 90 gallons of wine and 50 gallons of cheese with the resources available? Explain your answer.

_____

_____

_____ .

c. Graph the land and labor constraints on production in this economy.

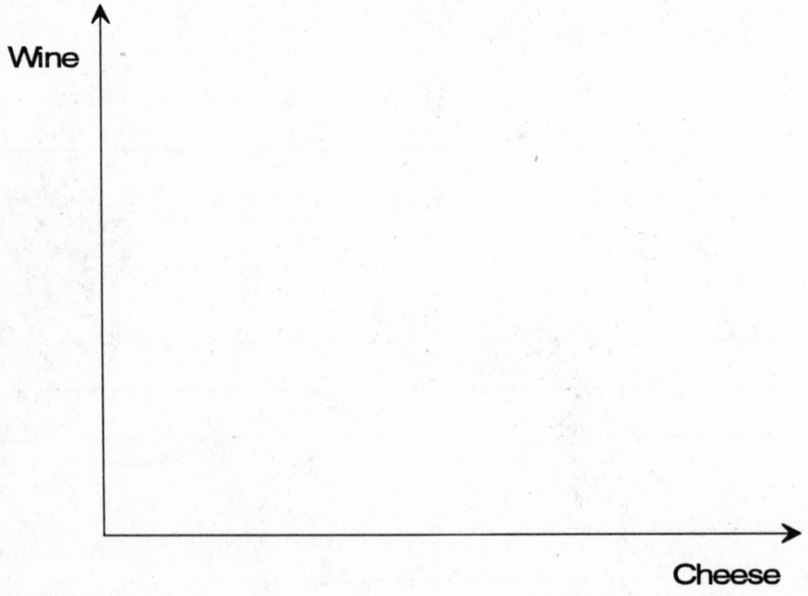

Wine

Cheese

d. How are these constraints affected by an increase in the supply of labor by 100 workers? Show this graphically in the diagram above .

_____

_____

_____ .

2.   Production of a bushel of wheat requires 9 units of land and 3 units of labor. Production of a yard of cloth requires 6 units of labor and only 1 unit of land. Suppose an economy is endowed with 120 units of labor and 180 units of land.

a. Draw the production possibilities frontier of this economy on the axis provided below.

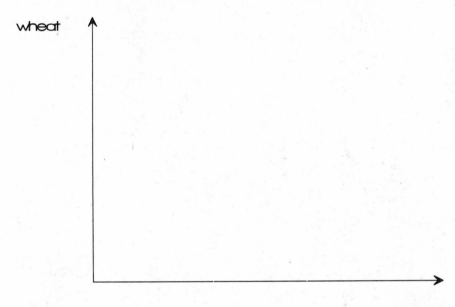

b. If the supply of land increases by 90 units, how does the production possibilities frontier change? What is the intuition behind this result?

_____

_____

_____.

3.   Television production is relatively labor-intensive, requiring 20 units of labor and 4 units of land. Televisions sell for $60 each. Rice, on the other hand, is a relatively land-intensive product, requiring 1 unit of labor and 4 units of land for every pound of rice produced. Rice sells for $4 per pound.

a. If Home has 120 million workers and 200 million acres, while Foreign has 40 million workers and 50 million acres, what is the pattern of trade between these countries that will be predicted by the factor proportions theory?

_____

_____

_____.

b. Under what conditions in the real world would the predictions of the factor proportions theory be contradicted?

_____

_____

_____

_____

_____.

c. Given the prices described above, graph the lines along which price equals production costs for rice and for television.

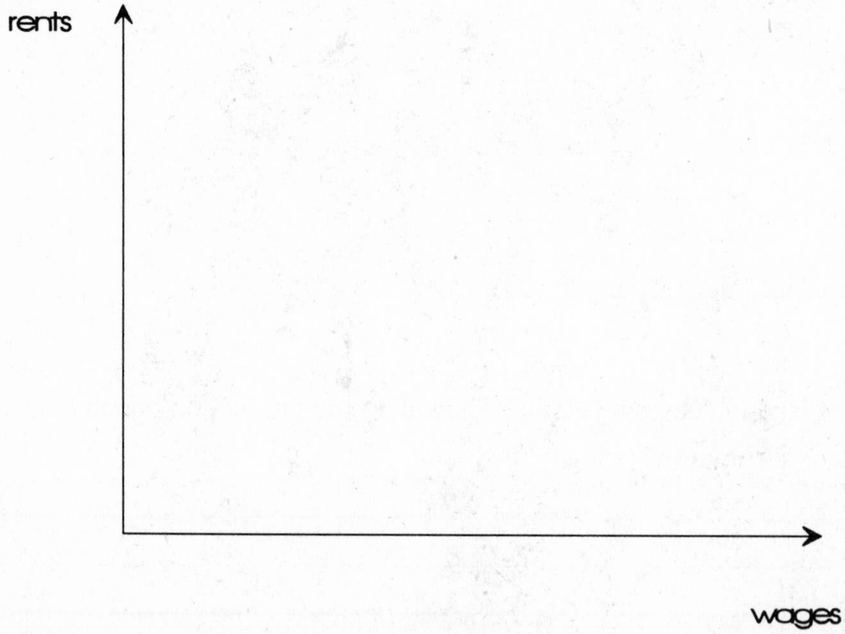

rents

wages

4. Suppose that production of wine requires 10 units of land and 5 units of labor per gallon, while the production of cheese requires 4 units of labor and 8 units of land per pound.

a. If the unit prices of wine and cheese are $30 and $16, respectively, show that unit wages and rent <u>cannot</u> be 2 and 3, respectively, in a competitive economy.

_____

_____

_____.

b. If the unit prices of wine and cheese are $30 and $16, respectively, graph the lines along which price equals marginal cost for each of these two goods.

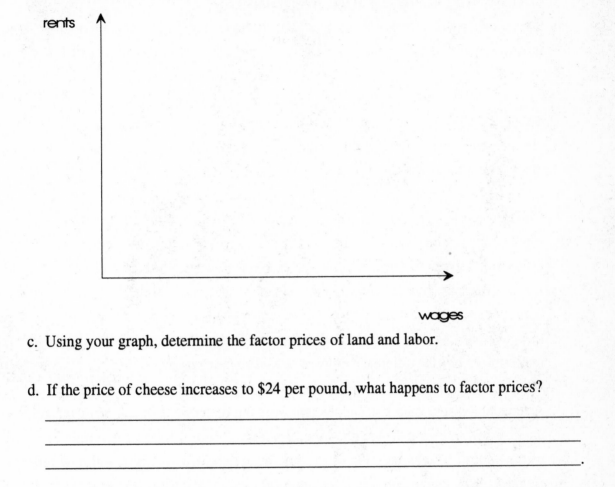

c. Using your graph, determine the factor prices of land and labor.

d. If the price of cheese increases to $24 per pound, what happens to factor prices?

_____

_____

_____.

e. How will the purchasing power of workers and landowners be affected by an increase in the price of cheese? Discuss your result.

_____

_____

_____

_____.

ANSWERS TO ODD-NUMBERED TEXT PROBLEMS

1. a. The labor constraint is a straight line intersecting the Steel axis at 10 tons and intersecting the Wheat axis at 50 tons. The land constraint is a straight line intersecting the Steel axis at 20 tons and intersecting the Wheat axis at 25 tons.

b. The PPF is defined by the segment of the land constraint from the Wheat axis to the intersection of the two constraints and the segment of the labor constraint from the Steel axis to the intersection of the two constraints.

c. The PPF extends outward in a biased fashion, favoring steel production. The intersection of the two constraints shifts towards greater steel output and less wheat output.

3.   This question is similar to an issue discussed in Chapter 2. What matters is not the absolute abundance of factors, but their relative abundance. Poor countries have an abundance of labor relative to capital when compared to more developed countries.

5.   Conditions necessary for factor price equalization include both countries (or regions) produce both goods, both countries have the same technology of production, and the absence of barriers to trade. The difference between wages different regions of the US may reflect all of these reasons; however, the barriers to trade are purely "natural" barriers due to transportation costs. US trade with Mexico, by contrast, is also subject to legal limits; together with cultural differences that inhibit the flow of technology, this may explain why the difference in wage rates is so much larger.

7.   A reduction in the supply of labor diminishes the dimensions of the labor market box diagram by decreasing the length of the labor axis. There will be a new origin for either of the goods. The intersection of the production expansion curves will now reflect a decrease in the amount of both labor and land used in the production of cloth, and thus a decline in the production of cloth. There will be more of each factor used in the production of food, and thus the food output of the economy rises.

CHAPTER 5

The Standard Trade Model

CHAPTER ORGANIZATION

KEY THEMES

Previous chapters have emphasized certain specific sources of comparative advantage which give rise to international trade, including differences in the productivity of labor or in the relative endowments of factors of production. This chapter presents a general model which admits previous models as special cases. This "standard trade model" can be viewed the workhorse of international trade theory and can be used to address a wide range of issues. Some of these issues, such as the welfare and distributional effects of economic growth, transfers between nations, and tariffs and subsidies on traded goods, are considered in this chapter.

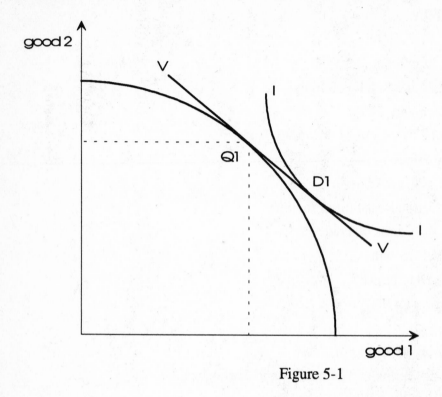

Figure 5-1

The standard trade model is based upon four relationships. *First*, an economy will produce at the point where the production possibilities curve is tangent to the relative price line VV (called the isovalue line). In Figure 5-1 the production point is Q_1. *Second*, indifference curves (II) describe the tastes of an economy and the consumption point for that economy is found at the tangency of the budget line and the highest indifference curve. This is point D_1 in the figure. Together, these two relationships yield the general equilibrium trade diagram for a small economy (one which takes as given the terms of trade) where the consumption point and production point are the tangencies of the isovalue line with the highest indifference curve and the production possibility frontier, respectively. Note that at the point D_1 food consumption occurs at higher levels than food production. By contrast, cloth consumption is at lower levels than cloth production. At the price shown, this economy is a net importer of food and a net exporter of cloth.

The *third* relationship is that an improvement in the terms of trade (an increase in the price of exports relative to the price of imports) increases welfare in the economy. The *fourth* relationship takes us from a small country analysis to a two country analysis by introducing a structure of world relative demand and supply curves which determine relative prices. As shown in figure 5-2, the higher is p_c/p_f, the larger the world supply of cloth relative to food (see the *RS* curve) and the lower the world demand for cloth relative to food (see the *RD* curve).

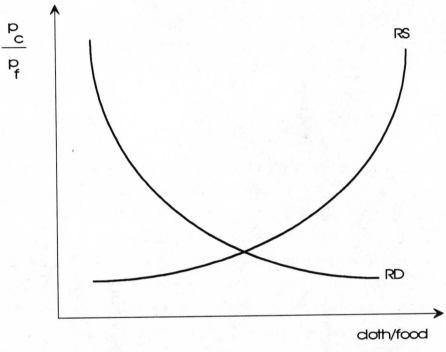

Figure 5-2

One application of the standard trade model deals with the popular arguments in the media that growth in Japan or Korea hurts the United States. The analysis presented in this chapter demonstrates that the *bias* of growth is more important for determining welfare effects than is the country in which growth occurs. The existence of biased growth causes a shift of the TT curve of figure 5-1 and of the *RS* curve of figure 5-2. The Relative Supply and Relative Demand curves provide a clear illustration of the effect of biased growth on the terms of trade. The new terms of trade line (determined by the point of intersection of the new *RS* curve and the existing *RD* curve) can be used with the general equilibrium analysis to find the welfare effects of growth. A general principle which emerges is that a country which experiences export-biased growth will have a deterioration in its terms of trade while a country which experiences import-biased growth has an improvement in its terms of trade. A case study points out that growth in the rest of the world has made other countries more like the U.S. This import-biased growth has worsened the terms of trade for the U.S.. The

41

theoretical possibility that a country's growth can lead it to a lower level of welfare is called immiserizing growth.

The second issue addressed in the context of the standard trade model is the effects of international transfers. The salient point here is the direction, if any, in which the relative demand curve shifts in response to the redistribution of income from a transfer. A transfer worsens the donor's terms of trade if the donor has a higher marginal propensity to consume its export good than the recipient. The presence of nontraded goods tends to reinforce the transfer related deterioration of terms of trade for the donor country.

The third area to which the standard trade model is applied are the effects of tariffs and export subsidies on welfare and terms of trade. The analysis proceeds by recognizing that tariffs or subsidies shift both the relative supply and relative demand curves. A tariff on imports improves the terms of trade, expressed in external prices, while a subsidy on exports worsens terms of trade. The size of this effect depends upon the size of the country in the world. Graphical analyses which illustrate these points are provided through the study guide problems. You should spend some time working through these problems and the end of chapter problems in the text. Tariffs and subsidies also impose distortionary costs upon the economy. Thus, if a country is large enough, there may be an optimum, non-zero tariff. Export subsidies, however, only impose costs upon an economy. Intranationally, tariffs aid import-competing sectors and hurt export sectors while subsidies have the opposite effect. An appendix presents offer curve diagrams and explains this mode of analysis.

KEY TERMS

Define the following key terms:

1. Terms of Trade _____
_____
_____
_____.

2. Import-Biased Growth_____
_____
_____
_____.

3. Import Tariff_____

_____

_____

_____.

4. Export Subsidy _____

_____

_____

_____.

5. Metzler Paradox _____

_____

_____

_____.

REVIEW QUESTIONS

1. Assume that a country produces two goods, wine (W) and cheese (C). Equilibrium output is at the point where the initial isovalue line (v_1v_1) is tangent to the production possibilities frontier. The relative price p_C/p_W at this point is equal to 4.

    a. Suppose the relative price of cheese increases to 6. Graph the new isovalue line (v_2v_2) in the figure below.

    b. Describe the new equilibrium output mix.

    _____

    _____

    _____.

    c. Suppose the relative price of cheese decreases to 2. What happens to the isovalue line? Describe the new equilibrium output mix.

    _____

    _____

    _____.

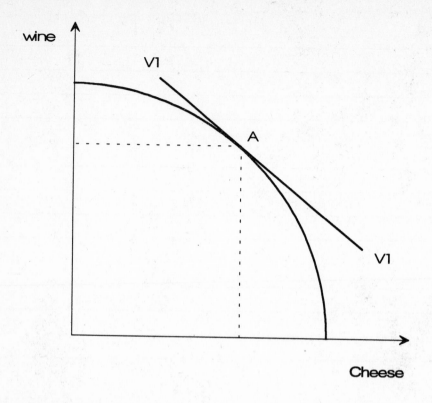

d. What is the relationship between the supply of cheese relative to wine and the relative price of cheese to wine?

_____

_____

_____.

2. Continuing with the example in problem 1, assume that the relative price of cheese to wine is 4 and that the economy exports wine and imports cheese.

a. Given these consumption preferences, describe the point at which the isovalue line is tangent to the highest indifference curve. Draw isoquants on the figure below to illustrate this tangency.

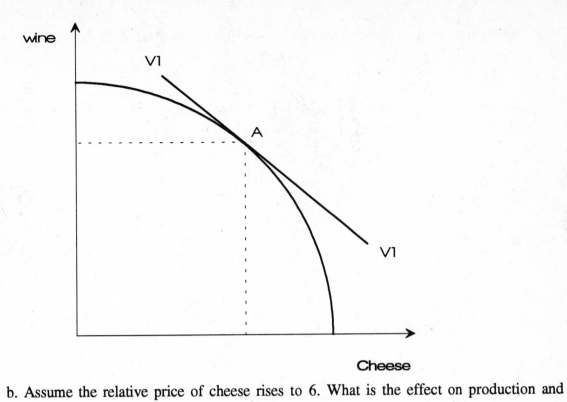

wine

V1

A

V1

Cheese

b. Assume the relative price of cheese rises to 6. What is the effect on production and consumption?

_____

_____

_____.

c. What are the welfare effects of this relative price change?

_____

_____

_____.

d. Discuss the income and substitution effects associated with this relative price change.

_____

_____

_____.

e. Assume that the relative price of cheese falls to 2. Discuss the effect on production, consumption, the terms of trade and the welfare of the economy.

_____

_____

_____.

3. Continuing with the same economy, suppose instead that the economy exports cheese and imports wine.

a. Use the tangency of the isovalue line, the production possibility frontier and the highest indifference curve to show the production and consumption points of this economy.

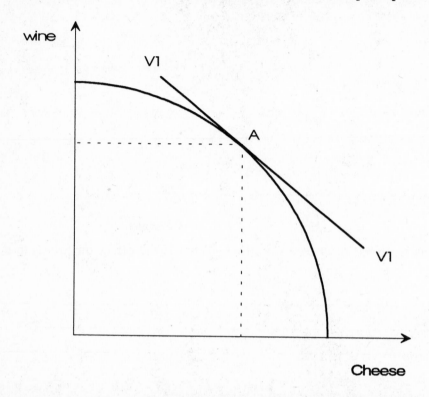

b. What are the effects on production of a decline in the relative price of cheese?

_____

_____

_____.

c. What are the effects on consumption of this decline in relative prices? Is this country better off or worse off?

_____

_____

_____.

d. Discuss the relationship between a country's terms of trade and its welfare.

_____

_____

_____.

4. Consider an economy which produces two goods, wine and cheese, whereby wine production is land -intensive and cheese production is labor -intensive.

a. Suppose the government decides to turn all public parks into land used in production, thereby increasing the supply of land available to producers. Show how this will affect the production possibilities of the economy. Discuss.

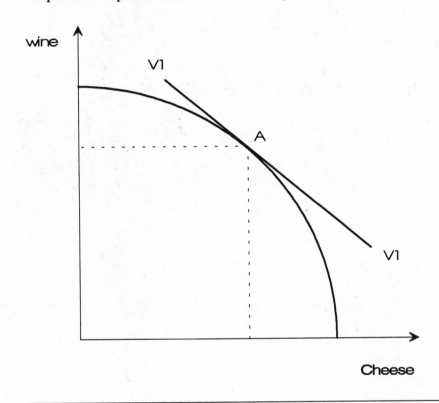

_____

_____

_____.

b. What is the theoretical basis for your answer to part a?

_____

_____

_____.

c. Suppose the relative price of cheese is unchanged following biased growth. Compare the new production mix with the original production mix.

_____

_____

_____.

d. If the government wants the output of cheese to remain constant, despite the biased growth, what must happen to the relative price of cheese? What types of policies could achieve this goal?

_____

_____

_____.

5. The Home economy produces labor-intensive sneakers and land-intensive beets. Suppose that demographic changes are strongly biased in favor of the export good, sneakers.

a. If this were a small country so that the relative price of sneakers was unchanged by this growth, what would be the effect of growth on the Home production mix?

_____

_____

_____.

b. If this were a medium to large country, what would be the effect on the world relative supply of sneakers to beets?

_____

_____

_____.

c. How does this growth affect Home terms of trade? Home welfare?

_____

_____

_____.

d. Suppose that biased growth had favored beet production instead. Discuss the impact on world relative supply, the terms of trade for the Home country, and the Home welfare.

_____

_____

_____.

6.   Assume that the Home country is an importer of wine and an exporter of cheese. The domestic government imposes a 25 percent tariff on wine imports.

a. How does the tariff affect the Home relative price of wine vis-a-vis the relative price of wine on world markets?

_____

_____

_____.

b. How does the tariff affect the world relative demand and supply for wine?

_____

_____

_____.

c. What is the impact of the tariff on Home's terms of trade?

_____

_____

_____.

d. Discuss the assumptions that are critical for your answer to part c.

_____

_____

_____.

ANSWERS TO ODD-NUMBERED TEXTBOOK PROBLEMS

1.   An increase in the terms of trade increases welfare when the PPF is right-angled. The production point is the corner of the PPF. The consumption point is the tangency of the relative price line and the highest indifference curve. An improvement in the terms

of trade rotates the relative price line about its intercept with the PPF rectangle (since there is no substitution of immobile factors, the production point stays fixed). The economy can then reach a higher indifference curve. Intuitively, although there is no supply response, the economy receives more for the exports it supplies and pays less for the imports it purchases.

3.　In terms of the relative demand and relative supply diagram where prices and quantities are expressed as manufactured goods relative to raw materials.

  a. The relative supply curve shifts out, decreasing the relative price of manufactured goods and deteriorating Japan's terms of trade.

  b. The relative supply curve shifts out, decreasing the relative price of manufactured goods and deteriorating Japan's terms of trade.

  c. The relative demand curve shifts out, increasing the relative price of manufactured goods and improving Japan's terms of trade. This occurs even if no fusion reactors are installed in Japan since world demand for raw materials falls.

  d. The relative supply curve shifts out, and the relative demand curve shifts in, decreasing the relative price of manufactured goods and deteriorating Japan's terms of trade.

5.　Immiserizing growth occurs when the welfare deteriorating effects of a worsening in an economy's terms of trade swamp the welfare improving effects of growth. For this to occur an economy must undergo very biased growth and the economy must be a large enough actor in the world economy such that its actions spill over to adversely alter the terms of trade to a large degree. This combination of events is unlikely to occur in practice.

7.　Given the difference in technological development between most Eastern European countries and the United States and Japan, the effects on Western European prices will depend in the short run on transfer problem issues and in the long run on the likely biases in Eastern Europe's growth. The transfer problem point is concerned with the consumption demands of countries which receive available international credit supplies. If loans to developing countries shift from availability to Latin American countries, which have a relatively high propensity to consume United States goods, to availability to Eastern European countries, which have a lower propensity to consume United States goods and a higher propensity to consume West German goods, the price of West German exports will rise relative to the price of United States exports. This would like to an improvement in the terms of trade of Germany and a worsening of the terms of trade of the United States. Note, however, that in the long term, the analysis of terms of trade effects should also consider whether the biases in economic growth in Eastern Europe will be in sectors of the economy more closely aligned with the export industries of West Germany or of the United States. The greater the similarity of the export oriented industrial push in Eastern European with the existing industries in West Germany, the greater the supply side reversal of the favorable West German terms of trade movement which had arisen from the demand side forces of the transfer problem.

CHAPTER 6

Economies of Scale, Imperfect Competition and International Trade

CHAPTER ORGANIZATION

KEY THEMES

In previous chapters trade between nations was motivated by their differences in *factor productivity* or in *relative factor endowments*. The type of trade which occurred, for example of food for manufactures, is based on comparative advantage and is called *interindustry trade*. This chapter introduces trade based on *economies of scale in production*. Such trade in similar productions is called *intraindustry trade*, and describes, for example, the trading of one type of manufactured good for another type of manufactured good. The chapter shows that trade can occur when there are no technological or endowment differences, but when there are economies of scale or increasing returns in production.

Economies of scale can either take the form of: 1) *external economies* whereby the cost per unit depends on the size of the industry but not necessarily on the size of the firm; or 2) *internal economies*, whereby the production cost per unit of output depends on the size of the individual firm but not necessarily on the size of the industry. Internal economies of scale give rise to imperfectly competitive markets: this departs from the assumption of perfectly competitive market structures made in earlier chapters. Forms of imperfect competition include monopoly and monopolistic competition.

In markets described by *monopolistic competition* there are a number of firms in an industry, each of which produces a "differentiated product" meaning that the product of one firm can be distinguished from the products of rival firms in the industry. Demand for a firm's good depends on the number of other similar products available and their prices. This type of model is useful for illustrating that trade improves the trade-off between scale and variety available to a country. In an industry described by monopolistic competition, a larger market -- such as that which arises through international trade-- lowers average price (by increasing production and lowering average costs) and makes available for consumption a greater range of goods. You should spend some time becoming comfortable with the equilibrium concepts associated with imperfectly competitive markets. The equilibrium conditions related the average cost of production in a typical firm and the price to be charged for the good to the number of firms in the industry Using the equations presented in the text, you can derive the equilibrium price and number of firms in an industry by setting price equal to average costs. Some of the review questions enable you to practice using these tools.

Given the predictions of models of international trade under imperfectly competitive markets, you can compare the distributional effects of trade when motivated by comparative advantage with those when trade is motivated by increasing returns to scale in production. When countries are similar in their factor endowments, and when scale economies and product differentiation are important, the income distributional effects of trade will be small. You should go through the thought exercises suggested in earlier chapters to convince yourself of this point.

Another important issue related to imperfectly competitive markets is the practice of price discrimination, namely charging customers in different markets different prices. One particularly controversial form of price discrimination is *dumping*, whereby a firm charges lower prices for exported goods than for goods sold domestically. This can occur only when domestic and foreign markets are segmented (domestic consumers can not easily purchase goods intended for export). The economics of dumping are illustrated in the text using the example of an industry which contains a single monopolistic firm selling in the domestic and foreign market. Reverse dumping can also occur, whereby a producer sells a product at lower prices in the domestic market than in the foreign market. While there is no good economic justification for the view that dumping is harmful, it is often viewed as an unfair trade practice.

The discussion has concentrated on the implications of *internal* economies of scale. The other type of economies of scale, *external* economies, has very different economic implications than internal economies. Since external economies of scale occur at the industry level rather than the firm level, it is possible for there to be many small competitors in an industry, in contrast to the structure which develops under internal economies of scale. This implies that, while models of imperfect competition may be appropriate for industries with internal economies of scale, the models of perfectly competitive markets may be more appropriate in markets characterized by external economies of scale Under external economies, trade may not be beneficial to all countries and there may be some justification for protectionism. Dynamic scale economies, which arise when unit production costs fall with cumulative production over time, rather than with current levels of production, also provide a potential justification for protectionism.

KEY TERMS

Define the following key terms:

1. Imperfect Competition _____

_____

_____

_____.

2. Intraindustry Trade _____

_____

_____

_____

3. Internal Economies of Scale _____

_____

_____

_____.

4. Price Discrimination _____

_____

_____

_____.

5. Infant Industry Argument _____

_____

_____

_____.

REVIEW QUESTIONS

1.   A downward sloping average cost curve reflects economies of scale since increased
      output of the firm lowers it's unit costs.

   a. Given that the firm's fixed costs are $20 and the marginal cost of production is $2 per
      unit, how do average costs change as production increases from 5 to 10 to 20 to 40
      units?

      _____

      _____

      _____.

b. Discuss the intuition behind your response to part a.

_____

_____

_____.

c. In the figure below, graph the relationship between output, and average and marginal costs.

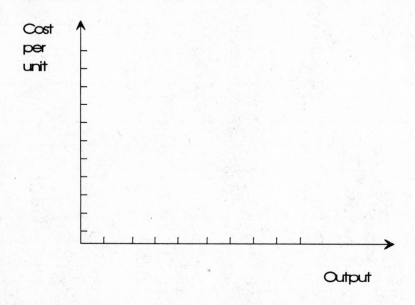

d. As output gets extremely large, what happens to average cost? Why?

_____

_____

_____.

e. What is the relationship between average cost and the number of firms in an industry?

_____

_____

_____.

2. Consider the production decision of a high-end producer of VCRs who behaves as a monopolistic competitor facing a demand curve with parameter b=1/8000. Fixed costs are $4,000,000 and the marginal cost of producing a VCR is $800. Suppose Home has annual VCR sales of 500,000 units.

a. Graph the PP and CC curves for the Home VCR industry.

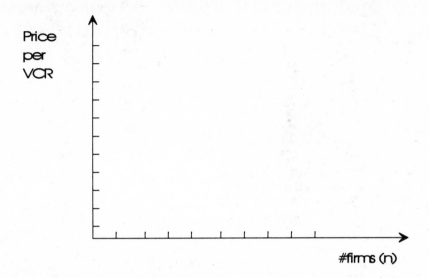

b. Discuss the significance of the PP and CC curves.

_____

_____

_____.

c. In the absence of trade, how many firms will produce VCRs?

_____

_____

_____.

d. What will be the profit of each of these firms?

_____

_____

_____.

e. What is the economic significance of points to the left of the PP/CC intersection?

_____

_____

_____.

3.   Assume that the monopolistic competitor produces tractors. He incurs fixed production costs of $120,000,000 and marginal costs of $8,000. The demand parameter is b=1/40,000. The total annual tractor sales in the Home market is 600,000 units.

a. Graph the PP and CC curves for the Home tractor industry.

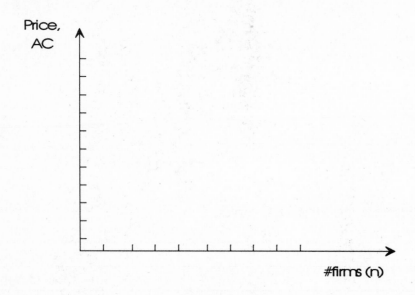

b. How many tractor firms will exist in equilibrium? What will be the equilibrium price of a tractor?

_____

_____

_____.

c. Confirm that this is a long run equilibrium.

_____

_____

_____.

4. a . What conditions give rise to economies of scale in production?

_____

_____

_____

_____

_____

_____.

b. What is the justification for trade based on economies of scale in production?

_____

_____

_____.

c. Does your response depend on the form of economies of scale in production (i.e. internal or external)?

_____

_____

_____.

ANSWERS TO ODD-NUMBERED TEXTBOOK PROBLEMS

1.   Cases *a* and *d* reflect external economies of scale since concentration of the production of an industry in a few locations reduces the industry's costs even when the scale of operation of individual firms remains small. External economies need not lead to imperfect competition. The benefits of geographical concentration may include a greater variety of specialized services to support industry operations and larger labor markets or thicker input markets. Cases *b* and *c* reflect internal economies of scale and occur at the level of the individual firm. The larger the output of a product by a particular firm, the lower its average costs. This leads to imperfect competition as in petrochemicals, aircraft and autos.

3.   By concentrating the production of each good with economies of scale in one country rather than spreading the production over several countries, the world economy will use the same amount of labor to produce more output. In the monopolistic competition model, such a concentration of labor benefits the host country, which can also capture some monopoly rents, while it may hurt the rest of the world which could then face higher prices on its consumption goods. In the external economies case, such monopolistic pricing behavior is less likely since imperfectly competitive markets are less likely.

5. a. The relatively few locations for production suggest external economies of scale in production. If these operations are large, there may also be large internal economies of scale in production.

59

b. Since economies of scale are important in airplane production it tends to be concentrated in certain areas.

c. External economies exist in the area around Silicon Valley and Boston's route 128, as well as in the area of Japan where chips are produced.

d. "True" scotch whiskey can only come from Scotland. The production of scotch whiskey requires a technique known to skilled distillers who are concentrated in the region. Also, soil and climactic conditions are favorable for grains used in local scotch production. This reflects comparative advantage.

e. France has a particular blend of climactic conditions and land that is difficult to reproduce elsewhere. This generates a comparative advantage in wine production.

7. The Japanese producers are price discriminating across United States and Japanese markets, so that the goods sold in the United States are much cheaper than those sold in Japan. It may be profitable for other Japanese to purchase these goods in the United States, incur any tariffs and transportation costs, and resell the goods in Japan. Clearly, the price differential across markets must be nontrivial for this to be profitable.

CHAPTER 7

International Factor Movements

CHAPTER ORGANIZATION

International Labor Mobility
    A One-Good Model without Factor Mobility
    International Labor Movement
    Extending the Analysis
    Box: International Labor Mobility in Practice: "Guest Workers" in Europe
International Borrowing and Lending
    Intertemporal Production Possibilities and Trade
    The Real Interest Rate
    Intertemporal Comparative Advantage
    Box: Changes in the Pattern of Capital Movements in the 1980s
Direct Foreign Investment and Multinational Firms
    The Theory of Multinational Enterprise
    Multinational Firms in Practice
    Case Study: Foreign Direct Investment in the United States
Appendix to Chapter 7: More on Intertemporal Trade

KEY THEMES

Trade in goods and services reflects one form of financial integration. This chapter introduces an additional aspect of economic integration, international factor movements, most notably labor and financial capital mobility across countries. Among the most important points emphasized in this chapter is that many of the same forces which trigger international trade in goods between countries, will, if permitted, trigger international flows of labor and finances. The chapter proceeds in three main sections. First, it presents a simple model of international labor mobility. Next, it analyzes intertemporal production and consumption decisions in the context of international borrowing and lending. Finally, it considers the role of multinational corporations in economic integration.

To demonstrate the forces behind international labor mobility, the chapter begins with a model which is quite similar to that presented in chapter 3. In each country of the world, the real return to labor, is equal to its marginal product. There are perfectly competitive markets in each of two countries which produce one good using two factors of production. Labor relocates until its marginal product is equalized across countries. While the redistribution of labor increases world output and provides overall gains, it also has important income distribution effects. Workers in the country that originally had higher wages are made worse off since wages fall with the inflow of additional workers; workers in the originally low wage country are made better off.

While labor mobility influences the levels of current production between countries, the analysis of international capital mobility influences consumption and production tradeoffs between current and future periods. An analysis of international capital movements involves the consideration of intertemporal trade. Analogous to the way in which real wage differentials were used to motivate the international mobility of workers, the important point here is that differences in the real rate of interest across countries motivates the international mobility of capital. These international factor movements provide gains to both borrowers and lenders.

When considering international capital mobility, instead of choosing between consumption of goods at any point in time, the analysis focuses on a one good world where the choice at a point in time is between future and present consumption. There is now a clear parallel to be drawn with the standard trade model developed in Chapter 5. Once international borrowing and lending is introduced, the relative price of future consumption is determined (which implies that the real interest rate is also determined) by the world relative demand for and supply of future consumption. An intertemporal production possibilities frontier replaces the PPF and the intertemporal price line replaces the relative price line. With these tools one can analyze the gains from intertemporal trade, the size of borrowing and lending, and the effects of taxes on capital transfers using techniques similar to those presented in previous chapters. (The appendix presents this model in greater detail.)

The final issue addressed in this chapter concerns the motives for and the effects of direct foreign investment and multinational firms. Direct foreign investment differs from the other types of capital transfers discussed above in that it involves the acquisition of control of a company. While the theory of multinational firms is not well developed, some of the key points of existing theory are that decisions concerning multinationals are based upon concerns involving a) location and b) internalization. Location decisions are based upon barriers to trade and transportation costs. Internalization decisions focus on vertical integration and technology transfers. Multinationals facilitate shifts in factors of production such that factor prices move in the direction which free trade would cause. One politically charged issue related to foreign direct investment is the associated income distributional effects. This theme is considered in further detail in Chapter 11 when the discussion specifically focuses on less developed countries (LDCs).

KEY TERMS

Define the following key terms:

1. Intertemporal Production Possibility Frontier _____
_____
_____
_____.

2. Real Interest Rate _____
_____
_____
_____.

3. Direct Foreign Investment _____
_____
_____
_____.

4. Technology Transfer _____
_____
_____
_____.

5. Vertical Integration _____
_____
_____
_____.

1. Assume that the Home country produces one good, food, using two factors of production, land and labor.

    a. Holding the supply of land fixed, what would the typical production function for food look like?

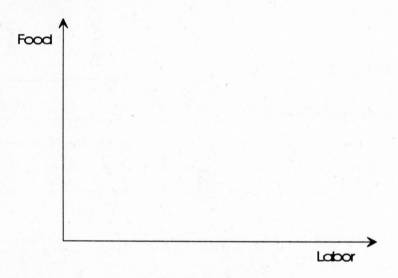

    b. Why is the production function shaped as it is?

    _____
    _____
    _____.

    c. Suppose that the marginal productivity of labor is described by the table below.

Labor	Marginal Product
1	$12
2	10
3	8
4	6
5	4
6	2

What does the real wage of labor depend upon?

_____

_____

_____.

d. If a landlord employs 2 workers on his land, what will be his wage bill? How could you determine the rent earned by the landlord?

_____

_____

_____.

e. How does the real wage, total wage bill and rental bill change if 4 more workers are hired?

_____

_____

_____.

2. Suppose the world consists of two countries, Home and Foreign, each of which have two factors of production, land and labor, and produce only one good, food. Consequently, trade is limited to the movement of labor between the two countries. Assume that Home is land abundant and Foreign is labor abundant. The figure below describes the MPL of each work force. The distance OO* represents the sum of the work-forces of the two countries.

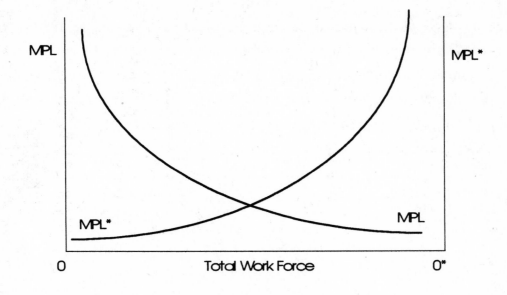

a. When would labor have an incentive to move between countries? Explain your answer.

_____

_____

_____.

b. Given that Home has a smaller work-force and hence higher MPL than Foreign, what would the initial allocation of labor look like in this figure?

_____

_____

_____.

c. If labor is permitted to move across borders, what would be the equilibrium allocation of labor, wages and labor marginal product in each country?

_____

_____

_____.

d. Who are the winners and losers when labor is permitted to move across countries?

_____

_____

_____.

3.   Consider the intertemporal production possibility frontier faced by most nations.

a. A common topic of discussion in the context of the Debt Crisis of the 1980s is the comparison between the Latin American debtors, often described as having squandered their borrowings on luxury and consumption goods, and the nations of Southeast Asia, often described as having invested their money wisely in future capacity. What does this statement imply about the position of each region on the intertemporal frontier?

_____

_____

_____.

b. Given the bias of each of these regions toward present versus future output, draw realistic intertemporal PPFs for each region.

Future consumption	SouthEast Asia		Latin America

Present Consumption C0   Present Consumption C0

c. In which country would you expect the relative price of future consumption to be higher?

_____
_____
_____.

d. What type of "trade pattern" would these differences in "prices" suggest?

_____
_____
_____.

e. Can you think of any other reasons why Latin American countries might be charged higher interest rates for their credit than Asian nations ?

_____
_____
_____.

4.   Which of the following represents direct foreign investment?

a. McDonald's corporation sets up a subsidiary in Moscow.

_____.

b. Canadian investor Campeau acquires the Bloomingdale's chain.

_____.

c. Japanese investors purchase a large share in Rockefeller Center in New York City.

_____.

d. The International Monetary Fund grants Russia $1 billion in aid.

_____.

e. The Union Carbide Corporation sets up a chemical manufacturing plant in India.

_____.

5.   How does direct investment differ from international borrowing and lending?

_____

_____

_____

_____

_____

_____.

6.   Discuss the following statement: Direct foreign investment can often achieve the same goals as international lending, so nations should be indifferent between the two methods of international transfers of funds.

_____

_____

_____

_____

_____

_____.

ANSWERS TO ODD-NUMBERED TEXTBOOK PROBLEMS

1.   The marginal product of labor in Home is 10 and in Foreign is 18. Wages are higher in Foreign, so workers migrate there to the point where the marginal product in both Home and Foreign is equated. This occurs when there are 7 workers in each country, and the marginal product of labor in each country is 14.

3.   The analogy between international borrowing and lending and ordinary international

trade can be made most directly by first introducing the concept of intertemporal trade. The analysis of intertemporal trade follows directly the analysis of trade of two goods. Substitute "future consumption" and "present consumption" for "cloth" and "food". The relevant relative price is the cost of future consumption compared to present consumption, which is the inverse of the real interest rate. Countries in which present consumption is relatively cheap (which have low real interest rates) will "export" present consumption (i.e. lend) to countries in which present consumption is relatively dear (which have high real interest rates). The equilibrium real interest rate after borrowing and lending occur lies between that found in each country before borrowing and lending take place. Gains from borrowing and lending are analogous to gains from trade--there is greater efficiency in the production of goods intertemporally.

5. a. $10 million is not controlling interest in IBM, so this does not qualify as direct foreign investment. It is international portfolio diversification.

   b. This is direct foreign investment if one considers the apartment building a business which pays returns in terms of rents.

   c. Unless particular U.S. shareholders will not have control over the new French company this will not be direct foreign investment.

   d. This is not direct foreign investment since the Italian company is an "employee", but not the ones which ultimately control, the company.

CHAPTER 8

ECONOMIC GEOGRAPHY

CHAPTER ORGANIZATION

What is a Country?
>How Governments Create National Economies
>From International to Interregional Trade
>Box: Food Wars in Europe

Comparing Regions and Nations
>Specialization and Trade
>Factor Mobility

Problems of Regional Economics
>Absolute versus Comparative Advantage
>Box: Anatomy of a Declining Region
>Uneven Development

KEY THEMES

Events of the past few years have dramatically demonstrated how national boundaries change. We have seen the creation of new national boundaries with the break-up of one country into separate sovereign states (as in the former Soviet Union or the former Czechoslovakia). We have also seen the disappearance of a national boundary as the former East Germany and the former West Germany were re-unified. In the former case, trade that was conducted within a country is now international trade while in the latter case, trade that had been classified as international is now taking place within one country. At a somewhat less dramatic level, trade agreements among countries, such as the North American Free Trade Agreement ("N.A.F.T.A.") or the Single European Act ("EC 1992") also make the distinction between regions and nations less clear.

The analysis developed in earlier chapters on international trade and patterns of international specialization is used in this chapter to address regional economic issues. The pattern of economic specialization may have little to do with political boundaries. There is often a closer economic profile between adjacent parts of different countries than between distant regions of the same country. Governments do have a potentially important influence, however, on the pattern of trade and specialization. Barriers to trade which are either explicit (such as tariffs or quotas) or less well-defined (such as national standards or regulations) influence the type and size of industries within a nation's regions. Government policies, national traditions and national institutions also make trade within nations easier to conduct than international trade. More extensive labor mobility within a nation than across nations also contributes to the greater economic integration across national regions than across nations.

Still, the difference between analyzing the economics of regions and the economics of nations is one of degree and not one of kind. This means that we can use the tools of international trade to address issues such as why regions specialize and why industries tend to cluster in a few areas. An important factor in regional specialization is the presence of economies of scale (or of external economies) which tend to make industries concentrate in a region. Transport cost (which broadly defined can include any types of impediments or barriers to trade) increase the incentive for industries to set up production near their markets and thus reduce the tendency of an industry to concentrate in only one region. Thus lower transport costs and more pronounced economies of scale or external economies contribute to geographic concentration and specialization.

Once the process of regional specialization begins it may take on its own dynamic and become self-reinforcing. This is called *cumulative causation*. Cumulative causation magnifies the effects of initial small advantages to the point where there is a high degree of specialization. The text provides an example where the location decision of a firm depends upon the location decision of other firms. The outcome of this example is that concentration in either of the two locations, once established, will be self-sustaining.

The self-reinforcing nature of regional development, as well as the importance of absolute rather than comparative advantage when factors of production are mobile across regions, raises the possibility of uneven development. Regional decline may be offset, at a national level, by the growth of other areas. At a less aggregate level, transfers which would compensate those in the declining region, which in theory could be made, in practice are seldom realized. Those left behind in the declining region suffer losses. Also, countries value their regional traditions as a part of the mosaic of their national identity. The cumulative causation mentioned above suggests that once regional decline begins it is difficult to reverse. On the other hand, the case of the United States where concentration has declined suggests that the forces that contribute to uneven development may not be as strong as they once were. Economies of scale may be less important and transport costs may be lower than in the past.

71

Define the following key terms:

1. Interregional Trade_____
_____
_____
_____.

2. Regional Economics_____
_____
_____
_____.

3. Barriers to Trade_____
_____
_____
_____.

4. Absolute Advantage_____
_____
_____
_____.

5. Uneven Development _____
_____
_____
_____.

6. Cumulative Causation_____
_____
_____
_____.

7. Agglomeration Economies_____
_____
_____
_____.

REVIEW PROBLEMS

1. In each of the following, circle whether the listed factors would tend to lead to more concentration or more dispersion of an industry. Briefly explain your answer.

a. (More dispersion / More concentration) would occur in the production of high-technology goods as the production process becomes more routine and standardized because _____
_____.

b. (More dispersion / More concentration) would occur in the metal fabrication industry as the rail lines and highways of a country become more extensive and better developed because_____
_____.

c. (More dispersion / More concentration) would occur in the aircraft industry as firms learn to take advantage of economies of scale because _____
_____.

d. (More dispersion / More concentration) would occur in the financial service sector with the development of FAX transmission and a nationwide "computer highway" because
_____
_____.

e. (More dispersion / More concentration) would occur in the European automobile industry with the easing of carrying goods across borders because of "1992" since
_____
_____.

2. In the book *Geography and Trade* (MIT Press, 1991; see the further readings at the end of the chapter) Paul Krugman proposes a way to measure regional or national divergence using employment data. Define $s_{1,A}$ as the share of manufacturing workers in industry 1 in region A as a proportion of all manufacturing workers in region A, $s_{2,A}$ as the share of workers in industry 2, etc. Also define $s_{1,B}$ as the share of workers in industry 1 in region B as a proportion of all manufacturing workers in region B, $s_{2,B}$ as the share of workers in industry 2, etc. Then the index of divergence between two regions is the sum of the absolute value of $(s_{1,A} - s_{1,B})$ plus the absolute value of $(s_{2,A} - s_{2,B})$, etc.

a. Suppose that we have two regions of a country, its North and its South. There are two industrial goods produced in that country, automobiles and bricks. Use Krugman's method to calculate the index of regional divergence under the three following circumstances;

Case I

Region	Automobile Workers	Brick Workers	Total Workers	Share of Workers in Production of Autos	Bricks
North	8 million	4 million	12 million	_____	_____
South	2 million	1 million	3 million	_____	_____

Case I: Regional Divergence Index = _____

Case II

Region	Automobile Workers	Brick Workers	Total Workers	Share of Workers in Production of Autos	Bricks
North	12 million	0	12 million	_____	_____
South	0	3 million	3 million	_____	_____

Case II: Regional Divergence Index = _____

Case III

Region	Automobile Workers	Brick Workers	Total Workers	Share of Workers in Production of Autos	Bricks
North	8 million	4 million	12 million	_____	_____
South	1 million	2 million	3 million	_____	_____

Case III: Regional Divergence Index = _____

b. Complete the following by filling in the blanks or circling the appropriate words:
The maximum value that the Regional Divergence Index can take is _____. The minimum value that the it can take is _____. These maximum and minimum values (do / do not) depend upon the number of industries used in the analysis. A larger value for the index implies that regions are (more similar / more different) in their industrial structure.

3. In *Geography and Trade*, Paul Krugman calculates regional divergence indices across the United States and between the United States and Europe (see question 2 above for a description of these indices). The following charts present the regional divergence indices for the United States in 1947 and in 1985 (in these charts, NE means Northeast, MW means Midwest, W means West and S means South).

1947

	NE	S	W
MW	.36	.61	.44
NE	---	.56	.50
S	---	---	.40

1985

	NE	S	W
MW	.22	.34	.18
NE	---	.25	.24
S	---	---	.27

a. The two regions that are the most similar in 1947 are _____ and _____. The two regions that are most dissimilar are _____ and _____.

b. The two regions that are the most similar in 1985 are _____ and _____.

The two regions that are most dissimilar are _____ and _____.

c. In general, the pattern of these indices across time shows (increasing / decreasing) regional differences. Some possible reasons for this include:

_____

_____

_____.

d. Krugman also presents an index of national divergence for four European countries: France (FR), West Germany (WG), Italy (IT) and the United Kingdom (UK) in 1985. The table of the national divergence indices for these countries is as follows;

European Countries, 1985

	WG	IT	UK
FR	.20	.20	.08
WG	---	.18	.18
IT	---	---	.18

Complete the following:

While it is difficult to directly compare the set of indices for Europe and for the United States, the pattern of divergence for the four European countries in 1985 and for the four regions of the United States in 1985 suggests that (the European countries / the regions of the United States) are more diversified. A possible reason for this is:

_____

_____.

4. The country of Floria has two states; Daisy and Rose. Everyone of the 12 million workers who live in Floria either works in agriculture or in factories. Agricultural workers, who grow flowers, are immobile while factory workers, who produce perfume, will move to wherever the factories are located. A factory in a particular region can costlessly transport perfume to consumers in that region, but must pay a shipping cost to send perfume to a consumer in the other region. The total sales of perfume from your factory will be 12 million bottles since each worker will purchase one bottle of perfume. Use the information below to decide whether to build one factory or two and in which region to to locate your factory. Base this decision on

minimizing the shipping costs or, if you build two factories, the additional cost of a second factory.

a. Suppose that there are 9 million flower growers split evenly between Daisy and Rose and transportation costs of shipping a bottle of perfume to the other region is $1 per bottle. The cost of building a second factory is an additional $5 million.

    i. Complete the following table if all factories are located in Daisy:

	In Daisy	In Rose
Sales to Farmers	_____	_____
Sales to Factory Workers	_____	_____
Shipping cost if locate factory in:	_____	_____

Location Decision:_____

    ii. Complete the following table if half of all factories are located in each region:

	In Daisy	In Rose
Sales to Farmers	_____	_____
Sales to Factory Workers	_____	_____
Shipping cost if locate factory in:	_____	_____

Location Decision: _____

b. Now suppose that advances in perfume-shipping-technology lower transportation costs to $0.50 per bottle, but all else is as described above.

    i. Complete the following table if all factories are located in Daisy:

	In Daisy	In Rose
Shipping cost if locate factory in:	_____	_____

Location Decision:_____

ii. Complete the following table if half of all factories are located in each region:

	In Daisy	In Rose
Shipping cost if locate factory in:	_____	_____

Location Decision: _____

iii. What do your answers imply about the effect of transportation costs on location decisions?_____

_____.

c. Now suppose that perfume production is made more routine and economies of scale fall. The cost of producing 12 million bottles of perfume in one factory is now only $2 million more than building two factories, each of which produces 6 million bottles of perfume. As in part (b), continue to assume that shipping costs are $0.50 per bottle. Do your location decisions in part (b) change in this case?

_____

_____.

What does your answers imply about the effect of economies of scale on location decisions?_____

_____.

ANSWERS TO ODD-NUMBERED PROBLEMS IN THE TEXT

1. Independence for Quebec may make trade between it and the rest of Canada more difficult than is presently the case. If Quebec becomes independent it would likely create its own currency and the uncertainty and risk that would then arise due to movements between the Canadian dollar and the Quebec currency would inhibit trade. French-language requirements in Canada might be relaxed if Quebec seceded, which would lead to a divergence in the language abilities of citizens of Quebec and citizens of what remained of Canada, which would further inhibit trade. Also, trade restrictions put in place by Quebec or the rest of Canada would inhibit trade, as would the possible divergence in national standards between Quebec and the other provinces that constitute Canada.

3. a. This problem can be solved using the analytical methods presented in Chapter 2. California has a comparative advantage in the production of wine while Nebraska has a comparative advantage in the production of cattle. The relative supply schedule is horizontal from 0 to 1 at the relative price $P_c/P_w = 1/5$, is vertical at the relative supply $Q_c/Q_w = 1$ from $P_c/P_w = 1/5$ to $P_c/P_w = 2$ and is horizontal again at $P_c/P_w = 2$ from $Q_c/Q_w = 1$ onwards. Setting demand equal to supply we find that the demand curve intersects the supply schedule at the relative price $P_c/P_w = 1/5$, and at the relative supply $Q_c/Q_w = 1/2$. At this point, California specializes in wine production and produces 1 million gallons of wine. Nebraska produces both wine and cattle. To determine the amount of wine production and cattle production in Nebraska, we use the fact that $Q_c/Q_w = 1/2$ and the unit labor requirements in Nebraska. Denoting labor used in producing cows in Nebraska as $L_{c,N}$, we solve $(L_{c,N}/1)/(1+[(1-L_{c,N})/5]) = 1/2$ which shows that the 6/11 of the labor force in Nebraska is in cattle production while 5/11 is in wine production. Solving this, and using the unit labor requirements, we find that Nebraska produces 6/11 million cows and 1/11 million gallons of wine. Thus, Nebraska exports cattle to California and imports wine from California.

b. If labor is mobile between the two regions then the climatic advantages dictates that absolute advantage determines where production occurs; California will produce wine and Nebraska will produce cattle. Labor mobility also insures that wages are equal in the two regions; therefore, then $P_c/a_{Lc} = P_w/a_{Lw}$. Since the unit labor requirements for wine in California and cattle in Nebraska are equal, the prices of cattle and wine must also be equal. Substituting the price ratio of 1 into the relative demand equation we find that $Q_c/Q_w = 1/10$. Since the unit labor requirements for both goods in this case are 1, we can find the number of workers in the production of cattle by solving $L_c/2 - L_c = 1/10$. This results in 2/11 of the total amount of workers (about 364,000) in cattle production in Nebraska and the remainder in the production of wine in California.

c. When workers are mobile, absolute advantage determines where production occurs; in this case, Nebraska produces both cattle and wine in the answer to (a) but only cattle in the answer to (b). Labor mobility leads to out-migration from Nebraska to California in this case.

5. a. We can construct the following tables:

Regional Sales

	Sales in East	Sales in West	Total Sales
All firms in East	5.5	4.5	10
All firms in West	1.5	8.5	10

Costs of Shipping

	Cost if Factory in East	Cost if Factory in West
All other factories in East	$4.5 million	$5.5 million
All other factories in West	$8.5 million	$1.5 million

If all other firms locate in the East, the low-cost production location is the East; likewise, if all other firms locate in the West, the low-cost production location is the West. Therefore, these are both self-sustaining outcomes.

b. The outcome that all firms locate in the West is a better outcome since less of the economies resources would be devoted to transportation costs.

OVERVIEW OF SECTION II: INTERNATIONAL TRADE POLICY

The second part of the textbook, Section II, has four chapters:

Chapter 9   The Instruments of Trade Policy
Chapter 10   The Political Economy of Trade Policy
Chapter 11   Trade Policy in Developing Countries
Chapter 12   Industrial Policy in Advanced Countries

Section II Overview: Trade policy issues figure prominently in current political debates and public policy discussions. The first two chapters of this section of the text introduce you to the instruments of trade policy and the arguments for free trade and managed trade. The second two chapters of this section consider the usefulness of trade policies in the context of specific sets of countries that face common problems. Throughout, the textbook presents a number of case studies which are real world examples that clearly illustrate the theoretical arguments.

Chapter 9 begins by defining various instruments of trade policy, including tariffs, quotas, export subsidies, voluntary export restraints and local content requirements. The effects of these policies on prices and trade volumes are determined. The chapter reviews the analytical tools of consumer and producer surplus, and uses these tools to consider the welfare effects of various protectionist measures. Specific incidents of trade restrictions are presented as case studies, including import quotas on sugar entering United States markets, voluntary export restraints on Japanese autos, and oil import quotas.

Chapter 10 presents the a set of ideas known as the political economy of trade theory. These ideas enable you to understand why certain trade restrictions exist, despite the force of general economic arguments which suggest that they reduce aggregate welfare. Possible motivations for trade restrictions are identified as those which increase national welfare, such as the optimum tariff, and those which foster either income redistribution or the preservation of status quo. While sometimes politically popular, these motivations for trade restrictions ignore the possibility of retaliation and usually fail tests based upon basic welfare analysis.

Chapter 11 considers the possible uses of trade policies to promote the growth of developing economies. The chapter reviews the relative successes of different development strategies, including import-substituting industrialization and programs of export promotion. The

81

phenomenon of economic dualism, referring to the coexistence of capital intensive industrial sectors and low wage traditional sectors, and of uneven development are considered. The chapter concludes with a discussion of the importance of multinational corporations and export cartels to developing countries.

Chapter 12 considers the theory and lessons from the history of industrial policy applications by developed economies. Industrial policy refers to the use of trade (and other) tools for channeling resources to sectors targeted for growth by industrial country governments. The first part of the chapter presents some commonly voiced arguments for intervention in particular sectors of the economy, and then shows how these arguments are critically flawed. The second part of the chapter introduces more sophisticated arguments for industrial policy. The most persuasive of these is the existence of some form of market failure. The chapter concludes by presenting a series of case studies on the use of industrial policy by developed countries.

CHAPTER 9

The Instruments of Trade Policy

CHAPTER ORGANIZATION

KEY THEMES

This chapter and the next three focus on international trade policy. These chapters will provided valuable insights into the causes of and implications of different types of protectionist policies. When you read newspapers you undoubtably see various arguments for and against restrictive trade practices in the media: some of these arguments are sound and some are clearly not grounded in fact. This chapter provides a framework for analyzing the economic effects of trade policies by describing the tools of trade policy and analyzing their effects on consumers and producers in domestic and foreign countries. Case studies discuss actual episodes of restrictive trade practices.

The analysis presented here takes a partial equilibrium view, focusing on demand and supply in one market, rather than the general equilibrium approach followed in previous chapters. Import demand and export supply curves are derived from domestic and foreign demand and supply curves. There are a number of trade policy instruments analyzed in this chapter using these tools. Some of the important instruments of trade policy include: *specific tariffs*, defined as taxes levied as a fixed charge for each unit of a good imported; *ad valorem tariffs*, levied as a fraction of the value of the imported good; *export subsidies*, which are payments given to a firm or industry that ships a good abroad; *import quotas*, which are direct restrictions on the quantity of some good that may be imported; *voluntary export restraints*, which are quotas on trading that are imposed by the exporting country instead of the importing country; and, *local content requirements* which are regulations that require that some specified fraction of a good is produced domestically.

The import supply and export demand analysis demonstrates that the imposition of a tariff drives a wedge between prices in domestic and foreign markets, and increases prices in the country imposing the tariff and lowers the price in the other country by less than the amount of the tariff. When you consider whether tariffs are actually achieving their goal of protecting produces, you must consider both the effects of tariffs on the final price of a good, and the effects of tariffs on the costs of inputs used in production. The actual protection provided by a tariff will not equal the tariff rate if imported intermediate goods are used in the production of the protected good. The proper measurement, *the effective rate of protection*, is described in the text and calculated for a sample problem.

The analysis of the costs and benefits of trade restrictions require tools of welfare analysis.

The text explains the essential tools of consumer and producer surplus. *Consumer surplus* on each unit sold is defined as the difference between the actual price and the amount that consumers would have been willing to pay for the product. Geometrically, consumer surplus is equal to the area under the demand curve and above the price of the good. Producer surplus is the difference between the minimum amount for which a producer is willing to sell his product and the price which he actually receives. Geometrically, producer surplus is equal to the area above the supply curve and below the price line. These concepts, along with measures of the consumption and production distortionary losses associated with tariffs and quotas, and the government revenues from tariff collection are shown in the figure below. Some of the problems in this chapter of the study guide provide the opportunity for you to practice these concepts for the case of the different tariffs, export subsidies, quotas and voluntary export restraints.

The costs of a tariff include distortionary efficiency losses in both consumption and production. A tariff provides gains from terms of trade improvement when and if it lowers the foreign export price. Summing the areas in a diagram of internal demand and supply provides a method for analyzing the net loss or gain from a tariff.

Other instruments of trade policy can be analyzed with this method. An export subsidy operates in exactly the reverse fashion of an import tariff. An import quota has similar effects as an import tariff upon prices and quantities but revenues, in the form of quota rents, accrue to foreign producers of the protected good. Voluntary export restraints are a form of quotas in which import licenses are held by foreign governments. Local content requirements raise the price of imports and domestic goods and do not result in either government revenue or quota rents.

Throughout the chapter the analysis of different trade restrictions are illustrated by drawing upon specific episodes. Europe's common agricultural policy provides and example of export subsidies in action. Voluntary export restraints are discussed in the context of Japanese auto sales to the U.S. The oil import quota in the U.S. in the 1960's provides an example of a local content scheme.

The United States often criticizes countries like Japan for restrictions imposed on imports of United States agricultural products. However, the United States also protects many of its industries. In the textbook, the case study corresponding to quotas describes trade restrictions on U.S. sugar imports.

Another example of quotas in the United States occurs in the peanut market. The United States maintains a federal program that limits the number of farmers who can sell peanuts in the United States and comes close to forbidding the import of peanuts. The government provides assurances to farmers that their production costs will be recovered each year, and also sees to it that the minimum quota price for the quota peanuts is about 50 percent higher than peanut prices in world markets. This reaps tremendous gains to peanut farmers at the expense of much higher prices on goods such as peanut butter and peanut oils.

There are two appendices to this chapter. Appendix I uses a general equilibrium framework to analyze the impact of a tariff, departing from the partial equilibrium approach taken in the chapter. When a small country imposes a tariff, it shifts production away from its exported good and toward the imported good. Consumption shifts toward the domestically produced goods. Both the volume of trade and welfare of the country declines. A large country imposing a tariff can improve its terms of trade by an amount potentially large enough to offset the production and consumption distortions. For a large country, a tariff may be welfare improving.

Appendix II discusses tariffs and import quotas in the presence of a domestic monopoly. Free trade eliminates the monopoly power of a domestic producer and the monopolist mimics the actions of a firm in a perfectly competitive market, setting output such that marginal cost equals world price. A tariff raises domestic price. The monopolist, still facing a perfectly elastic demand curve, sets output such that marginal cost equals internal price. A monopolist faces a downward sloping demand curve under a quota. A quota is not equivalent to a tariff in this case. Domestic production is lower and internal price higher when a particular level of imports is obtained through the imposition of a quota rather than a tariff.

KEY TERMS

Define the following key terms:

1. Consumer Surplus _____

_____

_____

_____.

2. Production Distortion Loss _____

_____

_____

_____.

3. Consumption Distortion Loss _____

_____

_____

_____.

4. Terms of Trade Gain _____

_____

_____

_____.

5. Effective Rate of Protection _____

_____

_____

_____.

REVIEW QUESTIONS

1.   Provided below is a chart of the Home country's domestic supply of and demand for wine at various price levels. Using this information, construct the Home country's import demand curve for wine. (Remember: the Home import demand is the excess of what Home consumers demand over what Home producers supply.)

Price per bottle	Demand	Supply	Home Import Demand
$ 5	95	25	_____
10	90	30	_____
15	70	50	_____
20	60	60	_____

87

2. Suppose a country, Home, wants to encourage the development of high resolution wide screen televisions. These are currently quite expensive, priced at $6500 per television. The component used in making such televisions cost $3000. Similar Foreign televisions can be imported at the world market price of $5000.

   a. Using an infant industry argument which claims that domestic manufacturers should be protected from foreign competition, would you recommend an ad valorem tariff? How large should it be?

   _____

   _____

   _____.

   b. At this level of tariff, what is the effective rate of protection on assembly of domestic high resolution televisions?

   _____

   _____

   _____.

   c. Who are the winners and who are the losers from this protection?

   _____

   _____

   _____.

3. Suppose that Home imports vodka from Foreign at a world price of $12 per bottle. The figure on the next page depicts the importing country's market for vodka.

   a. If Home decides to place a tariff on vodka imports such that it raises the domestic price to $15 and lowers the Foreign export price to $9, what is the impact on Home production and consumption?

   _____

   _____

   _____.

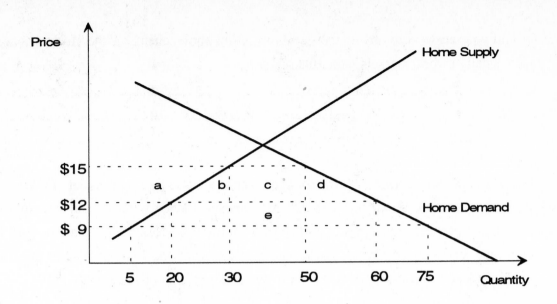

b. How are the benefits and costs of this tariff distributed among consumers and producers?

_____

_____

_____.

c. Assuming that the government is able to collect the full tariff revenues, calculate the direct government receipts from the tariff. Show this area on the preceding graph.

_____

_____

_____.

d. Suppose that vodka drinking consumers lobby against this restriction, but the government is unable to appeal the legislation. What other policy alternatives are available to the government?

_____

_____

_____.

e. Would your answers to any of the questions asked above change if the Home country were small in world markets rather than large?

_____

_____

_____.

4. Suppose that Home exports 50 tractors per year at a world trading price of $6000. The Home government, seeking to expand the domestic tractor industry and its exports, places a 15 percent ad valorem export subsidy on tractors. This results in an increase in the Home price of tractors to $6450 and a lowering of the Foreign market price to $5550. The figure below depicts the exporting country's tractor market.

a. Why doesn't the new price for tractors at home fully reflect the export subsidy?

_____

_____

_____.

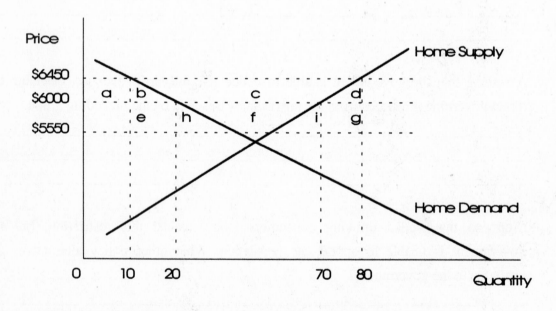

b. How are Home production and exports affected by the export subsidy?

_____

_____

_____.

c. What is the impact of the export subsidy on consumer surplus? producer surplus? government revenues?

_____

_____

_____.

d. In terms of the graph above, which areas depict consumer surplus, producer surplus, and government revenues?

_____

_____

_____.

e. What is the effect of the export subsidy on the Home terms of trade?

_____

_____

_____.

5. Suppose that the Home country wants to protect the domestic cheese industry. It imposes a quota on the import of cheese. Since we observe that the world supply of cheese is higher elastic, this implies that the Home country is small in would markets. Let the world price of cheese equal $3.60 per pound and the Home (guaranteed) support price is equal to $5.40 per pound. This implies that the right (license) to sell cheese in the Home market is worth $1.80 per pound ($5.40-$3.60). The Home cheese market is depicted in the figure below.

a. Compare the imports of cheese under free trade with the imports under this quota system.

_____

_____

_____.

b. In terms of the graph, what areas measure the changes of producer surplus and consumer surplus in Home markets?

_____

_____

_____.

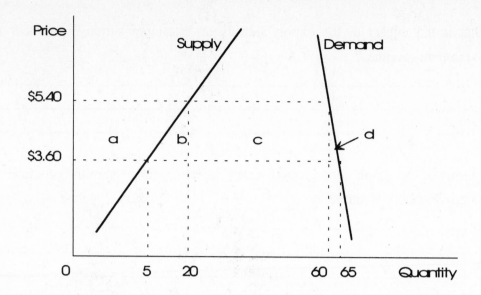

c. One way in which the imposition of a quota differs from that of a tariff is that, under a quota the quota revenues are collected by the holders of import licenses. Show the value of these quota rents in the graph.

ANSWERS TO ODD-NUMBERED TEXTBOOK PROBLEMS

1. The import demand equation, MD, is found by subtracting the home supply equation from the home demand equation. This results in MD = 80 - 40*P. Without trade, domestic prices and quantities adjust such that import demand is zero. Thus, the price in the absence of trade is 2.

3. a. The new MD curve is 80 - 40 * (P+t) where t is the specific tariff rate, equal to 0.5. (Note: in solving these problems you should be careful about whether a specific tariff or ad valorem tariff is imposed. With an ad valorem tariff, the MD equation would be expressed as MD=80-40*(1+t)p). The equation for the export supply curve by the foreign country is unchanged. Solving, we find that the world price is $1.25, and thus the internal price at home is $1.75. The volume of trade has been reduced to 10, and the total demand for wheat at home has fallen to 65 (from the free trade level of 70) while the total demand for wheat in Foreign has fallen to 55.

   b. and c. The welfare of the home country is best studied using the combined numerical and graphical solutions shown below.

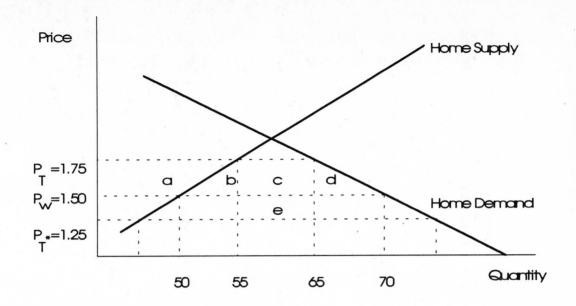

a: 55(1.75-1.50) -.5(55-50)(1.75-1.50)=13.125

b: .5(55-50)(1.75-1.50)=0.625

c: (65-55)(1.75-1.50)=2.50

d: .5(70-65)(1.75-1.50)=0.625

e: (65-55)(1.50-1.25)=2.50

Consumer surplus change: -(a+b+c+d)=-16.875. Producer surplus change: a=13.125. Government revenue change: c+e=5. Efficiency losses b+d are exceeded by terms of trade gain e. [Note: in the calculations for the a, b and d areas a figure of .5 shows up. This is because we are measuring the area of a triangle, which is one half of the area of the rectangle defined by the product of the horizontal and vertical sides.]

5.   The effective rate of protection takes into consideration the costs of imported intermediate goods. In this example, half of the the cost of an aircraft represents components purchased from other countries. Without the subsidy the aircraft would cost $60 million. The European value added to the aircraft is $30 million. The subsidy cuts the cost of the value added to purchasers of the airplane to $20 million. Thus, the effective rate of protection is (30 - 20)/20 = 50%.

7.   At a price of $10 per bag of peanuts, Acirema imports 200 bags of peanuts. A quota limiting the import of peanuts to 50 bags has the following effect:
   a) The price of peanuts rises to $20 per bag.
   b) The quota rents are ($20 - $10) * 50 = $500.

c) The consumption distortion loss is .5 * 100 bags * $10 per bag = $500.

d) The production distortion loss is .5 * 50 bags * $10 per bag = $250.

CHAPTER 10

The Political Economy of Trade Policy

CHAPTER ORGANIZATION

KEY THEMES

While the models presented in preceding chapters generally suggest that free trade maximizes national welfare, it has been clearly shown that free trade has income distributional effects. In the real world we observe that most governments maintain some form of restrictive trade practices. This chapter investigates reasons for the existence of impediments to free trade despite the general view that these impediments reduce national welfare. One set of reasons for the existence of trade restrictions is concerned with the particular circumstances under which restrictive trade practices increase national welfare. Another set of reasons concerns the manner in which the interests of different groups are weighed by governments. The chapter concludes with a discussion of the motives for international trade negotiations and a brief history of international trade agreements.

One recurring theme in the arguments in favor of free trade is the emphasis on related efficiency gains. As illustrated by the consumer/producer surplus analysis presented in the text of Chapter 10 and related study guide questions, nondistortionary production and consumption choices which occur under free trade provide one set of gains from eliminating protectionism. Another level of efficiency gains arise because of economies of scale in production.

Two additional arguments for free trade are introduced in this chapter. Free trade, as opposed to "managed trade", provides a wider range of opportunities and thus a wider scope for innovation. The use of tariffs and subsidies to increase national welfare (such as a large country's use of an optimum tariff), even where theoretically desirable, in practice may only advance the causes of special interests at the expense of the general public.

Next, consider some of the arguments voiced in favor of restrictive trade practices. These arguments that protectionism increases overall national welfare have their own caveats. The success of an optimum tariff or an optimum (negative) subsidy by a large country to influence its terms of trade depends upon the absence of retaliation by foreign countries. Another important set of arguments relies upon the existence of some form of market failure. The distributional effects of trade policies will differ substantially if, for example, labor cannot be easily reallocated across sectors of the economy as suggested by movements along the production possibility frontier.

Other proponents of protectionist policies argue that the key tools of welfare analysis, which apply demand and supply measures to capture social as well as private costs and benefits, are inadequate. They argue that tariffs may improve welfare when social and private costs or benefits diverge. In general, however, it is better to design policies which address these issues directly rather than using a tariff which has other effects as well. For example, you can think of a tariff as being like a combined tax and subsidy. A well targeted subsidy *or* tax leads to a confluence of social and private cost or benefit. A policy which combines *both* a subsidy *and* a tax has other effects which mitigate social welfare gains.

Actual trade policy often cannot be reconciled with the prescriptions of basic welfare analysis. Some reasons for this are that the social accounting framework of policy makers does not match that implied by cost-benefit analysis. For example, policy makers may apply a "weighted social welfare analysis" which weighs gains or losses differently depending upon which groups are affected. Of course, in this instance there is the issue of who sets the weights and on the basis of what criteria. Trade policy may end up being used as a tool of income redistribution. Inefficient existing industries may be protected to preserve the status quo.

Divergence between optimal theoretical and actual trade policy may also arise because of the manner in which policy is made. The benefits of a tariff are concentrated while its costs are diffused. Well-organized groups, whose individuals each stand to gain a lot by trade restrictions, have a better opportunity to influence trade policy than larger, less well-organized groups which have more to lose in the aggregate but whose members individually have little to lose.

Drawing upon these arguments, one would expect that you could generalize that countries with strong comparative advantage in manufacturing would tend to protect agriculture while countries with comparative advantage in agriculture would tend to protect manufacturing. For the U.S. however, this argument is not validated by the pattern of protection. The pattern of protectionism in the U.S. is concentrated in four disparate industries, autos, steel, sugar and textiles.

International negotiations led to mutual tariff reductions from the mid 1930's to about 1980. Negotiations which link mutually reduced protection across countries have the political advantage of playing off well-organized groups against each other rather than either against poorly organized consumers. International trade negotiations also help avoid trade wars. This is illustrated by an example of the Prisoner's dilemma as it relates to trade. The pursuit of self-interest may not lead to the best social outcome when each agent takes into account the other agent's decision. Indeed, in the example in the text, uncoordinated policy leads to the worst outcome since protectionism is the best policy for each country to undertake unilaterally. Negotiations result in the coordinated policy of free trade and the best outcome for each country.

The chapter concludes with a brief history of international trade agreements. The rules governing GATT (General Agreement on Tariffs and Trade) are discussed, as are the real threats to its future performance as an active and effective instrument for moving toward freer trade. Indeed, while GATT places constraints on the imposition of export subsidies, import quotas and tariffs, it does not govern the ever increasing incidence of voluntary export restraints (a country constrains its own exports) nor does it govern less explicit forms of barriers to trade.

The chapter also presents a discussion of preferential trading agreements, such as those in the European Community and the pact between the United States and Canada. Trade diverting and trade creating effects of such customs unions are demonstrated in an example.

An appendix proves that there is always an optimal positive tariff if a country's protectionist actions affect world prices. As was mentioned in Chapter 9, this arises when a country is large in world markets for a good.

KEY TERMS

Define the following key terms:

1. Efficiency Case for Free Trade _____
_____
_____
_____.

2. Political Argument for Free Trade _____
_____
_____
_____.

3. Terms of Trade Argument for Free Trade _____
_____
_____
_____.

4. Domestic Market Failure _____

_____

_____

_____.

5. Theory of the Second Best _____

_____

_____

_____.

6. Common Market _____

_____

_____

_____.

REVIEW QUESTIONS

1.   Assume that Foreign is a <u>small</u> country which produces automobiles for export and its
      own consumption. These autos are traded on the world markets at a price of $8000.

   a. If this small country imposes a specific tariff of 25 percent, what will be effect on
      automobile prices?

      _____

      _____

      _____.

   b. How does this differ from the effect of a large country imposing a similar tariff?

      _____

      _____

      _____.

   c. In what other ways is the small country affected by this tariff?

      _____

      _____

      _____.

d. Why are the costs of trade protection in the United States considered so low relative to national income?

_____

_____

_____.

2. An export subsidy reduces national welfare, as does a tariff imposed by a small country. However, it is possible that a large country's welfare can improve under certain circumstances when a tariff is imposed. The relationship between national welfare and the tariff rate for a large country is illustrated in the figure below.

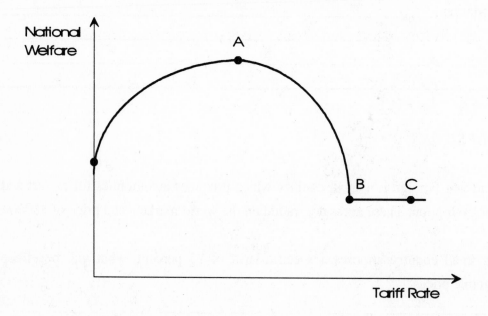

a. Up until what point is increasing the tariff rate beneficial to national welfare?

_____

_____

_____.

b. Discuss the intuition behind your response to part a.

_____

_____

_____.

c. What is the significance of point B on the graph?

_____

_____

_____.

d. Why would a large country be reluctant to use its optimal tariff despite the apparent gains to national welfare?

_____

_____

_____.

3. a. What is the relationship between the existence of domestic market failure and the use of trade policy?

_____

_____

_____.

b. Imagine an economy where production of textiles provides the additional marginal social benefit of innovations and technological spillovers into other industries. Such an economy is depicted in the figure on the next page. If this economy is a small country, what will be the effect of a tariff on production and consumption?

_____

_____

_____.

c. What does standard theory argue will be the efficiency and welfare effects of the tariff?

_____

_____

_____.

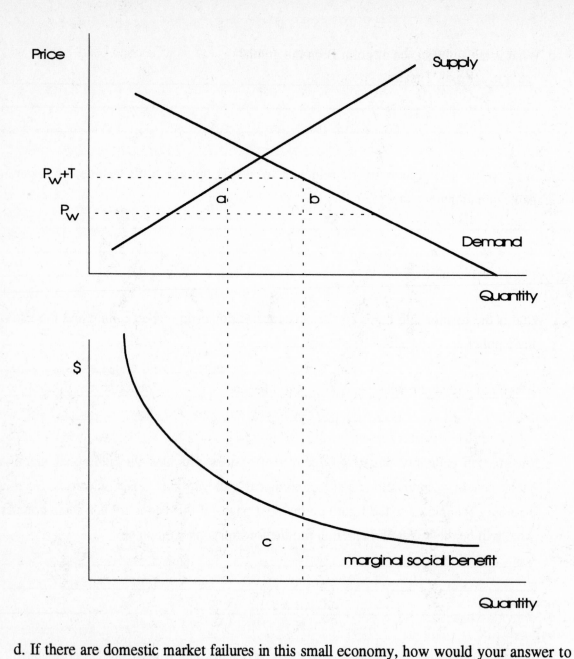

d. If there are domestic market failures in this small economy, how would your answer to part c change? Why?

_____
_____
_____
_____
_____.

e. If the application of the tariff to correct a market failure is a "second best" policy, what are examples of "first best" policies?

_____

_____

_____.

4.   Under most circumstances, a small country imposing a tariff or quota will not generate overall welfare gains.

a. Discuss the expected impact of a tariff or quota on a small country.

_____

_____

_____.

b. Graphically illustrate what would happen if the small nation depicted in the figure below imposes an ad valorem tariff of 100 percent on it imports of cloth. Assume that the relative price of cloth (to wine) on the world market is $P_C/P_W=1$, Home production is at point A and consumption is at point B.

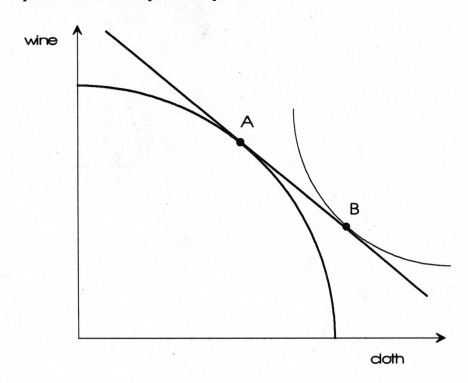

5. Assume that the demand and supply of cloth of a small country are described by the following schedule:

Price (p_c/p_w)	Cloth Supply	Cloth Demand
$2	20 yards	100 yards
$3	40 yards	80 yards
$4	60 yards	60 yards
$5	80 yards	40 yards

At free trade the relative price of cloth is $2.

a. Suppose this small country imposes a 50 percent ad valorem tariff on cloth imports. How will the new domestic price affect consumption, production and tariff revenues?

_____

_____

_____.

b. What types of forces or externalities would alter your conclusions to part a?

_____

_____

_____.

c. What would constitute a prohibitive tariff on cloth?

_____

_____

_____.

ANSWERS TO ODD-NUMBERED TEXTBOOK PROBLEMS

1. The arguments for free trade in this quote include;
    -Free trade allows consumers and producers to make decisions based upon the marginal cost and benefits associated with a good when costs and prices are undistorted by government policy.
    -The Philippines is "small", so it will have little scope for influencing world prices and capturing welfare gains through an improvement of its terms of trade.

-"Escaping the confines of a narrow domestic market" allows possible gains through economies of scale in production.

- Free trade "opens new horizons for entrepreneurship".

- Special interests may dictate trade policy for their own ends rather than for the general welfare. Free trade policies may aid in halting corruption where these special interests exert undue or disproportionate influence on public policy.

3.   Without tariffs, the country produces 100 units and consumes 300 units, thus importing 200 units.

a. A tariff of 5 per unit leads to production of 125 units and consumption of 250 units. The increase in welfare is the increase due to higher production of 25*10 minus the losses to consumer and producer surplus of (25*5)/2 and (50*5)/2, respectively, leading to a net gain of 62.5.

b. A production subsidy of 5 leads to a new supply curve of S = 50 + 5*(P+5). Consumption stays at 300, production rises to 125, and the increase in welfare equals the benefits from greater production minus the production distortion costs, 25*10 - (25*5)/2 = 187.5.

c. The production subsidy is a better targeted policy than the import tariff since it directly affects the decisions which reflect a divergence between social and private costs while leaving other decisions unaffected. The tariff has a double-edged function as both a production subsidy and a consumption tax.

d. The best policy is to have producers fully internalize the externality by providing a subsidy of 10 per unit. The new supply curve will then be S = 50 + 5*(P+10), production will be 150 units, and the welfare gain from this policy will be 50*10 - (10*50)/2 =250.

5.   The U.S. has a legitimate interest in the trade policies of other countries, just as other countries have a legitimate interest in U.S. activities. The reason is that uncoordinated trade policies are likely to be inferior to those based on negotiations. By negotiating with each other, governments are better able both to resist pressure from domestic interest groups and to avoid trade wars of the kind illustrated by the Prisoners' Dilemma example in the text.

7.   The potential economic costs associated with the entrance of Poland and Hungary into an expanded EC depend largely on whether their membership results in trade creation or trade diversion. In particular, Poland and Hungary will gain if they engage in new

trade with Western Europe although they might lose if trade within the European Community simply replaces trade which had been occurring with Eastern bloc countries. Furthermore, both of these nations will face at least higher structural unemployment during the transition period. Some of the negative effects on workers might be lessened if labor mobility is permitted across borders.

The Western nations should also be concerned on the trade creation versus trade diversion aspects of the entry of Poland and Hungary. For distributional and political reasons, they may be concerned about whether the prices of their own products will be driven down by competition or whether the entrants will simply bring to the Western markets an expanded variety of products and scope for additional scale economies of production. Workers in Western markets may be concerned that inflows of foreign labor drive down wages, although, as we have observed in previous chapters, the nominal wage shifts should be considered in light of changes in the prices of consumption goods.

Countries outside of the EC, such as the United States and Japan, would express concern if the supplies of products to the EC by Poland and Hungary substitute for goods previously supplied by the United States and Japan. The large outsiders, however, could reap substantial positive gains from having expanded access to the consumers of Poland and Hungary.

CHAPTER 11

Trade Policy in Developing Countries

CHAPTER ORGANIZATION

Trade Policy to Promote Manufacturing
    Why Manufacturing is Favored: The Infant Industry Argument
    How Manufacturing is Favored: Import-Substituting Industry
    Results of Favoring Manufacturing: Problems of Import-Substituting Industrialization
    Box: Trade Liberalization and Economic Growth: The Case of China
    Another Way to Favor Manufacturing: Industrialization Through Exports
Problems of the Dual Economy
    The Symptoms of Dualism
    Case Study: Economic Dualism in India
    Dual Labor Markets and Trade Policy
    Trade Policy as a Cause of Economic Dualism
Negotiations Between Developing and Advanced Countries: The North-South Debate
    Are Poor Nations Exploited?
    The Role of Foreign Capital and Multinational Firms in Development
    Raising the Export Prices of Developing Countries: Commodity Export Cartels
    Case Study: OPEC

KEY THEMES

The final two chapters on international trade, Chapters 11 and 12, discuss trade policy considerations in the context of specific sets of countries which face similar issues. Chapter 11 focuses on the use of trade policy in developing countries and Chapter 12 focuses on the application of industrial policy in advanced countries.

While there is great diversity among the developing countries, they share some common policy concerns. These include the development of domestic manufacturing industries, the uneven degree of development within the country, and the desire to promote changes in the international economic system. This chapter discusses both the successful and unsuccessful trade policy strategies which have been applied by developing countries in attempts to address these concerns.

Many LDCs pose the creation of a significant manufacturing sector as a key goal of economic development. One commonly voiced argument for protecting manufacturing industries is the *infant industry argument* which states that developing countries have a potential comparative advantage in manufacturing and can realize that potential through an initial period of protection. This argument assumes *market failure* in the form of imperfect capital markets or the existence of externalities in production: such a market failure makes the social return to production higher than the private return. This implies that a firm will not be able to recapture rents or profits that are in line with the contribution to welfare made by the product or industry establishment of the firm. Without some government support, the argument goes, the amount of investment which will occur in this industry will be less than socially optimal levels.

If a government chooses to develop through promoting manufacturing, the industries supported can either substitute for imported goods (known as an *import-substitution strategy*) or can produce for export (known as an *export promotion strategy*). Import substitution policies, fueled by vested interests and a skepticism concerning the ability to export, have been less successful than export promotion and have led to high levels of protection and inefficiently small scale production. By way of contrast, recent success stories of export promotion include Taiwan, Hong Kong, Singapore and South Korea. Drawing upon the lessons of history, most economists believe that export promotion is generally the preferred method of achieving growth and development.

Development often proceeds unevenly and results in a dual economy consisting of a modern sector and a traditional sector. The modern sector typically differs from the traditional sector in that it has a higher value of output per worker, higher wages, higher capital intensity, lower returns to capital, and persistent unemployment. For example, in India less than 1 percent of the population is employed in the manufacturing sector but this sector produces 15 percent of GNP. Wages in Indian manufacturing are six times those in agriculture.

Some argue that the existence of wage differentials in a dual economy demonstrates the failure of labor markets to work well (note: this argument falls under a market failure approach). Since wages are higher in manufacturing, it must be that society would benefit if workers moved from agriculture to manufacturing. A first best policy addresses the wage differential directly. Protectionism may be a second best solution, but one with the undesirable consequences of inducing both capital and labor into manufacturing. This raises the already too high capital intensity in the manufacturing sector. Further, an increase in the number of urban manufacturing jobs may exacerbate the problems of urban unemployment through migration from the countryside to the cities. This is a key theme of the Harris-Todaro model. It is possible that the medicine of trade policies worsens the illness of economic dualism.

The relationship between developing countries and advanced countries is termed the *North-South Debate*. This debate centers on three issues: the existence of exploitation by advanced countries; the role of foreign capital in development; and the pricing of commodity exports by developing countries. The charge of exploitation is taken to mean either an unequal exchange in terms of the value of developing countries' imports and exports (with value measured by labor hours) or the thwarting of development due to competition from already industrialized countries. Other concerns of the developing economy over foreign investment focus on issues of national sovereignty, the use of appropriate technology, and the degree of technology transfer from multinationals to developing countries.

Developing countries, which depend upon the export of commodities, may form cartels to attempt to swing terms of trade in their favor. This could conceivable occur in those sectors in which the colluding parties control a significant share of the market. While OPEC provides the most spectacular example of a successful cartel, it stands in stark contrast to the experience of most cartels.

KEY TERMS

Define the following key terms:

1. Imperfect Capital Markets _____

_____

_____

_____.

2. Import-Substituting Industrialization _____

_____

_____

_____.

3. Economic Dualism _____

_____

_____

_____.

4. Wage Differentials Argument _____

_____

_____

_____.

5. North-South Debate _____

_____

_____

_____.

6. Appropriate Technology _____

_____

_____

_____.

REVIEW QUESTIONS

1. a. Discuss the shortcomings of using traditional trade theory as a guide to LDC development strategy.

_____

_____

_____

_____

_____.

b. How would your arguments be countered by the proponents of traditional trade theory?

_____

_____

_____.

2. a. Discuss why international trade may not be the "engine of growth" sought by many of todays LDCs.

_____

_____

_____

_____

_____

_____.

b. Discuss some of the methods used by LDCs as they attempt to overcome their international trade difficulties.

_____

_____

_____

_____

_____

_____.

3. Assume that the developing country has a production and consumption mix as depicted in the figure below. Before trade and growth, the LDC production possibilities frontier is represented by TT, production and consumption both occur at point 1. Once trade begins, the LDC exchanges its goods (wine and cloth) at the world terms of trade, T_w. Production shifts toward cloth, and consumption of both wine and cloth rise to point 3. This represents attainment of a higher indifference level so trade has made this LDC better off.

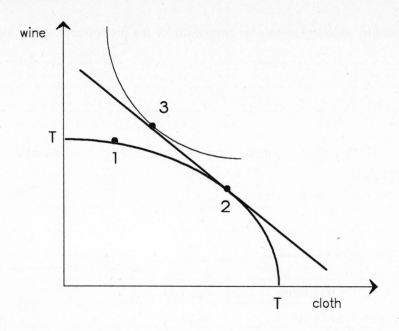

Show how an LDC can be made worse off with growth while it remains open to trade. Discuss your result.

_____

_____

_____.

4.   Multinational corporations have been both scorned and welcomed in LDCs.

  a. Discuss the arguments in favor of the activities of multinational corporations in LDCs.

_____

_____

_____.

  b. What are some the problems which multinational corporations allegedly create for LDCs?

_____

_____

_____.

SOLUTIONS TO ODD-NUMBERED TEXTBOOK PROBLEMS

1. The Japanese example gives pause to those who believe that protectionism is always disastrous. However, the fact of Japanese success does not demonstrate that protectionist trade policy was responsible for that success. Japan was an exceptional society that had emerged into the ranks of advanced nations before World War II, and was recovering from wartime devastation. It is arguable that economic success would have come anyway, so that the apparent success of protection represents a "pseudo-infant-industry" case of the kind discussed in the text.

3. There are larger markets in larger countries like Brazil and industries which benefit from import substituting policies could realize economy of scale advantages there which would not be available to industries producing solely for the market of Ghana.

5. Under these circumstances, workers are both "pulled" into the urban, "modern" sector by the lure of high wages and "pushed" from the rural areas due to stagnant conditions in the agricultural sector. To correct this problem of the bias toward the urban-manufacturing sector, explicit attention should be paid to making the agricultural sector more rewarding, In order to retain labor, the agricultural sector might be provided with wage subsidies so that the rural-urban wage gap is reduced. Policies can also be targeted at promoting light rural enterprise and agricultural investment which would increase wages through increasing worker productivity. In addition, development of the rural infrastructure and social services might increase the relative attractiveness of the countryside.

7. The unequal exchange doctrine maintains that the exports of developing countries embody more hours of labor than their imports and thus this trade represents an unequal exchange which favors advanced countries at the expense of developing countries. The uneven development doctrine maintains that the division of countries into advanced and developing is a historical accident not based upon endowments or other factors. Were this true, there would be a strong case for the infant industry argument since the development of manufacturing would only require temporary protection.

9. a. When each country produces 100 tons, the price per ton is 20 and profit for each firm is 1000. When output is limited by a cartel to 75 for each firm, the price rises to 25 and the profit of each firm is 1125.

   b. The price falls to 22.5. The profit for the firm which adheres to the agreement is 937.5 while the profit of the firm which cheats is 1250. Once again, the maxim that cheaters never prosper is shown to be false. In the aggregate, however, this maxim may hold. This situation is an example of the Prisoner's Dilemma. Individually, cheaters prosper, but only if the other country is honest.

CHAPTER 12

Industrial Policy in Advanced Countries

CHAPTER ORGANIZATION

Popular Arguments for Industrial Policy
      Encouraging Industries with High Value Added per Worker
      Encouraging Linkage Industries
      Promoting Industries with Future Growth Potential
      Countering the Effects of Other Countries' Industrial Policies
Sophisticated Arguments for Industrial Policy
      Technology and Externalities
      Imperfect Competition and Strategic Trade Policy
Industrial Policy in Practice
      The Industrial Policy of Japan
      Industrial Policy in Other Countries
Case Studies of Industrial Policy
      Japanese Targeting of Steel (1960 to early 1970s)
      European Support of Aircraft in the 1970s and 1980s
      Japanese Targeting of Semiconductors (mid 1970s to date)
      The HDTV Debate

KEY THEMES

Industrial policy has become a topic of discussion among pundits and politicians in the United States as a response to the ascent of Japan as a world economic power and in response to frustrations about the economic performance of the United States.   There are numerous arguments for industrial policy: while some are clearly lacking in economic rationale, other, more sophisticated arguments deserve careful consideration. Essentially, while there are some valid instances in which protectionism is warranted, the reasoning behind such protection is often very different and much narrower than the standard arguments voiced by the proponents of protectionism.   Also, the importance of the contribution of industrial policy to some economic successes may be quite overstated. For example, while it is frequently argued that industrial policy has been a crucial feature of the economic success of some countries, it remains unclear whether attributing the successes to industrial policy is warranted. This chapter considers the theoretical basis for the use of industrial policy in industrialized economies and reviews actual country experiences.

Industrial policy involves attempts by governments to channel resources into sectors viewed as important for future economic growth. These efforts assume that markets, left to themselves, would fail to adequately provide the correct incentives and signals for these sectors to advance. Four frequently cited criteria for selecting targets of policy are: (1) choosing industries which have high value added per worker; (2) choosing industries with extensive linkages to other industries; (3) determining which industries have future growth potential; and (4) defensively countering other countries' industrial policies. These popular and seemingly plausible criteria are flawed. They ignore the workings of the market. They also suffer from a limited view of the consequences of promoting one set of industries at the expense of the economy as a whole.

A better basis for determining whether to apply industrial policy is the presence of market failures. One important type of market failure involves externalities present in research and development. Existence of externalities associated with research and development make the private return to investing in this activity less than its social return. This means that the private sector will tend to invest less in research and development than is socially optimal. To address this market failure, the first best policy is to directly support research and development in all industries. A second best policy is to protect or subsidize those industries which, by their nature, suffer the most from this externality. The prime example is high-technology industries.

Another set of market failures arises when imperfect competition exists. Strategic trade policy by a government can work to deter investment and production by foreign firms and raise the profits of domestic firms. An example is provided in the text which illustrates the case where the increase in profits following the imposition of a subsidy can actually exceed the cost of a subsidy to an imperfectly competitive industry. While this is a valid theoretical argument for industrial policy, it is nonetheless open to criticism in choosing the industries which should be subsidized and the levels of subsidies to these industries. These criticisms are associated with the practical aspects of insufficient information and the threat of foreign retaliation.

The final section of the chapter presents some examples of industrial policy in practice. For instance, Japanese policy from the 1950's to early 1970 involved the rationing of credit and foreign exchange to industries, combined with a system of tariffs and import restrictions. Japanese industrial policy since that early episode involves more subtle and ambiguous government intervention. Yet, the success of the Japanese economy may or may not be due to Japanese industrial planning. Some industries which prospered, such as automobiles and consumer electronics, did so without having received government aid. Those industries which have received aid and prospered, such as steel or semiconductors, may have benefitted at the expense of the greater economy. It is not clear that the industrial policies were the critical force in the success of these industries. These doubts are accentuated by the presence of characteristics which would promote development anyway, such as a high savings rate, and good labor-management relations.

Industrial planning beyond the borders of Japan is not necessarily correlated with success. The development of the Concorde presents an example in which industrial planning targeted an industry which did not do well. The European Airbus fared better but is still dependent upon government subsidies. Finally, the debate currently rages over whether industrial policy in the United States should be targeted at the development of HDTV (high definition television). The first set of difficulties are associated with predicting the importance of HDTV as a potentially successful industry with high technological spillovers. If this point could be established, the second set of difficulties arise on a practical levels, when optimal degrees of industrial subsidies must actually be determined.

The message emerging from this chapter is that industrial policy should be evaluated in the context of its full range of benefits to society as well as its necessity. That which benefits an industry does not necessarily benefit the overall economy. Those policies which are successful may be redundant since a well functioning market may have channelled resources in those directions anyway. The existence of some form of market failures often is considered by economists to be a precondition for targeting sound industrial policy.

KEY TERMS

Define the following key terms:

1. Linkage Argument _____
_____
_____
_____.

117

2. Externalities _____

_____

_____

_____.

3. Excess Returns _____

_____

_____

_____.

4. Strategic Trade Policy _____

_____

_____

_____.

5. Beggar-Thy-Neighbor Policies _____

_____

_____

_____.

REVIEW QUESTIONS

1. Industrial policy encompasses attempts by a government to encourage the shift of resources into particular, targeted sectors of the economy. Since there are limited resources available to any economy, this implied that the expansion of targeted sectors will occur at the expense of the contraction of other sectors.

    a. What is the significance of the existence of market failures for the formation of industrial policy?

    _____

    _____

    _____.

b. What mistakes are commonly made when a government chooses the particular sectors to be targeted?

_____

_____

_____.

c. Should United States industrial policy target and encourage those industries which have been selected for promotion by other countries? Why?

_____

_____

_____

_____

_____.

2. The existence of market failures in labor, capital and final goods industries is more prevalent in less developed countries than in developed economies. In fact, the existence of market failures is much more difficult to establish for many industrialized nations.

a. Discuss the types of market failures which are identified as relevant to the industrialized nations and to the formation of industrial policy.

_____

_____

_____

_____

_____.

b. Discuss the meaning of knowledge creation as it relates to research and development in the high technology sector.

_____

_____

_____.

3.   Government intervention in the sphere of private sector activity is, at best, cautiously advised by most economists. Yet, the experience of Japan seems to suggest that a highly visible and activist industrial policy can lead to tremendous success and economic growth. Discuss the linkage between the growth experience of Japan and it's policies of industrial targeting.

_____

_____

_____

_____

_____

_____.

SOLUTIONS TO ODD-NUMBERED TEXTBOOK PROBLEMS

1.   If everyone knows that an industry will grow rapidly, private markets will funnel resources into the industry even without government support. There is need for special government action only if there is some market failure; the prospect of growth by itself isn't enough.

3.   The results of basic research may be appropriated by a wider range of firms and industries than the results of research applied to specific industrial applications. The benefits to the United States of Japanese basic research would exceed the benefits from Japanese research targeted to specific problems in Japanese industries.

5.   Because the economy has limited resources, a trade policy that conveys a strategic advantage on one industry necessarily puts other industries at some strategic disadvantage. It is not possible to achieve a strategic advantage in all industries. This point should be clear from the emphasis on movements along production possibility frontiers as illustrated in previous chapters. Korea's across-the-board subsidy probably has little net effect on the strategic position of the industries because while it provides each industry with a direct subsidy, it indirectly raises all industries' costs.

7.   Low rates of return to industries targeted by industrial policy tend to support the thesis that this policy, while benefitting a particular industry, hurts the economy as a whole. If there are externalities associated with the industry, however, the promotion of that

industry may benefit the economy as a whole even when the particular industry has a low rate of return. These externalities, specifically technological innovations which benefit a range of other industries, are more likely to be found in the semiconductor industry than in the steel industry.

OVERVIEW TO PART III

EXCHANGE RATES AND OPEN ECONOMY MACROECONOMICS

Section III of the textbook is comprised of six chapters:

SECTION III OVERVIEW

The presentation of international finance theory proceeds by building up an integrated model of exchange rate and output determination. Successive chapters in Part III construct this model step by step so you can acquire a firm understanding of each component as well as the manner in which these components fit together. The resulting model presents a single unifying framework admitting the entire range of exchange rate regimes from pure float to managed float to fixed rates. The model may be used to analyze both comparative static and dynamic time path results arising from temporary or permanent policy or exogenous shocks in an open economy.

The primacy given to asset markets in the model is reflected in the discussion of national income and balance of payments accounting in the first chapter of this section. Chapter 13 begins with a discussion of the focus of international finance. The discussion then proceeds to national income accounting in a closed economy. The extension to an open economy emphasizes the link between the current account and international asset flows. The chapter points out, in the discussion on the balance of payments account, that current account transactions must be financed by capital account flows from either central bank or noncentral bank transactions. A case study uses national income accounting identities to consider the link between government budget deficits and the current account.

Observed behavior of the exchange rate favors modeling it as an asset price rather than as a

122

goods price. Thus, the core relationship for short-run exchange-rate determination in the model developed in Part III is uncovered interest parity. Chapter 14 presents a model in which the exchange rate adjusts to equate expected returns on interest-bearing assets denominated in different currencies given expectations about exchange rates and the domestic and foreign interest rate. This first building block of the model lays the foundation for subsequent chapters that explore the determination of domestic interest rates and output, the basis for expectations of future exchange rates and richer specifications of the foreign-exchange market that include risk. An appendix to this chapter explains the determination of forward exchange rates.

Chapter 15 introduces the domestic money market, linking monetary factors to short-run exchange-rate determination through the domestic interest rate. The chapter begins with a discussion of the determination of the domestic interest rate. Interest parity links the domestic interest rate to the exchange rate, a relationship captured in a two-quadrant diagram. Comparative statics employing this diagram demonstrate the effects of monetary expansion and contraction on the exchange-rate in the short run. Dynamic considerations are introduced through an appeal to the long run neutrality of money that identifies a long run steady-state value toward which the exchange rate evolves. The dynamic time path of the model exhibits overshooting of the exchange-rate in response to monetary changes.

Chapter 16 develops a model of the long run exchange rate. The long-run exchange rate plays a role in a complete short-run macroeconomic model since one variable in that model is the expected future exchange rate. The chapter begins with a discussion of the law of one price and purchasing power parity. A model of the exchange rate in the long run based upon purchasing power parity is developed. A review of the empirical evidence, however, casts doubt on this model. The chapter then goes on to develop a general model of exchange rates in the long run in which the neutrality of monetary shocks emerges as a special case. In contrast, shocks to the output market or changes in fiscal policy alter the long run real exchange rate. This chapter also discusses the real interest parity relationship that links the real interest rate differential to the expected change in the real exchange rate.

Chapter 17 presents a macroeconomic model of output and exchange-rate determination in the short run. The chapter introduces aggregate demand in a setting of short run price stickiness to construct a model of the goods market. The exchange-rate analysis presented in previous chapters provides a model of the asset market. The resulting model is, in spirit, very close to the classic Mundell-Fleming model. This model is used to examine the effects of a variety of policies. The analysis allows a distinction to be drawn between permanent and temporary policy shifts since permanent policy shifts alter long-run expectations while temporary policy shifts do not. This distinction highlights the importance of exchange-rate expectations on macroeconomic outcomes. A case study of U.S. fiscal and monetary policy between 1979 and 1983 utilizes the model to explain recent events. The chapter concludes with a discussion of the links between exchange rate and import price movements which focuses on the J-curve and exchange-rate pass-through. An appendix to the chapter compares the IS-LM model to the model developed in this chapter. A second appendix discusses the Marshall-Lerner condition and estimates of trade elasticities.

The final chapter of this section discusses intervention by the central bank and the relationship of this policy to the money supply. This analysis is blended with the previous chapter's short-run macroeconomic model to analyze policy under fixed rates. The balance sheet of the central bank is used to keep track of the effects of foreign exchange intervention on the money supply. The model developed in previous chapters is extended by relaxing the interest parity condition and allowing exchange-rate risk to influence agents' decisions. This allows a discussion of sterilized intervention. Another topic discussed in this chapter is capital flight and balance of payments crises. The analysis also is extended to a two-country framework to discuss alternative systems for fixing the exchange-rate as a prelude to Part IV. An appendix to Chapter 18 develops a model of the foreign-exchange market in which risk factors make domestic-currency and foreign-currency assets imperfect substitutes. A second appendix explores the monetary approach to the balance of payments. The third appendix discusses the timing of a balance of payments crisis.

CHAPTER 13

National Income Accounting and the Balance of Payments

CHAPTER ORGANIZATION

KEY THEMES

This chapter introduces the international macroeconomics section of the text. In international macroeconomics we study "open" economies, that is economies that trade both assets and goods and services with the rest of the world. International macroeconomic theory focuses on issues such as unemployment, savings, trade imbalances, and money and the price level in open economies. Some of the issues that you might have read about in newspapers or magazines that are studied in international economics include the United States' trade deficit, the exchange rate of the dollar against other currencies, the international debt crisis, and the consequences of the low savings rate in the United States.

A major portion of this chapter is taken up with the presentation of the theory of national income accounting and the balance of payments account. You may have seen some of the material on national income accounting for a closed economy in previous economics courses. In those courses you learned that GNP can be considered the sum of different categories of spending or, alternatively, as the sum of different categories of payments to domestic workers, capital-owners, and land-owners. These two ways of adding up GNP give us the relationship for a closed economy that private savings minus investment equals government expenditures minus government tax revenues; that is, net private saving equals net government dissaving.

This relationship must be modified in an open economy to include the current account which represents exports minus imports or, alternatively, net lending by an economy to the rest of the world. The current account equals net private savings (private savings minus private investment) plus government savings (tax receipts minus government expenditures). The case study on the current account imbalances of the United States and Japan in the 1980s allows you to consider the relationship among the United States budget deficit, savings in Japan and the United States, and the current account of the United States and Japan in a consistent framework.

It is useful, when studying balance of payments accounting, to keep in mind the rule that there is a debit in either the current account or the capital account of a country when payment for an item classified in that account is flowing out of a country. For example, a car is a good and thus is a current account item. When a car produced by Toyota in Japan is sold to a United States resident, there is a payment from the United States and thus the import of the car is recorded as a current account debit. If the Toyota company uses the payment for the car to

126

increase the size of its checking account in the United States, then this purchase of a capital account item (the checking account) by Toyota represents a credit in the United States' capital account. This example brings up the important point that balance of payment accounting is a form of double-entry bookkeeping since each transaction enters the accounts twice, once as a credit and once as a debit. In reality, as discussed in the box in this chapter, there are large statistical discrepancies between the current and capital accounts. These discrepancies reflect some real-world difficulties in measuring international payments.

The chapter concludes with a discussion of official reserve transactions. The important point to keep in mind now is that these official capital flows play the same role as other capital flows from the standpoint of financing the current account. There are, however, additional macroeconomic implications of central-bank foreign asset transactions. These will be studied in detail in Chapter 18.

KEY TERMS

Define the following key terms:

1. Gross national product _____

_____

_____

_____.

2. Balance of payments _____

_____

_____

_____.

3. National saving _____

_____

_____

_____.

4. Official international reserves:_____

_____

_____

_____.

5. Current account_____

_____

_____ .

6. Capital account _____

_____

_____

_____ .

REVIEW QUESTIONS

1. Fill in the blanks below.

    i. For a Closed Economy;

        a. Spending approach $Y = \underline{\quad} + \underline{\quad} + G$

        b. Income approach $Y = \underline{\quad} + SP + \underline{\quad}$

          combining (a) and (b) $SP - \underline{\quad} = G - \underline{\quad}$

    ii. For an Open Economy

        c. Spending approach $Y = \underline{\quad} + \underline{\quad} + G + \underline{\quad} - IM$

        d. Income approach $Y = \underline{\quad} + SP + \underline{\quad}$

        e. Current Account Definition $CA = \underline{\quad} - \underline{\quad}$

          combining (c), (d) and (e) $SP - \underline{\quad} = G - \underline{\quad} + \underline{\quad}$

2.   The following chart lists savings, investment, the government budget surplus and the current account surplus, all relative to GNP, for a number of hypothetical countries.

    a. Fill in the missing entries in the chart.

Country	S/GNP	I/GNP	(G-T)/GNP	CA/GNP
Oceania	0.22	0.20	0.02	___
Armansk	___	0.15	-0.01	0.08
Vantu	0.17	0.22	___	- 0.05
Klingon	0.21	___	0.05	0.01

b. In the graph below, plot the line that represents all points where the budget deficit equals the current account deficit. Then plot the points corresponding to the appropriate values for the four hypothetical countries. Do you see a relationship between budget deficits and current account deficits? Why or why not?

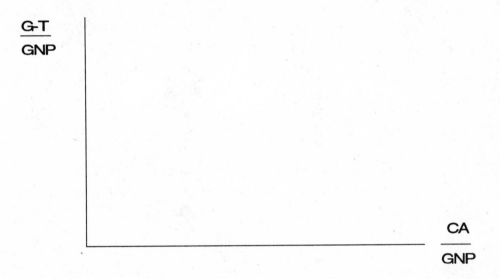

c. Below are values for the budget surpluses or deficits, and the current account surpluses or deficits for a number of countries (all data are for 1986, and are expressed as percent of GNP). Plot these points.

Country:	Korea	Philippines	Italy	Indonesia	Germany	Switzerland
(G-T)/GNP:	00	.05	.12	.03	.01	-.01
CA/GNP:	06	.06	.00	-.02	.06	.01

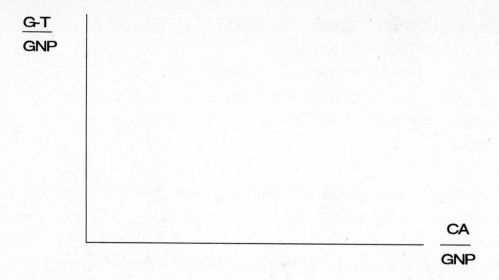

$\dfrac{G-T}{GNP}$

$\dfrac{CA}{GNP}$

Do you find a relationship between budget deficits and current account deficits for these countries? Why or why not?

_____

_____

_____.

3. Below is a roster of transactions for the mythical economy of Freedonia. Use this roster of transactions to complete the balance of payments chart which follows. (all transactions are in millions of Freedonian dollars)

Description	Amount
a. Sale of stock in the Freedonian Balloon Company to U.S. investors	$ 8
b. Payment of dividends to Italian shareholders in Freedonia Balloon Co.	$ 9
c. Purchase of British tea sets	$ 5
d. Purchase of American cowboy hats	$ 8
e. Sale of Freedonian cigars to Belgium	$ 3
f. Sale of Freedonia's largest hotel to Japanese investors	$14
g. Purchase of IBM stock by several Freedonian investors	$10
h. Sale of Freedonian harps to Switzerland	$22
i. Purchase of Canadian hockey sticks	$ 5
j. Rental of hotel rooms by German tourists in Freedonia	$ 3
k. Sale of Freedonian croquet mallets to Great Britain	$11
l. Purchases of French Francs by Freedonian Central Bank	$18

130

m. Foreign aid to Freedonia from Bolivia	$ 5
n. Purchases of beef from Argentina	$ 4
o. Sale Freedonian dollars to the U.S. Federal Reserve	$ 8
p. Remittance of dividends to Freedonian shareholders of Chrysler stock	$ 3
q. Purchase of cars from Yugoslavia	$12
r. Sale of socks to Australia	$ 6
s. Sale of a large Freedonian farm to a British citizen	$ 2
t. Purchase of restaurant meals in Israel by Freedonian tourists	$ 1
u. Freedonian foreign aid to Mongolia	$ 1

The Freedonia Balance of Payments Account (millions of Freedonia Dollars)

Current Account

1. Exports _____

   of which:

2. Merchandise _____

3. Investment Income Received _____

4. Imports _____

   of which:

5. Merchandise _____

6. Investment Income Paid _____

7. Net Unilateral Transfers _____

8. Balance on Current Account _____

Capital Account

9. Freedonian assets held abroad _____

   (increase -)

   of which:

10. Official Reserve Assets _____

11. Other assets _____

12. Foreign assets held in Freedonia _____

   of which:

13. Official reserve assets _____

14. Other assets _____

15. Balance on Capital Account _____

16. Statistical Discrepancy _____

1.   The reason for including only the value of final goods and services in GNP, as stated in the question, is to avoid the problem of double counting. Double counting will not occur if intermediate imports are subtracted and intermediate exported goods are added to GNP accounts. Consider the sale of U.S. steel to Toyota and to General Motors. The steel sold to General Motors should not be included in GNP since the value of that steel is subsumed in the cars produced in the U.S. The value of the steel sold to Toyota will not enter the national income accounts in a more finished state since the value of the Toyota goes towards Japanese GNP. The value of the steel should be subtracted from GNP in Japan since U.S. factors of production receive payment for it.

3. a. The purchase of the German stock is a debit in the U.S. capital account. There is a corresponding credit in the U.S. capital account when the American pays with a check on his Swiss bank account because his claims on Switzerland fall by the amount of the check. This is a case in which an American trades one foreign asset for another.

   b. Again, there is a U.S. capital account debit as a result of the purchase of a German stock by an American. The corresponding credit in this case occurs when the German seller deposits the U.S. check in her German bank and that bank lends the money to a German importer (in which case the credit will be in the U.S. current account) or to an individual or corporation that purchases a U.S. asset (in which case the credit will be in the U.S. capital account). Ultimately, there will be some action taken by the bank which results in a credit in the U.S. balance of payments.

   c. The foreign exchange intervention by the French government involves the sale of a U.S. asset, the dollars it holds in the U.S., and thus represents a debit item in the U.S. capital account. The French citizens who buy the dollars may use them to buy American goods, which would be an American current account credit, or an American asset, which would be an American capital account credit.

   d. Suppose VISA uses a checking account in France to make payments. When VISA pays the French restaurateur for the meal, its payment represents a debit in the U.S. current account. VISA must sell assets (deplete its checking account in France) to make this payment. This reduction in the French assets owned by VISA represents a credit in the American capital account.

   e. There is no credit or debit in either the capital or the current account since there has been no market transaction.

   f. There is no recording in the U.S. balance of payments of this off-shore transaction.

5. a. Since non-central bank capital inflows fell short of the current-account deficit by $500 million, the balance of payments of Pecunia (official settlements balance) was -$500 million. The country as a whole somehow had to finance its $1 billion current-account deficit, so Pecunia's net foreign assets fell by $1 billion.

   b. By dipping into its foreign reserves, the central bank of Pecunia financed the portion of the country's current-account deficit not covered by private capital inflows. Only if foreign central banks had acquired Pecunian assets could the Pecunian central bank have avoided using $500 million in reserves to complete the financing of the current account. Thus, Pecunia's central bank lost $500 million in reserves, which would appear as an official capital inflow (of the same magnitude) in the country's balance of payments accounts.

   c. If foreign official capital inflows to Pecunia were $600 million, the country had a balance of payments surplus of $100 million. Put another way, the country needed only $1 billion to cover its current-account deficit, but $1.1 billion flowed into the country. The Pecunian central bank must therefore have used the extra $100 million in foreign borrowing to increase its reserves. Purchases of Pecunian assets by foreign central banks enter their countries' balance of payments accounts as outflows, which are debit items. The rationale is that the transactions result in foreign payments to the Pecunians who sell the assets.

   d. Along with non-central bank transactions, the accounts would show an increase in foreign official reserve assets held in Pecunia of $600 million (a capital-account credit, or inflow) and an increase Pecunian official reserve assets held abroad of $100 billion (a capital-account debit, or outflow). Of course, total net capital inflows of $1 billion just cover the current-account deficit.

7. The official settlements balance, also called the balance of payments, shows the net change in international reserves held by United States government agencies, such as the Federal Reserve and the Treasury, relative to the change in dollar reserves held by foreign government agencies. This account provides a partial picture of the extent of intervention in the foreign exchange market. One reason that the U.S. balance of payments data do not provide a complete characterization of the purchase and sale of dollars in currency markets is because these data do not capture changes in dollar asset holdings among the central banks of different foreign countries. For example, a trade of dollars for deutschemarks between Germany and France will not appear in the United States official settlements balance because it does not represent a net change in

133

dollar holdings by central banks outside the United States, even though it does reflect the use of dollars in an official exchange. In a similar fashion, transactions that involve foreign central banks may not appear in the balance of payments account for the United States if the foreign central banks undertake transactions with foreign private banks, foreign exporters, or foreign importers. Finally, the official settlements balance reflects only net flows. A given net flow could represent very different gross flows in reserves, and thus very different levels of purchases and sales of dollars by foreign central banks.

CHAPTER 14

Exchange Rates and the Foreign Exchange Market: An Asset Approach

CHAPTER ORGANIZATION

KEY THEMES

Exchange rates translate the price of goods denominated in different currencies to common units. Exchange rates also represent the relative price of foreign and domestic currencies. An introduction to these two functions of the exchange rate serves as the main points in this chapter. This chapter shows you how to use exchange rates to convert the prices of goods denominated in different currencies into common units. This chapter also begins our discussion on the determination of exchange rates in the asset market. These two points are of central importance for your understanding of all of the material that follows in the international macroeconomics course.

The main players in the foreign exchange market are large organizations such as commercial banks, corporations, nonbank financial institutions and central banks. These organizations are able to trade deposits quickly and at low cost, which ensures that common exchange rates are offered worldwide. Financial instruments such as forward foreign exchange contracts, foreign-exchange futures contracts and foreign-exchange options play an important part in currency market activity. The chapter describes how these financial instruments provide a low-cost way to eliminate short- term exchange rate risk, although, as discussed in a box, longer- run risk remains difficult to guard against.

The determination of exchange rates follows from the role they play in bringing about equilibrium in asset markets. Equilibrium in asset markets requires an equalization of nominal returns of assets that differ only in the currency in which they are denominated, when these returns are expressed in a common currency. (Differences in the riskiness or liquidity of different assets may affect this equilibrium relationship.) It is very important to understand how to compare expected returns on assets denominated in domestic and foreign currency. There are two parts of the expected return on a foreign-currency asset (measured in domestic-currency terms): the interest payment and the change in the value of the foreign currency relative to the domestic currency over the period in which the asset is held.

Setting equal the return on a domestic-currency asset and the expected return on a foreign-currency asset gives us the interest parity condition. The foreign exchange market is in equilibrium only when the interest parity condition holds. Thus, for given interest rates and given expectations about future exchange rates, interest parity determines the current equilibrium exchange rate. The interest parity diagram introduced in this chapter is instrumental in later chapters in which a more general model is presented.

The result that a dollar appreciation makes foreign currency assets more attractive and that dollar depreciation makes foreign currency assets less attractive may strike you as strange -- why does a stronger dollar reduce the expected return on dollar assets? The key to explaining this point is that, when the expected value of the future exchange rate is constant and when interest rates remain unchanged, an appreciation of the dollar today implies a future depreciation of the dollar. Thus when the dollar appreciates today, American investor can expect to gain not only the foreign interest payment but also the extra return due to the dollar's future depreciation.

The following diagram illustrates this point. In this diagram, the exchange rate at time t+1 is expected to be equal to E. If the exchange rate at time t is also E then expected depreciation is 0. If, however, the exchange rate depreciates at time t to E' then it must appreciate to reach E at time t+1. If the exchange rate appreciates today to E" then it must depreciate to reach E at time t+1. Thus, with a given expected future exchange rate, a depreciation in period t to E' implies an expected appreciation during the time from t to t+1 (as the exchange rate moves during this time from E' to E). Conversely, an appreciation in period t to E" implies that the exchange rate depreciates over the period t to t+1 as it moves from E" to E.

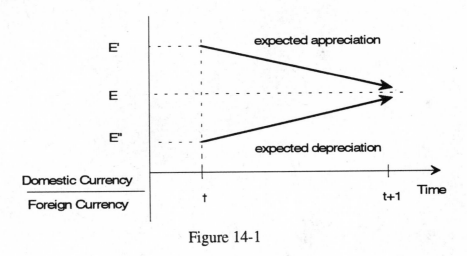

Figure 14-1

This diagram helps provide some further intuition behind the interest parity relationship. Suppose that the domestic and foreign interest rates are equal. Interest parity then requires that expected depreciation is equal to zero and that the exchange rate today and next period is equal to E. If the domestic interest rate rises, people will want to hold more domestic-currency deposits. The resulting increased demand for domestic currency drives up the price of domestic currency, causing the exchange rate to appreciate. How long will this continue? The answer is that the appreciation of the domestic currency continues until the expected depreciation that is a consequence of the domestic currency's appreciation today just offsets the interest differential.

The Appendix describes the covered interest parity relationship. The covered interest parity relationship differs from the uncovered interest parity relationship only in the use of the forward exchange rate in the covered interest parity relationship, rather than the (unobservable) expected future exchange rate, which is used in the uncovered interest parity relationship. Covered interest parity explains the determination of forward rates and also helps explain why spot exchange rates and forward exchange rates move together.

KEY TERMS:

Define the following key terms:

1. Spot exchange rate_____
_____
_____
_____.

2. Forward exchange rate _____
_____
_____
_____.

3. Arbitrage _____
_____
_____
_____.

4. Interest parity condition _____
_____
_____.

5. Risk _____
_____
_____
_____.

6. Liquidity _____
_____
_____
_____.

REVIEW PROBLEMS

1. i. Look up the following exchange rates in today's newspaper;

        U.S. Dollars per German Deutschemark   _____

        U.S. Dollars per British Pound   _____

        U.S. Dollars per Japanese Yen   _____

        U.S. Dollars per Canadian Dollar   _____

  ii. Use these exchange rates to calculate the following cross-rates;

        German Deutschemarks per British Pound   _____

        Japanese Yen per Canadian Dollar   _____

        Canadian Dollar per German Deutschemark   _____

        British Pound per Japanese Yen   _____

2. a. Suppose you start the Totally Cool International Shirt (TCIS) Company, a business that imports authentic college t-shirts from foreign universities and sells them on campuses in the United States. You need to translate the foreign prices of the shirts into dollars. Do this for the t-shirts from the following universities by filling in the table:

University (Country)	Price of T-shirt	Exchange Rate	Dollar Price
Sorbonne (France)	60.0 Francs	6.0	Francs/$ _____
Delhi University (India)	153.0 Rupees	17.0	Rupees/$ _____
Seoul National Univ. (Korea)	8050.0 Wons	700.0	Wons/$ _____
Hebrew Univ.(Israel)	21.0 Shekels	2.0	Shekels/$ _____
Trinity College (Ireland)	4.75 Punts	0.5	Punts/$ _____

b. Suppose that a month from now the exchange rates are given below. State whether these new exchange rates represent an appreciation or a depreciation of each currency against the dollar. Also, without calculating the actual dollar prices of t-shirts, state whether the dollar price will fall or rise.

Currency	Franc	Rupee	Won	Shekel	Punt
Exchange Rate	5 F/$	15 R/$	770 W/$	1.5 S/$	0.45 P/$

Appreciation or
Depreciation?   ____   ____   ____   ____   ____

Dollar Price
Rise or Fall?   ____   ____   ____   ____   ____

3. Upon graduating from college, you take the proceeds from your successful shirt company and begin a company that sells foreign securities in the United States (to save money on stationery, you keep the same acronym by calling your new company Traditional Client Investment Service (TCIS) Company). Part of your task is to provide a newsletter to clients discussing the return on foreign securities. Fill in the blanks in the following newsletter.

TCIS NEWSLETTER

Currently, a one-year bond denominated in dollars pays an interest rate of 8%. A bond that is denominated in lira, and has similar characteristics in terms of risk and liquidity, pays 9%. This means that the implicit forecast by the foreign exchange market is that the dollar will (appreciate / depreciate) against the lira over the next year by ___%.

This month, it takes 1500 Italian Lira to buy one dollar. TCIS forecasts that next year at this time it will take 1575 lira to purchase a dollar. This represents (an appreciation / a depreciation) of the dollar against the lira of ____%.

Based upon our forecast, (we advise against / we advise) purchasing lira-denominated securities. The reason for this is that _____

_____

_____.

For example, if you used $1000 to purchase a dollar-denominated bond, a year from now you would have $_____. If you took the same $1000 and purchased a lira-denominated bond, a year from now you would have $_____.

Some of you may be concerned that we have focused on nominal returns and thus have ignored real returns. We do this because _____

_____

_____.

4. Use the covered interest parity condition to fill in the following table.

U.S. Interest Rate	U.K. Interest Rate	Spot Exchange Rate	Forward Exchange Rate
10%	5%	2 $/£	____$/£
8%	__%	2 $/£	2.04 $/£
10%	0%	__ $/£	2.10 $/£
__%	9%	2 $/£	1.98 $/£

5. i. Consider a case where the interest rate on a one-year dollar-denominated bond is 9% and the expected value of the yen one year from now is 180 yen to the dollar. Plot the points that satisfy the interest parity relationship between the yen/dollar exchange rate and the Japanese interest rate in the Graph 1, where the yen/dollar exchange rate is on the vertical axis and the Japanese interest rate is on the horizontal axis.

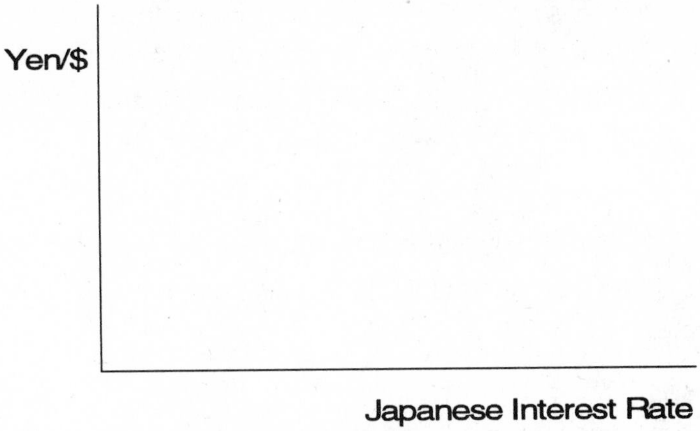

Yen/$

Japanese Interest Rate

Graph 1

Determine the spot ¥/$ exchange rates when the Japanese interest rate is 8%. Also determine the ¥/$ exchange rate when the Japanese interest rate is 11%.

ii. In Graph 2, plot the interest parity relationship, but this time for a U.S. interest rate of 11%.

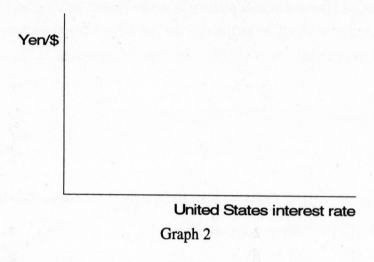

Graph 2

iii. Now go back to the case of a U.S. interest rate of 9%, but suppose the expected value of the ¥/$ exchange rate one year from now is 190 yen to the dollar. Plot the interest parity relationship under these assumptions in Graph 3.

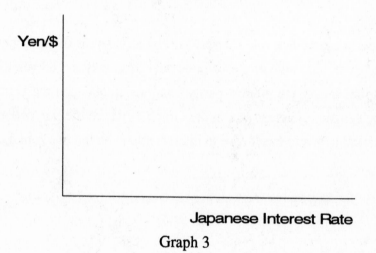

Graph 3

Again determine the spot ¥/$ exchange rates when the Japanese interest rate is 8% and when the Japanese interest rate is 11% and compare your answers here to your answers in part i.

iv. What can you conclude about the direction of the effect of changes on the ¥/$ exchange rate of the following, holding everything else unchanged?

142

a. A fall in the Japanese interest rate. _____.

b. A rise in the U.S. interest rate._____.

c. A rise in the expected future value of the ¥/$ exchange rate._____.

ANSWERS TO ODD-NUMBERED PROBLEMS IN THE TEXT

1. At an exchange rate of 50 cents per DM, the price of a bratwurst in terms of hot dogs is 1 hot dog per bratwurst. After a dollar appreciation to 40 cents per DM, the relative price of a bratwurst falls to 0.8 hot dogs per bratwurst.

3. The dollar rates of return are as follows:
    a. ($250,000 - $200,000)/$200,000 = 0.25.
    b. ($216 - $180)/$180 = 0.20.
    c. There are two parts of this return. One is the loss involved due to the appreciation of the dollar; the dollar appreciation is ($1.38 - $1.50)/$1.50 = -0.08. The other part of the return is the interest paid by the London bank on the deposit, 10%. (The size of the deposit is immaterial to the calculation of the rate of return.) In terms of dollars, the realized return on the London deposit is thus 2% per year.

5. The current equilibrium exchange rate must equal its expected future level since, with equality of nominal interest rates, there can be no expected increase or decrease in the dollar/pound exchange rate in equilibrium. If the expected exchange rate remains at $1.52 per pound and the pound interest rate rises to 10%, then interest parity is satisfied only if the current exchange rate changes such that there is an expected appreciation of the dollar equal to 5%. This will occur when the exchange rate rises to $1.60 per pound (a depreciation of the dollar against the pound).

7. The analysis will be parallel to that in the text. As shown in the accompanying diagrams, a movement down the vertical axis in the new graph, however, is interpreted as a deutschemark appreciation and dollar depreciation rather than the reverse. Also, the horizontal axis now measures the deutschemark interest rate. Diagram 14.2 demonstrates that, given the expected future exchange rate, a rise in the deutschemark interest rate from i_0 to i_1 will lead to a deutschemark appreciation from E_0 to E_1. Diagram 14.3 shows that, given the deutschemark interest rate of i, the expectation of a stronger deutschemark in the future leads to a leftward shift of the downward-

sloping curve from II to I'I' and a deutschemark appreciation (dollar depreciation) from E to E'. A rise in the dollar interest rate causes the same curve to shift rightward, so the DM depreciates against the dollar. This simply reverses the movement in diagram 14.3, with a shift from I'I' to II, and a depreciation of the deutschemark from E' to E. All of these results are the same as in the text when using the diagram for the dollar rather than the deutschemark.

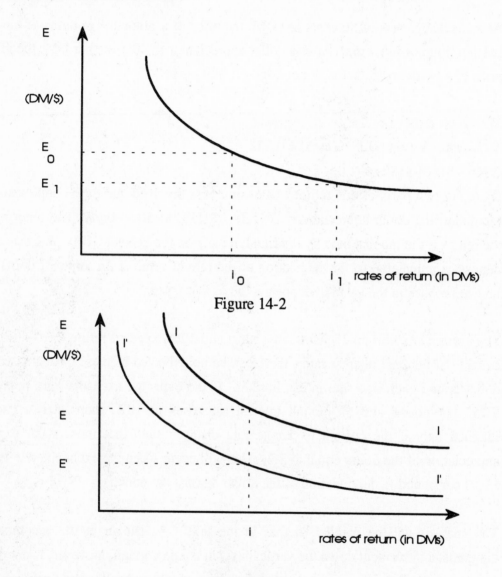

Figure 14-2

Figure 14-3

9.   The DM is less risky for you. When the rest of your wealth falls, the DM tends to appreciate, cushioning your losses by giving you a relatively high payoff in terms of dollars. Losses on your DM assets, on the other hand, tend to occur when they are least painful, that is, when the rest of your wealth is unexpectedly high. Holding the

DM therefore reduces the variability of your total wealth.

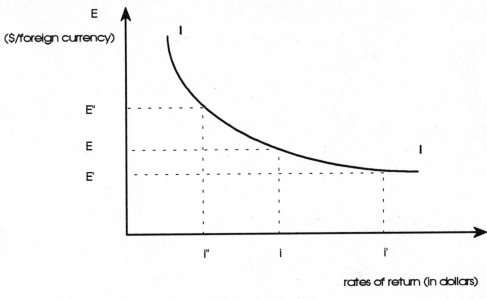

Figure 14-4

11. Greater fluctuations in the dollar interest rate lead directly to greater fluctuations in the exchange rate using the model described here. The movements in the interest rate can be investigated by shifting the vertical interest rate curve. As shown in diagram 14.4, these movements lead directly to movements in the exchange rate. For example, an increase in the interest rate from i to i' leads to a dollar appreciation from E to E'. A decrease in the interest rate from i to i" leads to a dollar depreciation from E to E". This diagram demonstrates the direct link between interest rate volatility and exchange rate volatility, given that the expected future exchange rate does not change.

13. The forward premium can be calculated as described in the appendix. In this case, we find the forward premium on DM to be (0.38 - 0.362)/0.362 = 0.5. The interest-rate difference between one-year dollar deposits and one-year DM deposits will be 5% because the interest difference must equal the forward premium on DM against dollars when covered interest parity holds.

CHAPTER 15

Money, Interest Rates, and Exchange Rates

CHAPTER ORGANIZATION

This chapter combines the foreign exchange market model of the previous chapter with an analysis of the demand for and supply of money to provide a more complete analysis of exchange rate determination in the short run. The chapter also introduces the concept of the long-run neutrality of money which states that, in the long-run, changes in money supply will have no permanent effect on real variables such as the real GNP, interest rates, or the real exchange rate. Combining the short-run analysis with the long-run neutrality of money allows us to examine the dynamics of the exchange rate, that is the movement of the exchange rate over time.

The chapter begins by reviewing the roles played by money. Money facilitates transactions, and an important part of the demand for it reflects this. Since money is demanded for the purchasing power it provides, money demand is a demand for real money balances, which are nominal balances divided by the price level (M/P). An increase in GNP reflects an increase in the number or size of transactions that people want to undertake, and thus money demand rises with GNP. Money also serves as a way to store wealth over time, but in this role it is overshadowed by other ways to store wealth that pay interest. As the interest rate rises, the opportunity cost of holding money rather than other assets also rises, and so money demand decreases with an increase in the interest rate.

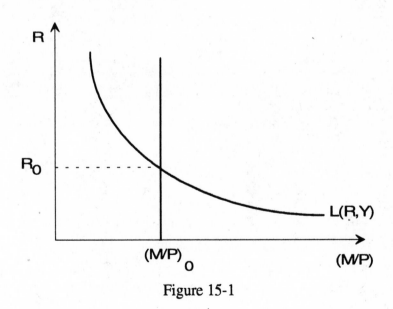

Figure 15-1

These two effects are summarized in the function L(R,Y) which increases with an increase in Y and decreases with an increase in R. The supply of nominal money balances is determined by the central bank. Money-market equilibrium--the equality of real money demand and the supply of real money balances--determines the equilibrium interest rate, as shown in the money market equilibrium diagram 15-1 where the equilibrium interest rate, R_0, reflects the interaction of money demand, $L(R,Y)$, and the supply of money equal to (M_0/P_0).

Combining the diagram portraying money-market equilibrium with the interest rate parity diagram presented in the previous chapter gives us a model of monetary influences on exchange rate determination, as shown below. The domestic interest rate, determined in the domestic money market, affects the exchange rate through the interest parity mechanism. Thus, an increase in domestic money supply from (M_0/P_0) to (M_1/P_0) leads to a fall in the domestic interest rate from R_0 to R_1. The home currency depreciates from E_0 to E_1. At this new equilibrium, interest parity holds; with a fixed future exchange rate, the exchange rate depreciation implies an expected future appreciation and this expected appreciation equates expected returns on interest-bearing assets denominated in domestic currency and in foreign currency. By simply reversing the steps of this argument, you can see how a contraction in the money supply leads to an exchange rate appreciation.

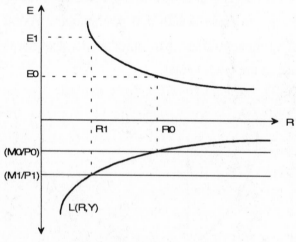

Figure 15-2

The chapter next describes the movement in the exchange rate over time in response to a permanent change in the money supply. The long-run neutrality of money is used to tie down the ultimate effect of monetary changes. The long-run neutrality of money is a condition that states that all else equal, a permanent increase in the money supply affects only the general price level--and not interest rates, relative prices, or real output--in the long run. Money prices, including, importantly, the money prices of foreign currencies, move in the long run in proportion to any change in the money supply's level. Thus, an increase in the money supply

148

ultimately results in a proportional exchange rate depreciation and a decrease in the money supply ultimately results in a proportional exchange rate appreciation.

The long-run neutrality of money is instrumental in understanding an important difference between permanent and temporary changes in money supply. Since a permanent increase in the money supply ultimately changes the long-run value of the exchange rate, it also has an effect on today's expectation of the future exchange rate. We saw in the previous chapter how expectations of the future value of the exchange rate affect its value today; for example, when the expected future value of the exchange rate becomes more depreciated, the interest parity curve shifts out and to the right, and, at any interest rate, the exchange rate depreciates today. Incorporating these types of effects in our model enables us to consider exchange rate dynamics.

One dynamic result which emerges from our model is exchange rate overshooting in response to a permanent change in the money supply. For example, consider a permanent money-supply expansion. There are two immediate effects of this; the interest rate falls due to the increase in real balances from (M_0/P_0) to (M_1/P_0) and expectations of a proportional long-run currency depreciation shift the interest parity curve out from I_0 to I_1. Thus the immediate effect is a depreciation of the exchange rate from its initial value of E_0 to E_1 as the equilibrium point in the top half of the diagram moves from point 0 to point 1. Foreign-exchange market equilibrium requires an initial depreciation of the currency large enough to equate expected returns on foreign and domestic bonds and since the domestic interest rate falls in the short run from R_0 to R_1, the currency must actually appreciate beyond (and thus overshoot) its new expected long-run level to maintain interest parity. Over time, money neutrality tells us that real balances must return to their original level, so in the long-run the permanent change in the money supply has no effect on real balances or on the interest rate, while the nominal exchange rate is more depreciated (at the level E_2). The real exchange rate does not change in the long run since the more depreciated value of the nominal exchange rate is matched by a higher long-run price level.

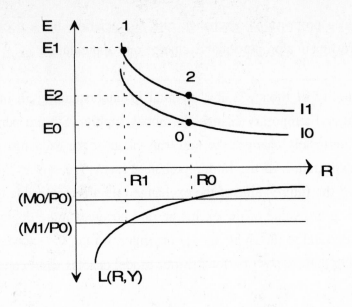

Figure 15-3

KEY TERMS

Define the following key terms:

1. Money supply _____
_____
_____
_____.

2. Aggregate money demand_____
_____
_____
_____.

3. Short run _____
_____
_____
_____.

4. Long run_____

_____

_____

_____.

5. Exchange-rate overshooting_____

_____

_____

_____.

REVIEW PROBLEMS

1. The following data is for the small country of Lilliput:

Year	Money Supply	Price Level	Nominal Interest Rate	Nominal GNP
1985	1000	100	8%	1000
1986	1500	100	6%	1200
1987	1500	150	8%	1000
1988	1500	200	12%	700
1989	2000	200	8%	1000

a. Draw a money demand schedule and a money supply schedule for Lilliput in 1985 in Graph 1 below. Make sure that the equilibrium corresponds to the data given in the table.

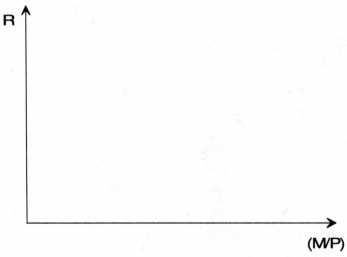

151

b. Now use a dashed line to draw, in Graph 1, the money demand and money supply schedules for 1986. Be sure that the intersection of the money demand and money supply schedules correspond to the equilibrium level of real money balances and the nominal interest rate given in the Lilliput data.

c. Would you need to draw another money demand schedule and money supply schedule in Graph 1 to depict the situation in Lilliput in 1987? Discuss why or why not, noting that the values of at least some of the variables in 1987 differ from their values in both 1985 and 1986.

_____

_____

_____.

d. In Graph 2, draw a money demand and money supply schedule for Lilliput for 1988, using a solid line for each. Then use a dashed line to show the money demand and money supply schedules for 1989.

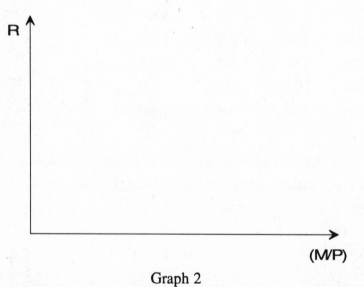

Graph 2

2. Graphs 2.1 through 2.3 represent initial schedules for the money demand, money supply, and interest parity schedules such that the equilibrium interest rate is $\underline{R}$ in each graph and the equilibrium exchange rate is $\underline{E}$ in each graph. Change one or more lines in the graph, as needed, to represent each of the following.

   i. A temporary increase in the money supply

   ii. An increase in the price level

   iii. A decrease in expected future exchange rates.

152

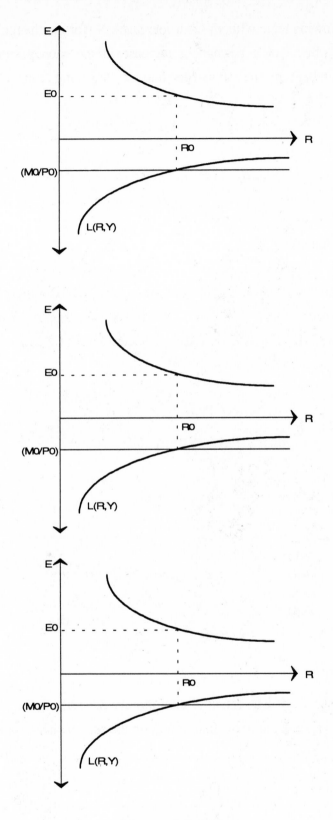

Figures 2.1-2.3

153

3.   Fill in the following table with an I (for increase), N (for no change) or D (for decrease) to show the effects of a permanent increase in the money supply on each of the following variables in the short-run and in the long run. ("Exchange Rate" is represented by "E.R.".)

	Short-run Effect	Long-run Effect
Prices	_____	_____
Output	_____	_____
Nominal E.R.	_____	_____
Real E.R.	_____	_____
Real Money Balances	_____	_____

4.   Graph 4.1 demonstrates an equilibrium where the money supply is $400 million, the U.S. price level is equal to 100, the U.S. interest rate is 7% and the U.S. dollar/ U.K. pound exchange rate equals its long-run expected level of 2. Not shown in the graph is the U.K. price level, which is equal to 50.

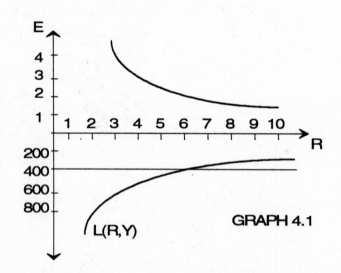

i. Demonstrate the immediate effect of a temporary decrease in the money supply to $300 in graph 4.1. Discuss the immediate effect on the real exchange rate.

_____

_____

_____.

ii. Now suppose instead that the decrease in the money supply to $300 million is permanent rather than temporary. How does the immediate effect of this permanent change differ from the immediate effect of the temporary change discussed in your answer to part (i)?

_____

_____

_____.

iii. What is the long run value of the U.S. price level, the U.S. interest rate, and the dollar/pound exchange rate in response to the permanent decrease in the U.S. money supply to $300 million?

_____

_____

_____.

iv. Continuing with your analysis of the effects of a permanent decrease in the money supply, show what happens in graph 4.1 over time. Use the information you obtain in your analysis to fill in the time graphs 4.3 and 4.4 when the money supply follows the permanent change shown in the time graph 4.2.

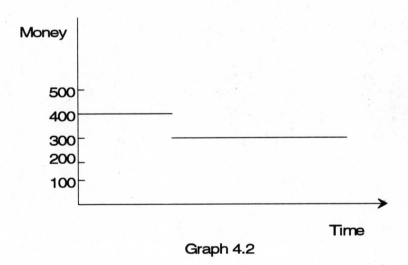

Graph 4.2

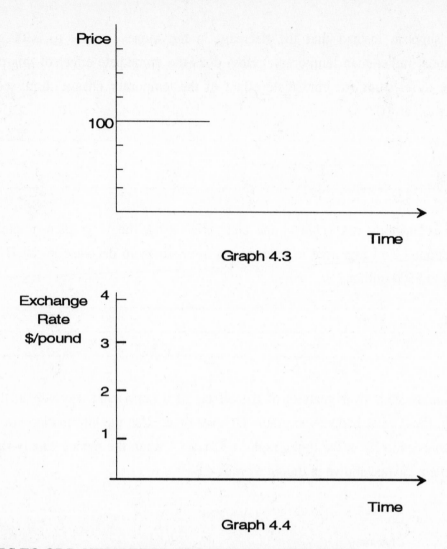

Price

100

Time

Graph 4.3

Exchange
Rate
$/pound

4

3

2

1

Time

Graph 4.4

ANSWERS TO ODD-NUMBERED PROBLEMS IN THE TEXT

1.   A reduction in real money demand has the same effects as an increase in the nominal money supply. In Diagram 15.4, the reduction in money demand is depicted as a backward shift in the money demand schedule from L_1 to L_2. The immediate effect of this is a depreciation of the exchange rate from E_1 to E_2, if the reduction in money demand is temporary, or a depreciation to E_3 if the reduction is permanent. The larger impact effect of a permanent reduction in money demand arises because this change also affects the future exchange rate expected in the foreign exchange market. In the long run, the price level rises to bring the real money supply into line with real money demand, leaving all relative prices, output, and the nominal interest rate the same and depreciating the domestic currency in proportion to the fall in real money demand. The long-run level of real balances is (M/P_2), a level where the interest rate in the long-run equals its initial value. The dynamics of adjustment to a permanent reduction in money

156

demand are from the initial point 1 in the diagram, where the exchange rate is E_1, immediately to point 2, where the exchange rate is E_3 and then, as the price level falls over time, to the new long-run position at point 3, with an exchange rate of E_4.

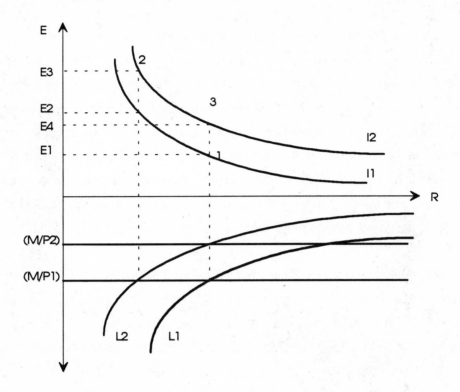

Figure 15-4

3. Equation 15-4 is $M^d/P = L(R,Y)$. The velocity of money, $V = Y/(M/P)$. Thus, when there is equilibrium in the money market such that money demand equals money supply, $V = Y/L(R,Y)$. When R increases, $L(R,Y)$ falls and thus velocity rises. When Y increases, $L(R,Y)$ rises by a smaller amount (since the elasticity of aggregate money demand with respect to real output is less than one) and the fraction $Y/L(R,Y)$ rises. Thus, velocity rises with either an increase in the interest rate or an increase in income. Since an increase in interest rates as well as an increase in income cause the exchange rate to appreciate, an increase in velocity is associated with an appreciation of the exchange rate.

5. Just as money simplifies economic calculations within a country, use of a vehicle currency for international transactions reduces calculation costs. More importantly, the more currencies used in trade, the closer the trade becomes to barter, since someone who receives payment in a currency she does not need must then sell it for a currency

she needs. This process is much less costly when there is a ready market in which any nonvehicle currency can be traded against the vehicle currency, which then fulfills the role of a generally accepted medium of exchange.

7. The interest rate at the beginning and at the end of this experiment are equal. The ratio of money to prices (the level of real balances) must be higher when full employment is restored than in the initial state where there is unemployment: the money-market equilibrium condition can be satisfied only with a higher level of real balances if GNP is higher. Thus, the price level rises, but by less than twice its original level. If the interest rate were initially below its long-run level, the final result will be one with higher GNP and higher interest rates. Here, the final level of real balances may be higher or lower than the initial level, and we cannot unambiguously state whether the price level has more than doubled, less than doubled, or exactly doubled.

9. Velocity is defined as real income divided by real balances or, equivalently, nominal income divided by nominal money balances ($V=P*Y/M$). Velocity in Brazil in 1985 was 13.4 (1418/106.1) while velocity in the United States was 6.3 (4010/641). These differences in velocity reflected the different costs of holding cruzados compared to holding dollars. These different costs were due to the high inflation rate in Brazil which quickly eroded the value of idle cruzados, while the relatively low inflation rate in the United States had a much less deleterious effect on the value of dollars.

CHAPTER 16

Price Levels and the Exchange Rate in the Long Run

CHAPTER ORGANIZATION

KEY THEMES

Our focus shifts to a longer time horizon in this chapter with an analysis of the determinants of the long-run value of the exchange rate. As you learned in earlier chapters, the expected future value of the exchange rate affects today's spot exchange rate -- therefore, an analysis of the determination of the long-run exchange rate is required for the completion of the short-run exchange rate model. In this chapter we divide the types of factors that affect the long-run exchange rate into two categories, monetary factors and real factors. Monetary factors include money supply and money demand, while real factors include the demand for and supply of goods and services. The ultimate goal of this chapter is to develop a general model of the determination of the exchange rate in the long run. In our path towards this goal, we touch on a number of related issues, including the effect of ongoing inflation on the exchange rate, the Fisher effect, and the role of tradable and nontradable goods. We also consider a number of empirical topics, such as the failure of purchasing power parity to explain the movement of the real exchange rate during the past twenty years and why prices are low in less developed countries.

It makes sense to think that similar goods sell for the same price, as expressed in a common currency, in different countries when there are no transport costs or trade restrictions. If this did not hold, sellers would sell more in the high-price country and less in the low-price country, forcing the prices in each country to move towards one another. This concept is behind the law of one price which is represented algebraically as $P_i = E \cdot P_i^*$ where P_i represents the price of a particular good in the home country, P_i^* represents its price in the foreign country, and E is the exchange rate. If we extend the law of one price from holding for one good to holding for a wide set of goods, we have the absolute purchasing power parity relationship, $P = EP^*$, where P represents the aggregate price level at home, and P^* represents the aggregate price level in the foreign country. Relative purchasing power parity relates changes in exchange rates to changes in relative price levels and may be valid even when absolute PPP is not. Relative purchasing power parity is expressed algebraically as $\pi = d + \pi^*$ where π is domestic inflation, π^* is foreign inflation, and d is the rate of depreciation of the currency.

Purchasing power parity provides a cornerstone of the monetary approach to the exchange rate, which serves as the first model of the long-run exchange rate developed in this chapter. In this framework, the purchasing power parity relationship is used to express the exchange rate as the price level in the home country relative to the price level in the foreign country, that is $E = P/P^*$. The money market equilibrium relationship is used to substitute money supply divided by money demand for the price level (that is, $P = L(R,Y)/M$, with a similar relationship for the foreign country). The Fisher relationship, which states that the nominal interest rate equals the real interest rate plus expected inflation (in symbols, $R = r + \pi^e$) allows us to substitute expected inflation for the nominal interest rate. The real interest rate, which is assumed to be the same in both countries, drops out when we subtract R^* from R. The resulting relationship models the long-run exchange rate as a function of relative money supplies, the inflation differential and relative output in the two countries;

$$E = (M/M^*) \cdot \lambda(\pi^e - \pi^{*e}, (Y^*/Y))$$

The lambda function represents the ratio of foreign to domestic money demand. It is important to understand why an increase in either $\pi^e - \pi^{*e}$, or in (Y^*/Y) increases the lambda function. The key is to remember that the lambda function represents foreign money demand divided by home money demand. An increase in inflation at home means higher home interest rates (through the Fisher equation) and lower home money demand, thus an increase in the lambda function. An increase in domestic output raises domestic money demand and causes the value of the lambda function to fall. The opposite results hold for changes in foreign expected inflation or for foreign output.

One result from this flexible price model that you may find confusing at first concerns the relationship between the long run exchange rate and the nominal interest rate. The model in this chapter provides an example of an increase in the interest rate associated with exchange rate depreciation. In contrast, the short-run analysis in the previous chapter provides an example of an increase in the domestic interest rate associated with an appreciation of the currency. These different relationships between the exchange rate and the interest rate reflect different causes for the rise in the interest rate as well as different assumptions concerning price rigidity. In the analysis of the previous chapter, the interest rate rises due to a contraction in the level of the nominal money supply. With fixed prices, this contraction of nominal balances is matched by a contraction in real balances. Excess money demand is resolved through a rise in interest rates which is associated with an appreciation of the currency to satisfy interest parity. In this chapter, the discussion of the Fisher effect demonstrates that the interest rate will rise in response to an anticipated increase in expected inflation due to an anticipated increase in the rate of growth of the money supply. A rise in interest rates would cause money demand to fall short of money supply. When prices are perfectly flexible, this excess money supply (which is an excess supply of real balances) is eliminated by an increase in the price level. Through PPP, this price level increase implies a depreciation of the exchange rate. Thus, with perfectly flexible prices (and its corollary PPP), an increase in the interest rate due to an increase in expected inflation is associated with a depreciation of the currency.

Empirical evidence presented in the chapter suggests that both absolute and relative PPP perform poorly for the period since 1971. Even the law of one price fails to hold for specific groups of commodities. The rejection of these theories is related to trade impediments (which help give rise to nontraded goods and services), to shifts in relative output prices and to imperfectly competitive markets. Since PPP serves as a cornerstone for the monetary approach, its rejection suggests that a convincing explanation of the long-run behavior of exchange rates must go beyond the doctrine of purchasing power parity.

The chapter concludes by presenting a more general model of the long-run behavior of exchange rates. This model differs from the monetary model because the more general model allows shifts in the demand and supply of goods and services to play a role. The real exchange rate will respond to shifts in the demand and supply of a country's goods and services, and thus in this model we drop the assumption of a constant real exchange rate. The real exchange rate, q, is the ratio of the foreign price index, expressed in domestic currency, to the domestic price index. If, for example, there is a balanced increase in productivity, the real exchange rate depreciates. If tastes shift and there is an increase in the demand for a country's goods, then the country's real exchange rate appreciates.

KEY TERMS

Define the following key terms:

1. Law of one price _____
_____
_____
_____.

2. Absolute purchasing power parity _____
_____
_____
_____.

3. Relative purchasing power parity _____
_____
_____
_____.

4. Fisher effect _____
_____
_____
_____.

5. Real interest rate _____
_____
_____
_____.

6. Real interest parity _____
_____
_____
_____.

7 Monetary approach to the exchange rate _____
_____
_____
_____.

REVIEW PROBLEMS

1. In this question you will use data to judge for yourself how well purchasing power parity performs in two different periods.

    a. Calculate the dollar/pound real exchange rate for 1961-1967 and for 1980-1987 using the following data for the consumer price index in each country and for the dollar/pound exchange rate. Then answer the following questions;

    b. What does absolute purchasing power parity predict for the value of the real exchange rate across time?

    _____
    _____
    _____.

c. Does the data seem to support the theory of purchasing power parity in the 1960s? In the 1980s?

_____

_____

_____.

d. What institutional factor might help explain the difference in the explanatory power of purchasing power parity across the two time periods?

_____

_____.

Year	U.S. CPI	British CPI	$/£ Nominal Exchange Rate	$/£ Real Exchange Rate
1961	36.3	19.3	2.80	_____
1962	36.7	20.1	2.81	_____
1963	37.2	20.5	2.80	_____
1964	37.6	21.2	2.79	_____
1965	38.3	22.2	2.80	_____
1966	39.4	23.0	2.79	_____
1967	40.5	23.6	2.75	_____
1980	100.0	100.0	2.33	_____
1981	110.4	111.9	2.03	_____
1982	117.2	121.5	1.75	_____
1983	120.9	127.1	1.52	_____
1984	126.1	133.5	1.34	_____
1985	130.6	141.6	1.30	_____
1986	133.1	146.4	1.47	_____
1987	137.9	152.5	1.64	_____

2. What does relative purchasing power parity predict for the behavior of real exchange rates? Use the data in question 1 to calculate whether relative purchasing power parity held for the dollar/pound exchange rate in the 1980s.

_____

_____

_____.

3. The chapter defines the real exchange rate, q, as the ratio EP^*/P where E is the exchange rate (domestic currency per unit of foreign currency), P^* is the foreign price level and P is the domestic price level. An equivalent way to define the real exchange rate is the price of tradable goods divided by the price of nontradable goods.

Defining the domestic price index as the weighted sum of tradable goods and nontradable goods in the domestic country, $P = aP_n + (1-a)P_t$. Define the foreign price index as the sum of tradables and nontradables in the foreign country, $P^* = bP^*_n + (1-a)P^*_t$. Assuming that purchasing power parity holds for traded goods, so $E = P_t/P^*_t$. Show how the definition $q = EP^*/P$ is related to the ratio of the price of traded to nontraded goods in the domestic economy, given the ratio of the price of traded to nontraded goods in the foreign economy.

_____

_____

_____

_____.

4. Consider the definition of the real exchange rate as the ratio of traded to nontraded goods, as discussed in the previous question. Discuss the real exchange rate effects of the following events.

a. A large loan is made to Jamaica expressly for the purpose of spending on health services in that country.

_____

_____.

b. Chile, which is a major copper exporter, finds that there is a fall in the world demand for copper.

_____

_____.

c. Colombia enjoys a particularly good coffee harvest.

_____

_____.

d. Nigeria, a major oil exporter, feels the effects of a fall in the world price of oil.

_____

_____.

e. The monetary authorities of Bolivia double the country's money supply.

_____

_____.

5. Productivity growth has slowed in the United States relative to other countries. This has implications for the real exchange rate as well as for the long-run nominal exchange rate.

a. What happens to the United States' real exchange rate if United States has a one-time decrease in productivity relative to that of another country? What happens to its nominal exchange rate?

_____

_____

_____.

b. How does the effect on the nominal exchange rate differ if, instead of a one-time drop in productivity, United States productivity relative to that of another country continues to decline for a very long time?

_____

_____

_____.

6. What is the effect on the long-run nominal dollar/DM exchange rate of a rise in the expected future rate of real dollar/DM depreciation? Explain the result in terms of the effects on nominal interest rates. Assume that all other things, including the current level of the real exchange rate, stay the same.

_____

_____

_____.

7. Use the real interest parity relationship to calculate the difference between the real interest rates in the United States and Japan in the late 1970s and 1980s. (assume that the actual inflation rate equals the expected inflation rate).

Year	U.S. CPI	Japanese CPI	$/¥	$/¥ Real Exch. Rate	Real Interest Rate Differential
1977	73.6	81.2	.0037	_____	_____
1978	79.2	79.1	.0048	_____	_____
1979	88.1	84.9	.0046	_____	_____
1980	100.0	100.0	.0044	_____	_____
1981	110.4	105.0	.0045	_____	_____
1982	117.2	107.8	.0040	_____	_____
1983	120.9	109.9	.0042	_____	_____
1984	126.1	112.3	.0042	_____	_____
1985	130.6	114.6	.0042	_____	_____
1986	133.1	115.3	.0059	_____	_____
1987	137.9	115.4	.0069	_____	_____

ANSWERS TO ODD-NUMBERED PROBLEMS IN THE TEXT

1. Relative PPP predicts that inflation differentials are matched by changes in the exchange rate. Under relative PPP, the guilder/cruzeiro exchange rate would fall by 95% with inflation rates of 100% in Brazil and 5% in Holland.

3. a. An tilt of spending towards nontraded products causes the real exchange rate to appreciate as the price of nontraded goods relative to traded goods rises (the real

exchange rate can be expressed as the price of tradables to the price of nontradables).

b. A shift in foreign demand towards domestic exports causes an excess demand for the domestic country's goods which causes the relative price of these goods to rise; that is, it causes the real exchange rate of the domestic country to appreciate.

5. The real effective exchange rate series for Britain shows an appreciation of the pound from 1977 to 1981, followed by a period of depreciation. Note that the appreciation is sharpest after the increase in oil prices starts in early 1979; the subsequent depreciation is steepest after oil prices soften in 1982. An increase in oil prices increases the incomes received by British oil exporters, raising their demand for goods. The supply response of labor moving into the oil sector is comparable to an increase in productivity which also causes the real exchange rate to appreciate. Of course, a fall in the price of oil has opposite effects. (Oil is not the only factor behind the behavior of the pound's real exchange rate. This was also a period in which there was stringent monetary policy.)

7. A permanent shift in the real money demand function will alter the long-run equilibrium nominal exchange rate, but not the long-run equilibrium real exchange rate. Since the real exchange rate does not change, we can use the monetary approach equation, $E = (M/M^*) \cdot \{L(R^*, Y^*)/L(R, Y)\}$. A permanent increase in money demand at any nominal interest rate leads to a proportional appreciation of the long-run nominal exchange rate. Intuitively, the level of prices for any level of nominal balances must be lower in the long run for money market equilibrium. The reverse holds for a permanent decrease in money demand. The real exchange rate, however, depends upon relative prices and productivity terms which are not affected by general price-level changes.

9. With no changes in monetary conditions in the two countries the franc would appreciate against the DM in nominal terms as well as in real terms.

11. The balanced expansion in domestic spending will increase the amount of imports consumed in the country that has a tariff in place, but imports cannot rise in the country that has a quota in place. Thus, in the country with the quota, there would be an excess demand for imports if the real exchange rate appreciated by the same amount as in the country with tariffs. Therefore, the real exchange rate in the country with a quota must appreciate by less than in the country with the tariff.

13. Suppose there is a temporary fall in the real exchange rate in an economy, that is the exchange rate appreciates today and then will depreciate back to its original level in the future. The expected depreciation of the real exchange rate, by real interest parity, causes the real interest rate to rise. If there is no change in the expected inflation rate then the nominal interest rate rises with the rise in the real exchange rate. This event may also cause the exchange rate to appreciate if the effect of a current depreciation dominates the effect of the expected depreciation of the real exchange rate, which would work in the opposite direction.

15. The initial effect of a reduction in the money supply in a model with sticky prices is an increase in the nominal exchange rate and an appreciation of the nominal exchange rate. The real interest rate, which equals the nominal interest rate minus expected inflation, rises by more than the nominal interest rate since the reduction in the money supply causes the nominal interest rate to rise and deflation occurs during the transition to the new equilibrium. The real exchange rate depreciates during the transition to the new equilibrium (where its value is the same as in the original state). This satisfies the real interest parity relationship which states that the difference between the domestic and the foreign real interest rate equals the expected depreciation of the domestic real exchange rate -- in this case, the initial effect is an increase in the real interest rate in the domestic economy coupled with an expected depreciation of the domestic real exchange rate. In any event, the real interest parity relationship must be satisfied since it is simply a restatement of the Fisher equation, which defines the real interest rate, combined with the interest parity relationship, which is a cornerstone of the sticky-price model of the determination of the exchange rate.

17. Combining the Fisher relationship with the interest parity condition we find that expected depreciation of the dollar/Swiss franc exchange rate equals the difference between U.S. and Swiss inflation rates less the difference between U.S. and Swiss real interest rates. The question states that the ex post difference between U.S. and Swiss real interest rates was positive between 1976 and 1980. Inspecting the data presented in figure 16-1 in the text demonstrates that U.S. inflation was consistently higher than Swiss inflation over this period. We thus expect that this period saw a consistent expected and actual depreciation of the dollar relative to the Swiss franc. Between 1981 and 1982 this pattern reverses with very high real U.S. interest rates, and comparable U.S. and Swiss inflation rates. This corresponds to the beginning of the dramatic appreciation of the dollar in 1981.

The actual data are as follows: the average Swiss franc/dollar exchange rate in 1978 was 1.79, for 1979 1.66, for 1980 1.68, for 1981 1.96 and for 1982 2.03. Thus we see an appreciation of the Swiss franc between 1978 and 1980 followed by a dramatic depreciation of the Swiss franc from 1981 to 1982.

CHAPTER 17

Output and the Exchange Rate in the Short Run

CHAPTER ORGANIZATION

Determinants of Aggregate Demand in an Open Economy

      Determinants of Consumption Demand

      Determinants of the Current Account

      How Real Exchange Rate Changes Affect the Current Account

      How Disposable-Income Changes Affect the Current Account

The Equation of Aggregate Demand

      The Real Exchange Rate and Aggregate Demand

      Real Income and Aggregate Demand

How Output is Determined in the Short-Run

Output-Market Equilibrium in the Short-Run: The DD Schedule

      Output, the Exchange Rate, and Output-Market Equilibrium

      Deriving the DD Schedule

      Factors that Shift the DD Schedule

Asset-Market Equilibrium in the Short Run: The AA Schedule

      Output, the Exchange Rate, and Asset-Market Equilibrium

      Deriving the AA Schedule

      Factors that Shift the AA Schedule

      Short-Run Equilibrium for the Economy: Putting the DD and AA Schedules Together

Temporary Changes in Monetary and Fiscal Policy

      Monetary Policy

      Fiscal Policy

      Policies to Maintain Full Employment

      Some Problems of Policy Formulation

Permanent Shifts in Monetary and Fiscal Policy

      A Permanent Increase in the Money Supply

      Adjustment to a Permanent Increase in the Money Supply

      A Permanent Fiscal Expansion

Macroeconomic Policies and the Current Account

      Case Study: U.S. Monetary Policy and Fiscal Policy in Action, 1979 - 1983

Gradual Trade-Flow Adjustment and Current-Account Dynamics

KEY THEMES

In Chapters 14 and 15, we focused on exchange rate determination taking output as given. In this chapter we develop a macroeconomic model that allows us to solve for output and the exchange rate through the interplay of an aggregate demand schedule and an asset market equilibrium schedule. This model enables us to determine the effects a number of factors, most importantly monetary and fiscal policies, on both the level of output and the exchange rate. The chapter also discusses different effects of temporary and permanent policies. The chapter concludes with some issues that have recently gained a good deal of attention; the possibility of a J-curve response of the current account to currency depreciation and exchange rate pass-through, that is the response of import prices to exchange rate movements.

The development of the model begins by developing an output market schedule. In a Keynesian-cross diagram, the aggregate demand function shifts up with a depreciation of the nominal exchange rate since this causes exports to rise and imports to fall, given foreign and domestic prices, fiscal policy, and investment levels. When we translate this into a diagram with the exchange rate on the vertical axis and output on the horizontal axis, we obtain a positively sloped output-market equilibrium (DD) schedule. The asset-market equilibrium (AA) schedule, which completes the model, has a negative slope. The derivation of this schedule follows from the analysis of previous chapters. If you have already taken intermediate macroeconomics, you may have noted that the intuition behind the slope of the AA curve is identical to that of the LM schedule with the additional relationship of interest parity providing the link between the closed-economy LM schedule and the open-economy AA schedule. As with the LM curve, higher income increases money demand and raises the home-currency interest rate (given real balances). In an open economy, higher interest rates require currency appreciation to satisfy interest parity (for a given future expected exchange rate). Appendix I discuss the relationship between the IS-LM model and the analysis in this chapter.

Expectations about how long certain policies will be in place are important in understanding the effects of these policies. The DD-AA model enables us to understand how the effects of temporary policies differ from those of permanent policies. Temporary policies have no effect on the expected future exchange rate while permanent policies shift the expected future exchange rate in line with the effects identified in Chapter 16. Temporary policies only have short-run effects, since the policies are reversed (by definition) before the long-run arrives. Permanent policies, on the other hand, have both short-run and long-run effects. In the long-run, prices change in response to monetary factors to clear markets.

Both temporary and permanent increases in money supply expand output in the short run through exchange rate depreciation. The long-run analysis of a permanent monetary change once again shows how the overshooting result can occur. Temporary expansionary fiscal policy raises output in the short run and causes the exchange rate to appreciate. Permanent fiscal expansion,however, has no effect on output even in the short run. The reason for this is that, given the assumptions of the model, the currency appreciation in response to permanent fiscal expansion completely "crowds out" exports. In terms of the mechanics of the model, the outward shift of the DD curve due to the fiscal expansion is just offset by an inward shift of the AA curve due to an appreciation of the expected exchange rate. A case study of U.S. fiscal and monetary policy between 1979 and 1983 allows you to apply the model to a historical episode. The model explains the recession of 1982 and the appreciation of the dollar as a result of tight monetary and loose fiscal policy.

The chapter concludes with some discussion of real-world modifications of the basic model. Recently, we have seen evidence that argues against a tight, unvarying relationship between movements in the nominal exchange rate and shifts in competitiveness and thus between nominal exchange rate movements and movements in the trade balance. Instead, we have seen that exchange rate pass-through is less than complete and thus nominal exchange rate movements are not translated one-for-one into changes in the real exchange rate. Also,the current account may worsen immediately after currency depreciation. This J-curve effect occurs because of time lags in deliveries and because of different demand effects in the short-run as compared to the long-run. The chapter contains a discussion of the way in which the analysis of the model would be affected by the inclusion of incomplete exchange rate pass-through and time-varying elasticities. Appendix II provides further information on trade elasticities with a presentation of the Marshall-Lerner conditions and a reporting of estimates of the impact, short-run and long-run elasticities of demand for international trade in manufactured goods for a number of countries.

KEY TERMS

Define the following key terms:

1. Monetary policy _____
_____
_____
_____.

2. Fiscal policy _____
_____
_____
_____.

3. J-curve _____
_____
_____
_____.

4. Exchange-rate pass-through _____
_____
_____
_____.

5. Beachhead effect _____
_____
_____
_____.

6. Marshall-Lerner condition _____
_____
_____
_____.

REVIEW PROBLEMS

1. a. Discuss how a temporary increase in output in a foreign economy affects the DD schedule:

   _____

   _____

   _____.

   b. Discuss how a temporary rise in the foreign interest rate affects the AA schedule:

   _____

   _____

   _____.

   c. The response of the interest rate and output for a closed economy to a fiscal expansion is:

   _____

   _____

   _____.

   The response to a monetary expansion is:

   _____

   _____

   _____.

   d. We can compare the effects of a foreign fiscal expansion to a foreign monetary expansion (hint: you will need to use your results from parts (a), b) and (c). Do not worry about additional feedback effects from the domestic economy to the foreign economy). In comparing these results, we find:

   _____

   _____

   _____.

2. a. Suppose the following headline appears in today's newspaper; "Congress Agrees to Tax Cut Next Year." What would you expect the effect of this headline to be on output and the exchange rate today?

Output:_____.

Exchange Rate:_____.

b. Suppose this headline appears in today's newspaper instead; "Federal Reserve Announces It Will Raise Money Supply Next Year." What would you expect the effect of this headline to be on output and the exchange rate today?

Output:_____.

Exchange Rate:_____.

c. Suppose both of these headlines appear in today's newspaper. Would you still necessarily expect to find an effect on output and the exchange rate?

_____

_____

_____.

3. Consider the following comment:

"The current account depends upon income and the real exchange rate. If income rises, consumption of imports is high, and the current account worsens. Thus, if monetary policy is the only tool that authorities can respond with quickly, a worsening of the current account due to a rise in income (say because of a tax cut) requires a monetary contraction to moderate the rise in income and stop the deterioration of the current account."

a. Use the DD-AA diagram on the next page to analyze the effects of a tax cut on income and the current account.

b. Do you find that the current account worsens and that income rises, as suggested in the comment?

_____

_____

_____.

176

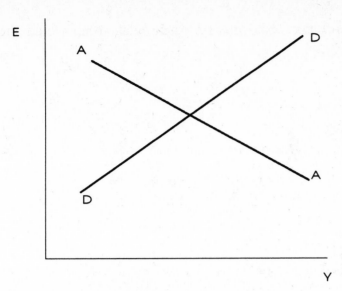

c. Now consider a monetary contraction. Use the following DD-AA diagram to show its effects on income and the current account.

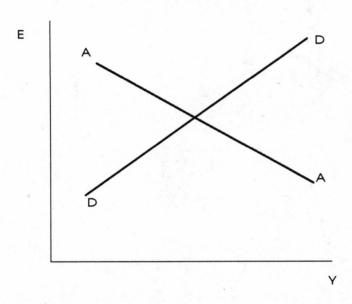

d. Does this monetary policy response moderate the rise in income? Does it reverse the deterioration of the current account?

_____

_____

_____.

4.   Many countries impose taxes or controls on holding foreign assets. One way to model this is to modify the interest parity equation by including a tax term. Since the return to foreign bonds is mitigated by the tax, the domestic interest rate need not be as high as it

would be if there were not a tax. The interest parity relationship would thus be modified as follows;

$$R = R^* + (E^e - E)/E - T$$

a. How does this modification in the interest parity relationship alter the DD-AA diagram?

_____

_____

_____.

b. Show the effects of a temporary increase in T, the tax on foreign assets, in the following diagram.

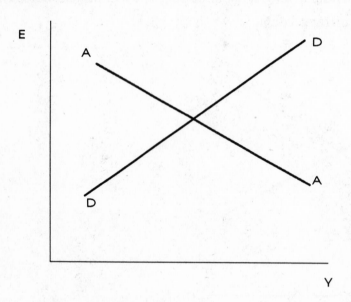

5.   We have been assuming that the expected exchange rate equals the rate predicted by the analysis in Chapter 16. Suppose instead that people always expect the exchange rate in the future to equal its value today.

a. Draw the DD- AA diagram under this assumption.

E

Y

b. Compare the effects of a temporary increase in the money supply on the exchange rate and output under these two different assumptions about E^e.

E

Y

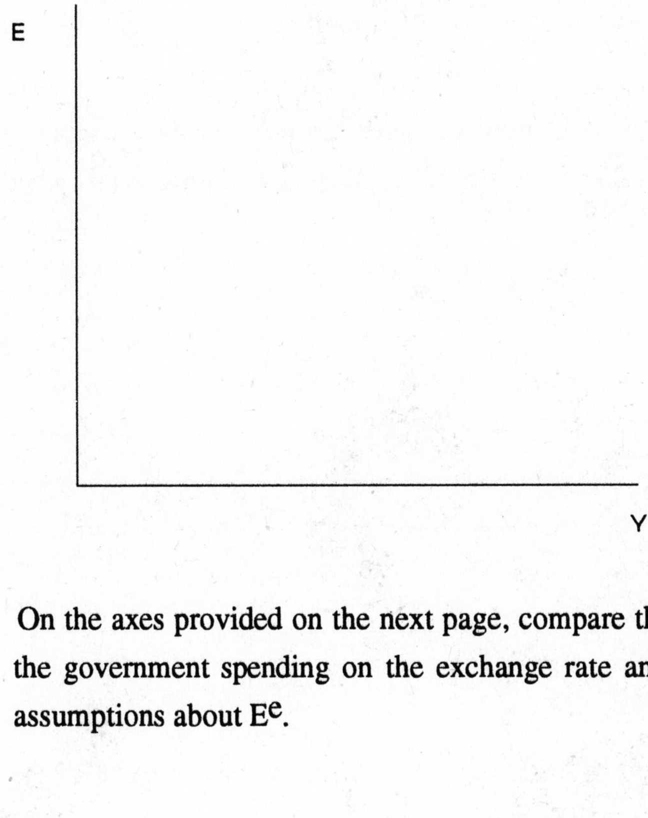

c. On the axes provided on the next page, compare the effects of a temporary increase in the government spending on the exchange rate and output under these two different assumptions about E^e.

E

Y

6. Firms may increase their prices when faced with an increase in demand for their goods. An increase in demand in an economy may be due to either a fiscal or a monetary expansion. Discuss how the pass-through relationship which links changes in exchange rates to changes in prices depends upon the source of the movement of the exchange rate when prices respond to demand.(hint: consider the way in which exchange rates and output move together when there is a fiscal expansion as compared to when there is a monetary expansion.)

_____

_____

_____

_____

_____

_____

_____

_____.

ANSWERS TO ODD-NUMBERED PROBLEMS IN THE TEXT

1. A decline in investment demand decreases the level of aggregate demand for any level of the exchange rate. Thus a decline in investment demand causes the DD curve to shift to the left.

3. A temporary fiscal policy shift affects employment and output, even if the government maintains a balanced budget. An intuitive explanation for this relies upon the different

180

propensities to consume of the government and of taxpayers. If the government spends $1 more and finances this spending by taxing the public $1 more, aggregate demand will have risen because the government spends the entire $1 while the public reduces its spending by less than $1 (choosing to reduce its saving as well as its consumption). The ultimate effect on aggregate demand is even larger than this first round difference between government and public spending propensities, since the first round generates subsequent spending (Of course, currency appreciation still prevents permanent fiscal shifts from affecting output in our model.)

5. Diagram 17.1 can be used to show that any permanent fiscal expansion worsens the current account. In this diagram, the schedule XX represents combinations of the exchange rate and income for which the current account is in balance. Points above and to the left of XX represent current account surplus and points below and to the right represent current account deficit. A permanent fiscal expansion shifts the DD curve to D'D' and, because of the effect on the long run exchange rate, the AA curve shifts to A'A'. The equilibrium point moves from 0, where the current account is in balance, to 1, where there is a current account deficit. If, instead, there was a temporary fiscal expansion of the same size, the AA curve would not shift and the new equilibrium would be at point 2 where there is a current account deficit, although it is smaller than the current account deficit at point 1.

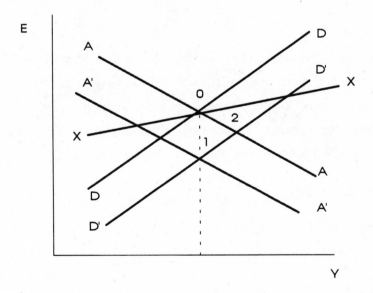

Figure 17-1

7.   A currency depreciation accompanied by a deterioration in the current account balance could be caused by factors other than a J-curve. For example,a fall in foreign demand for domestic products worsens the current account and also lowers aggregate demand, depreciating the currency. In terms of diagram 17.2, DD and XX undergo equal vertical shifts, to D'D' and X'X', respectively,resulting in a current account deficit as the equilibrium moves from point 0 to point 1. To detect a J-curve, one might check whether the prices of imports in terms of domestic goods rise when the currency is depreciating,offsetting a decline in import volume and a rise in export volume.

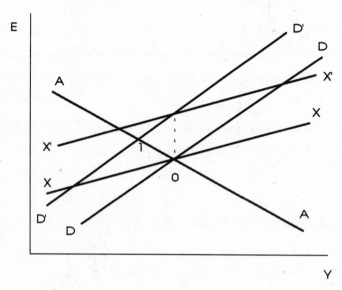

Figure 17-2

9.   If exchange rate pass-through is incomplete in the short-run then the DD curve becomes steeper; a given appreciation of the exchange rate crowds out less imports because the foreign currency price of these imports falls concurrent with the appreciation of the currency. In this case, a permanent fiscal expansion both shifts out the DD curve and, because of pricing behavior by foreign exporters, makes it steeper. This results in an increase in output along with a current account deficit, as depicted in diagram 17.3 by a shift from DD to D'D' which shifts the equilibrium point from 0 to 1. Over time, as the foreign currency price of imports rise, the slope of the DD returns to its original value, which reduces output and offsets, to some extent, the current account deficit. In the diagram, this is depicted as a movement from point 1 to point 2 with a flattening of the output market curve from D'D' to D"D". Thus, low government and private savings caused the current account deficit, but incomplete pass-through exacerbated the initial effect on the current account.

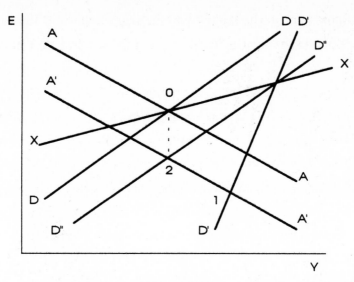

Figure 17-3

11. The derivation of the Marshall-Lerner condition uses the assumption of a balanced current account to substitute EX for (q x EX*). We cannot make this substitution when the current account is not initially zero. Instead, we define the variable z = (q x EX*)/EX. This variable is the ratio of imports to exports, denominated in common units. When there is a current account surplus, z will be less than 1 and when there is a current account deficit z will exceed 1. It is possible to take total derivatives of each side of the equation CA = EX - q EX* and derive a general Marshall-Lerner condition as n + z n* > z, where n and n* are as defined in the appendix. The balanced current account (z=1) Marshall-Lerner condition is a special case of this general condition. A depreciation is less likely to improve the current account the larger its initial deficit when n* is less than 1. Conversely, a depreciation is more likely to cause an improvement in the current account the larger its initial surplus, again for values of n* less than 1.

13. An increase in the risk premium shifts the asset market curve out and to the right, all else equal. A permanent increase in government spending shifts the asset market curve in and to the right since it causes the expected future exchange rate to appreciate. A permanent rise in government spending also causes the goods market curve to shift down and to the right since it raises aggregate demand. In the case where there is no risk premium, the new intersection of the DD and AA curve after a permanent increase in government spending is at the full-employment level of output since this is the only level consistent with no change in the long-run price level. In the case discussed in this question, however, the nominal interest rate rises with the increase in the risk premium.

Therefore, output must also be higher than the original level of full-employment output; as compared to the case in the text, the AA curve does not shift by as much so output rises.

15. The text shows output cannot rise following a permanent fiscal expansion if output is initially at its long-run level. Using a similar argument, we can show that output cannot fall from its initial long-run level following a permanent fiscal expansion. A permanent fiscal expansion cannot have an effect on the long-run price level since there is no effect on the money supply or the long-run values of the domestic interest rate and output. When output is initially at its long-run level, R equals R* and Y equals Y^f and real balances are unchanged in the short run. If output did fall, there would be excess money supply and the domestic interest rate would have to fall, but this would imply an expected appreciation of the currency since the interest differential (R - R*) would then be negative. This, however, could only occur if the currency appreciates in real terms as output rises and the economy returns to long-run equilibrium. This appreciation, however, would cause further unemployment and output would not rise and return back to Y^f. As with the example in the text, this contradiction is only resolved if output remains at Y^f.

CHAPTER 18

Fixed Exchange Rates and Foreign Exchange Intervention

CHAPTER ORGANIZATION

KEY THEMES

Although we use the same equations (and thus, the same model) to characterize the goods market and the money market whether an economy has fixed or flexible exchange rates, in some important ways the analysis of an economy that has a fixed exchange rate reverses the analysis of an economy with a floating exchange rates. Under fixed exchange rates, an analysis considers the effects policies have on the balance of payments (and the domestic money supply), taking the exchange rate as given. Conversely, under flexible exchange rates with no official foreign-exchange intervention, the balance of payments equals zero, the money supply is a variable chosen by policy-makers, and analysis focuses on exchange rate determination. In the intermediate case of managed floating, both the money supply and the exchange rate become, to an extent which is determined by central-bank policies, variables that are outcomes of the model.

This chapter analyzes various types of monetary policy regimes under which the degree of exchange-rate flexibility is limited. It has been more than twenty years since the United States stopped participating in the fixed-exchange rate Bretton Woods system, but the analysis presented in this chapter has current relevance. Many industrial economies attempt to manage their exchange rates through foreign-exchange intervention. Fixed exchange rates are prevalent among developing countries. Regional currency arrangements, most notably the European Monetary System, represent an important institutional arrangement. Finally, there are recurrent calls for a new international monetary regime based upon more aggressive exchange-rate management.

The chapter begins with an analysis of a stylized central bank balance sheet to show the link between the balance of payments, official foreign-exchange intervention, and the domestic money supply. An important point to remember here is that any change in the holdings of an asset by the central bank must be balanced by an offsetting change in the central bank's liabilities or by its holdings of another asset. When the central bank's liabilities change there is a change in the economy's money supply. Combining this link between the central bank's liabilities and the money supply with the exchange-rate determination analysis of Chapter 15 demonstrates how a central bank alters the money supply to peg the nominal exchange rate. A key point here is that if the central bank's focus is to peg the exchange rate then it must devote monetary policy to this goal, giving up the use of monetary policy for other purposes. Thus under fixed exchange rates the central bank does not control the money supply since it must fix the exchange rate.

The model developed in Chapter 17 is used to demonstrate some important characteristics of a fixed exchange rate regime. Monetary policy cannot be used separately from its goal of maintaining a fixed exchange rate. Fiscal policy, on the other hand, is very effective since the monetary authorities must react to fiscal policy expansion in a way that cancels the "crowding out" effects of an appreciation that occur under floating exchange rates. An additional policy tool that is available under a fixed exchange rate regime is a change in the exchange rate, which is called a devaluation if the currency is made less valuable and a revaluation if it is made more valuable. The short-run and long-run effects of devaluation and revaluation are examined. In the short-run, a devaluation makes an economy's exports more competitively priced which improves the trade account, expands output and raises the economies money supply (remember that a trade account surplus causes a balance of payments surplus and this, in turn, increases the money supply). Over a longer time horizon, however, prices will rise in the domestic economy and the real exchange rate (which equals $E \cdot P^*/P$), having depreciated because of the devaluation, appreciates back to its original value. This is just another example of how, in the long-run, a purely monetary change (such as an increase in the money supply under flexible exchange rates) has no lasting effect on output.

An expected devaluation of a currency can prompt a balance of payments crisis. Such an expectation causes private capital flight as people attempt to buy foreign currency at a relatively good rate and then, after the devaluation, trade the foreign currency back for domestic currency and realize a profit (note that even if the devaluation does not occur trading foreign currency back for domestic currency at the original exchange rate does not cause a loss to speculators; thus speculators have a "one-way bet"). The central bank loses reserves as people attempt to exchange their domestic currency for foreign currency. If the central bank runs out of foreign reserves then it will no longer be able to maintain the exchange rate at its initial level. Appendix III to this chapter contains a detailed analysis of the timing of a balance of payments crisis.

Managed floating represents a more realistic intermediate case than the polar cases of fixed and floating rates. An important issue in the study of managed exchange rates is sterilized foreign-exchange intervention. We discussed above how a central bank may intervene in the foreign exchange market by changing its asset holdings and, by so doing, altering its liabilities and thus affecting the money supply. A central bank may alternatively trade one type of asset for another, such as a domestic-currency bond for a foreign-currency bond, which does not change in its total amount of assets and thus does not affect the economy's money supply. This sterilized intervention changes the composition of interest-bearing assets held by the central bank, and thus also by the public. The theory of imperfect asset substitutability suggest why this type of policy may affect the exchange rate, even though the money supply has not changed. When we include a risk premium in the model governments have some scope to run independent exchange rate and monetary policies in the short run. As discussed in the chapter, however, attempts to demonstrate empirically the effectiveness of sterilized foreign-exchange operations are generally negative. Intervention may also play another role, as a "signal" of future policy actions, and thus may affect the exchange rate in this capacity.

While we have focused on the distinction between fixed and flexible exchange rate systems, it is important to note that not all fixed exchange rate systems are the same. The gold standard and a reserve-currency system represent two different fixed exchange rate systems. A key distinction between these systems is the asymmetry between the center country and the rest of the world under a reserve-currency system compared to the symmetric adjustment among all countries under the gold standard. Under a reserve-currency system, the reserve center country's currency is "as good as gold," which gives it exclusive control over world monetary conditions (at least when interest parity links countries' money markets). Under a gold standard only gold is "as good as gold" and thus no one country can control world monetary conditions. The chapter discusses some of the pros and cons of the gold standard and the gold-exchange standard.

Appendix I presents a more detailed model of exchange-rate determination with imperfect asset substitutability. Appendix II describes the monetary approach to the balance of payments and its usefulness as a tool of policy analysis. Appendix III provides an analysis of the timing of balance of payments crises.

KEY TERMS

Define the following key terms.

1. Sterilized foreign-exchange intervention _____
_____
_____
_____.

2. European Monetary System _____
_____
_____
_____.

3. Imperfect asset substitutability _____
_____
_____
_____.

4. Gold standard _____
_____
_____
_____.

5. Gold-exchange standard_____
_____
_____
_____.

6. Risk premium _____
_____
_____
_____.

7. Balance of payments crisis _____

_____

_____

_____.

REVIEW PROBLEMS

1. The tropical country of Humidor exports cigars and imports air conditioners. In 1992, Humidor exported H$10 million worth of cigars and imported H$9 million worth of air conditioners, where H$ represents the national currency, called the Humid dollar.

    a. Fill in the following balance of payments equation if the central bank does not intervene in the foreign exchange market, neither buying nor selling foreign currency, and if there are no autonomous private capital flows.

    Balance of Payments = Current Account Surplus + Capital Account Surplus

    H$_____-_____ = H$_____-_____ + H$_____-_____

    b. The balance sheet for the central bank of Humidor at the end of 1991 is given below. Under the assumption given in part (a) demonstrate how this balance sheet changes, and thus what happens to the money supply of Humidor, by the end of 1992 (assume that the central bank does not undertake any open market operations unrelated to the balance of payments).

    Balance Sheet of the Central Bank   Balance Sheet of the Central Bank
    on December 31, 1991   on December 31, 1992

	Assets	Liabilities
Domestic		
	H$100 mil.	H$_____mil.
Foreign		
	H$ 20 mil.	

	Assets	Liabilities
Domestic		
	H$ 120 mil	H$_____mil.
Foreign		
	H$_____mil.	

190

c. Now fill in the following balance of payments equation if Humidor has a fixed exchange rate and again there are no private capital flows.

Balance of Payments = Current Account Surplus + Capital Account Surplus

H$_____-_____ = H$_____-_____ + H$_____-_____

d. Under the assumptions that Humidor has a fixed exchange rate and that there are no private capital flows, demonstrate how the balance sheet of the central bank changes, and thus what happens to the money supply of Humidor, between the end of 1991 and the end of 1992.

Balance Sheet of the Central Bank
on December 31, 1991

	Assets	Liabilities
Domestic		
	H$100 mil.	
		H$ 120 mil.
Foreign		
	H$ 20 mil.	

Balance Sheet of the Central Bank
on December 31, 1992

	Assets	Liabilities
Domestic		
	H$_____mil.	
		H$_____mil.
Foreign		
	H$_____mil.	

2. While in practice the task of maintaining a fixed exchange rate falls to a country's monetary authority, in theory fiscal policy could be set to maintain the fixed exchange rate system, thus enabling monetary policy to pursue other goals. In this problem consider the country of Fiscalia which has a fixed exchange rate equal to E_0 that is maintained through government spending and tax policy.

a. Suppose there is a sudden, unexpected increase in investment demand in Fiscalia. Demonstrate in the diagram on the next page how this would affect the exchange rate if there were no government intervention. Discuss what must happen to government spending or taxes in Fiscalia under fixed exchange rates when this increase in investment demand occurs.

_____

_____

_____.

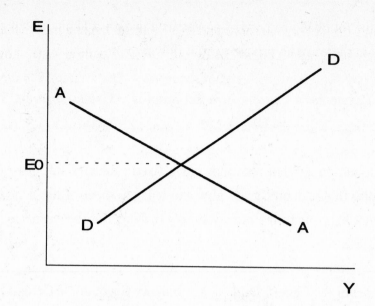

b. Suppose there is an unexpected fall in money demand in Fiscalia. Demonstrate this effect in the diagram below and the required fiscal response.

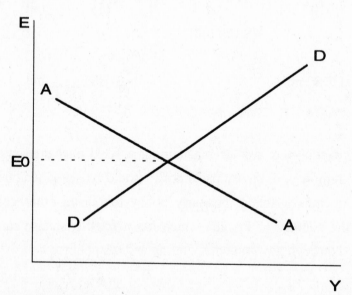

c. Is fiscal policy effective in altering output in Fiscalia? Does monetary policy have any effect? If your results differ from the standard case studied in the chapter, try to explain the source of this difference.

_____

_____

_____

_____.

3. Suppose that the Federal Reserve and the Bank of Japan agree that it is necessary to have the yen appreciate against the dollar. Neither central bank, however, wishes to have its money supply change as a consequence of this foreign exchange intervention.

a. Below is a simplified balance sheet of the Federal Reserve in which its assets include dollar-denominated bonds and yen-denominated bonds. Show how the Fed might alter its asset holdings to achieve an appreciation of the yen while keeping the United States money supply fixed.

Balance Sheet of the Federal
Reserve Before Intervention

Assets	Liabilities
Domestic	
$500 bil.	
	$600 bil.
Foreign	
$100 bil.	

Balance Sheet of the Federal
Reserve After Intervention

Assets	Liabilities
Domestic	
$____bil.	
	$____bil.
Foreign	
$____bil.	

b. Below is a simplified balance sheet of the Bank of Japan. Show how it might alter its asset holdings to depreciate the dollar while keeping the Japanese money supply fixed.

Balance Sheet of the Bank of
Japan Before Intervention

Assets	Liabilities
Domestic	
¥2000 bil.	
	¥2800 bil.
Foreign	
¥800 bil.	

Balance Sheet of the Bank of
Japan After Intervention

Assets	Liabilities
Domestic	
¥____bil.	
	¥____bil.
Foreign	
¥____bil.	

c. Demonstrate how the risk premium on U.S. bonds changes with the policy described in part (a) in the diagram on the right. Demonstrate how the risk premium on Japanese bonds changes with the policy described in part (b) in the diagram on the right.

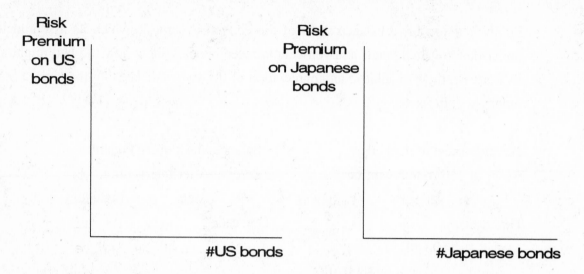

d. Use the diagram on the right below to show the effects on the dollar/yen exchange rate of the change in asset holdings by the Federal Reserve, and the diagram on the left to show the effect of the change in asset holdings by the Bank of Japan.

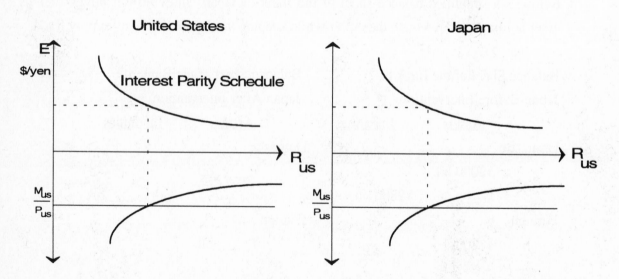

4. In the appendix describing the timing of a balance of payments crisis, the crisis occurs (that is, the central bank looses all its reserves) at the time when the line representing the shadow floating exchange rate crosses the fixed rate. In the diagram on the next page, this is at time T_0.

a. The slope of the shadow floating exchange rate represents the rate of growth of the money supply. Demonstrate in the diagram how the time when the balance of payments crisis occurs is affected by a slowing of the rate of growth of the money supply.

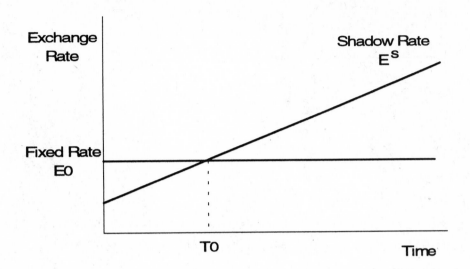

b. Is there a positive rate of growth of the money supply that will be small enough such that there is never a balance of payments crisis?

_____

_____

_____.

c. The y-intercept of the shadow floating exchange rate schedule decreases with an increase in the initial holdings of foreign reserves by the central bank. Show how an increase in initial reserve holdings by the central bank affects the timing of the speculative attack using the diagram on the next page.

d. If there is a positive rate of growth of the money supply, is there a level of reserves large enough to avoid ever having a balance of payments crisis?

_____

_____

_____.

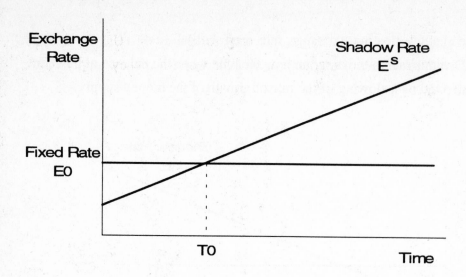

5. A politically charged issue in Britain at the end of the 1980s and in the early 1990s was potential membership in the exchange rate mechanism of the European Monetary System (EMS). Opponents of membership said that it would force British monetary policy to be the same as German monetary policy, curtailing British autonomy.

a. In the diagram below, demonstrate how an expansion of the money supply in Britain would affect the pound/deutschemark exchange rate and discuss why, as members of the (mostly) fixed rate EMS Britain would have less latitude for conducting monetary policy.

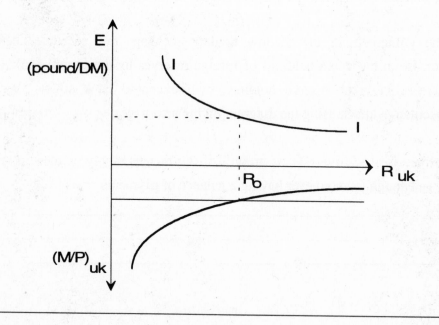

b. The deutschemark appears to be the reserve currency for the EMS. Use the diagram below to demonstrate the effect of a contraction of the German money supply on the policy of the British monetary authorities.

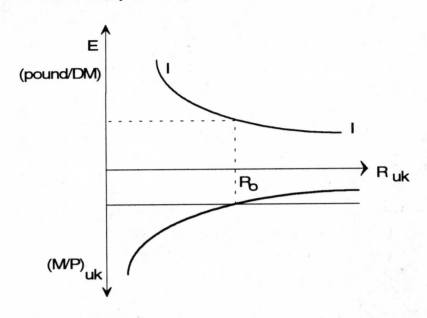

6. a. Using the monetary approach to the balance of payments, described in Appendix II of this chapter, discuss the effect of an increase in output on the level of foreign reserves held by the central bank. What is the net effect on the domestic money supply?

_____

_____

_____.

   b. Again using the monetary approach to the balance of payments discuss the effect of on the balance of payments of an increase in the rate of growth of domestic-currency assets held by the central bank. What is the effect of this increase in the rate of growth of domestic currency assets held by the central bank on the rate of growth of the domestic money supply?

_____

_____

_____.

c. Discuss the effects of maintaining balance of payments equilibrium using monetary tools in the face of a fall in money demand. Then discuss the effects of maintaining balance of payments equilibrium using monetary tools when there is an economic downturn due to a fall in investment. Do you expect unemployment to be similar or different in these two examples?

_____

_____

_____

_____

_____

_____.

ANSWERS TO ODD-NUMBERED PROBLEMS IN THE TEXT

1. An expansion of the central bank's domestic assets leads to an equal fall in its foreign assets, with no change in the bank's liabilities (or the money supply). The effect on the balance-of-payments accounts is most easily understood by recalling how the fall in foreign reserves comes about. After the central bank buys domestic assets with money there is initially an excess supply of money. The central bank must intervene in the foreign exchange market to hold the exchange rate fixed in the face of this excess supply: the bank sells foreign assets and buys money until the excess supply of money has been eliminated. Since private residents acquire the reserves the central bank loses, there is a non-central bank capital outflow (a capital-account debit) equal to the increase in foreign assets held by the private sector. The offsetting credit is the reduction in central bank holdings of foreign assets, an official capital inflow.

3. A one-time unexpected devaluation initially increases output; the output increase, in turn, raises money demand. The central bank must accommodate the higher money demand by buying foreign assets with domestic currency, a step that raises the central bank's liabilities (and the home money supply) at the same time as it increases the bank's foreign assets. The increase in official foreign reserves is an official capital outflow; it is matched in the balance of payments accounts by the equal capital outflow associated with the public's own reduction in net foreign asset holdings. (The public must exchange foreign assets for the money it buys from the central bank, either by selling foreign assets or by borrowing foreign currency abroad. Either course of action is a

198

capital inflow.)

A more subtle issue is the following: When the price of foreign currency is raised, the value of the initial stock of foreign reserves rises when measured in terms of domestic currency. This capital gain in itself raises central-bank foreign assets (which were measured in domestic currency units in our analysis)--so where is the corresponding increase in liabilities? Does the central bank inject more currency or bank-system reserves into the economy to balance its balance sheet? The answer is that central banks generally create fictional accounting liabilities to offset the effect of exchange-rate fluctuations on the home-currency value of international reserves. These capital gains and losses do not automatically lead to changes in the monetary base.

5. a. Germany can clearly change the dollar/DM exchange simply by altering its money supply. The fact that "Billions of dollars worth of currencies are traded each day" is irrelevant because exchange rates equilibrate markets for stocks of assets, and the trade volumes mentioned are flows.

b. One must distinguish between sterilized and nonsterilized intervention. The evidence regarding sterilized intervention suggests that its effects are limited to the signaling aspect. This aspect may well be most important when markets are "unusually erratic"; and the signals communicated may be most credible when the central bank is not attempting to resist clear-cut market trends (which depend on the complete range of government macroeconomic policies, among other factors). Nonsterilized intervention, however, is a powerful instrument in affecting exchange rates.

c. The "psychological effect" of a "stated intention" to intervene may be more precisely stated as an effect on the expected future level of the exchange rate.

d. A rewrite might go as follows:

To keep the dollar from falling against the West German mark, the European central banks would have to sell marks and buy dollars, a procedure known as intervention.

Because the available stocks of dollar and mark bonds are so large, it is unlikely that sterilized intervention in the dollar/mark market, even if carried out by the two most economically influential members of the European Community--Britain and West Germany--would have much effect. The reason is that sterilized intervention changes only relative bond supplies and leaves national money supplies unchanged. Intervention by the U.S. and Germany that was not sterilized, however, would affect those countries' money supplies and have a significant impact on the dollar/mark rate.

Economists believe that the direct influence of sterilized intervention on exchange rates is small compared with that of nonsterilized intervention. Even sterilized intervention can affect exchange rates, however, through its indirect influence on market expectations about future policies. Such psychological effects, which can result from just the stated intention of the Community's central banks to intervene, can disrupt the market by confusing traders about official plans. The signaling effect of intervention is most likely to benefit the authorities when their other macroeconomic policies are already being adjusted to push the exchange rate in the desired direction.

7. By raising output, fiscal expansion raises imports and thus worsens the current-account balance. The immediate fall in the current account is smaller than under floating, however, because the currency does not appreciate and crowd out net exports.

9. By expanding output, a devaluation automatically raises private saving, since part of any increase in output is saved. Government tax receipts rise with output, so the budget deficit is likely to decline, implying an increase in public saving. We have assumed investment to be constant in the main text. If investment instead depends negatively on the real interest rate (as in the IS-LM model), investment rises because devaluation raises inflationary expectations and thus lowers the real interest rate. (The nominal interest rate remains unchanged at the world level.) The interest-sensitive components of consumption spending also rise, and if these interest-rate effects are strong enough, a current-account deficit could result.

11. If the market expects the devaluation to "stick," the home nominal interest rate falls to the world level afterward, money demand rises, and the central bank buys foreign assets with money to prevent excess money demand from appreciating the currency. The central bank thus gains official reserves, according to our model. Even if another devaluation was to occur in the near future, reserves might be gained if the first devaluation lowered the depreciation expected for the future and, with it, the home nominal interest rate. An inadequate initial devaluation could, however, increase the devaluation expected for the future, with opposite effects on the balance of payments.

13. A bimetallic standard is a system under which currencies can be converted, at a fixed price, into either of two metals, usually gold and silver. This implies that the price of gold in terms of silver must also be fixed through triangular arbitrage. Generally, however, market forces change the equilibrium relative price of the metals from the one set by the central bank. If the market relative price of silver rises, for example, people will buy silver from the central bank at what has become a below-market price, melt

silver coins down, etc., until there is no silver left in the money supply or in the central bank's stockpile.

15. An ESF intervention to support the yen involves an exchange of dollar-denominated assets initially owned by the ESF for yen-denominated assets initially owned by the private sector. Since this is an exchange of one type of bond for another there is no change in the money supply and thus this transaction is automatically sterilized. This transaction increases the outstanding stock of dollar-denominated assets held by the private sector, which increases the risk premium on dollar-denominated assets.

OVERVIEW TO PART IV

INTERNATIONAL MACROECONOMIC POLICY

Part IV of the text is comprised of four chapters:

SECTION OVERVIEW

This final section of the book, which discusses international macroeconomic policy, provides historical and institutional background to complement the theoretical presentation of the previous section. These chapters also provide an opportunity for you to hone your analytic skills and intuition by applying and extending the models learned in Part III to a range of current and historical issues.

The first two chapters of this section discuss various international monetary arrangements. These chapters describe the workings of different exchange rate systems through the central theme of internal and external balance. The model developed in the previous section provides a general framework for analysis of gold standard, reserve currency, managed floating, and floating exchange-rate systems.

Chapter 19 chronicles the evolution of the international monetary system from the gold standard of 1870 - 1914, through the interwar years, and up to and including the post-war Bretton Woods period. The chapter discusses the price-specie-flow mechanism of adjustment in the context of the discussion of the gold standard. Conditions for internal and external balance are presented through diagrammatic analysis based upon the short-run macroeconomic model of Chapter 17. This analysis illustrates the strengths and weaknesses of alternative fixed exchange rate arrangements. The chapter also draws upon earlier discussion of balance of payments crises to make clear the interplay between "fundamental disequilibrium" and speculative attacks. There is a detailed analysis of the Bretton Woods system that includes a case study of the experience during its decline beginning in the mid-1960s and culminating with its collapse in 1973.

Chapter 20 focuses on recent experience under floating exchange rates. The discussion is couched in terms of current debate concerning the advantages of floating versus fixed exchange rate systems. The theoretical arguments for and against floating exchange rates frame two case studies, the first on the experience between the two oil shocks in the 1970s and the second on the experience since 1980. The transmission of monetary and fiscal shocks is analyzed using a two-country model developed in this chapter. Discussion of the experience in the 1980s points out the shift in policy toward greater coordination in the second half of the decade. The two-country model developed in this chapter provides the background for analysis in an appendix that illustrates losses arising from uncoordinated international monetary policy.

The European Monetary System (E.M.S.), the subject of Chapter 21, provides a particular example of a fixed exchange rate system. The chapter discusses the history of the E.M.S. and its precursors. The early years of the E.M.S. were marked by capital controls and frequent realignments. By the end of the 1980s, however, there was marked inflation convergence among member countries, few realignments and the removal of capital controls. The stage seemed to be set for the eventual establishment of a single European currency as outlined in the Maastricht Treaty. The single currency was viewed as an important part of the E.C. 1992 initiative which called for the free flow within Europe of labor, capital, goods and services. A single currency both imposes costs as well as confers benefits. The theory of optimum currency areas suggests conditions which affect the relative benefits of a single currency. The chapter provides a way to frame this analysis using the GG-LL diagram which compares the gains and losses from a single currency. Events since 1991, however, have called into doubt the likelihood of a single European currency by the end of the century. In the Autumn of 1992 the pound and lira dropped out of the exchange rate mechanism. Most recently, in the summer of 1993, the 2.25 percent bands were abandoned for 15 percent bands. An appendix to the chapter uses the IS-LM model to explain divergent macroeconomic outcomes between Germany and Britain. The tensions resulting from this divergence fueled the speculation which brought down the E.M.S.

The international capital market is the subject of Chapter 22. This chapter draws an analogy between the gains from trade arising from international portfolio diversification and international goods trade. There is discussion of institutional structures that have arisen to exploit these gains. The chapter discusses the Eurocurrency market and the creation of Eurocurrencies, the regulation of offshore banking and the role of international financial supervisory cooperation. The chapter also considers evidence of how well the international capital market has performed by focusing on issues such as the efficiency of the foreign exchange market, the extent of intertemporal trade and the existence of excess volatility of exchange rates.

Chapter 23 discusses issues facing developing countries, including the international debt crisis. The chapter begins by identifying characteristics of the economies of developing countries, characteristics that include undeveloped financial markets, pervasive government involvement, and a dependence on commodity exports. The macroeconomic analysis of previous chapters again provides a framework for analyzing relevant issues, such as inflation in developing countries. A case study discusses orthodox and heterodox stabilization programs in Latin America. Borrowing by developing countries is discussed as an attempt to exploit gains from intertemporal trade and is put in historical perspective with a discussion of international capital flows during the gold standard and the interwar years. The origins of the current debt crisis are outlined, followed by a discussion of the evolution of the policy response to this problem and the current state of affairs.

The text concludes with Chapter 24, which introduces some of the adjustment problems confronting the formerly communist countries of Eastern Europe and the former Soviet Union. The pre-1989 regional concentration of production and trade is discussed, as are the pricing distribution system, the use of barter exchanges, and the type of monetary regime in place. Given this background, the chapter outlines some of the reasons for the sharp collapse of output in most of these countries, emphasizing massive terms-of-trade and demand shocks. The monetary problems of the region also are reviewed, including the problems of a disintegrating monetary union and the timing of new currency introductions by the newly independent countries. The chapter concludes with a discussion of regional prospects.

CHAPTER 19

The International Monetary System, 1870-1973

CHAPTER ORGANIZATION

From the Gold Crisis to the Collapse: 1968-1973

Worldwide Inflation and the Transition to Floating Rates

KEY THEMES

This is the first of four international monetary policy chapters. These chapters complement the preceding theory chapters in several ways. They provide the historical and institutional background that allows you to place the theory you have learned in a useful context. The chapters also allow you, through study of historical and current events, to sharpen your grasp of theory and to develop your intuition. If you find that certain theoretical points used in these chapters are not clear, do not hesitate to look back at the earlier chapters to master the points you may have been missed on the first pass.

Chapter 19 chronicles the evolution of the international monetary system from the gold standard of 1870-1914, through the interwar years, and up to and including the post-World War II Bretton Woods that ended in March 1973. The central focus of the chapter is how each system addressed, or failed to address, the requirements of internal and external balance for its participants. A country is in internal balance when its resources are fully employed and there is price level stability. A country enjoys external balance when its current account is at an appropriate level, and, over the long run, the current account is in balance. External balance does not require current account balance year-to- year since there are good reasons to run temporary current account deficits or surpluses. For example, particularly good investment opportunities call for current account deficits which will be repaid in the future with current account surpluses when the investment opportunities bear fruit.

The price-specie-flow mechanism described by David Hume shows how the gold standard could ensure convergence to external balance. There are three key relationships that together cause this mechanism to work. The first relationship is that the gold holdings of the central bank are directly related to a country's money supply when the government follows the "rules of the game." These rules require governments to contract their monetary bases when gold reserves are falling (corresponding to a current-account deficit) and expand when gold reserves are rising (the surplus case). The second relationship is that the price level rises when the money supply expands, and the price level falls when the money supply contracts. The third relationship relates the current account to the real exchange rate. The real exchange rate, which you recall is defined as $(E \cdot P^*/P)$, depreciates with a fall in P and appreciates with a rise in P (E is given in this fixed exchange rate system and P* can be assumed to be constant for purposes of our analysis). Thus, a current account deficit, for example, would cause a country's money supply to fall as its gold reserves are depleted. This depresses prices in the country, causing a real exchange rate depreciation that makes its exports more attractive and reverses the current account deficit. In theory a country with expanding gold reserves due to a current account surplus would have just the reverse occur, but in practice there was little incentive for countries with expanding gold reserves to follow these rules. This increased the contractionary burden shouldered by countries with persistent current account deficits. The gold standard also subjugated internal balance to the demands of external balance. Research suggests price-level stability and high employment were attained no more consistently under the gold standard than in the post-1945 period.

The interwar years were marked by severe economic instability. The monetization of war debt and of reparation payments led to episodes of hyperinflation in Europe. An ill-fated attempt to return to the pre-war gold parity for the pound led to stagnation in Britain. Competitive devaluations and protectionism were pursued in a futile effort to stimulate domestic economic growth during the Great Depression. These beggar-thy-neighbor policies provoked foreign retaliation and led to the disintegration of the world economy.

Determined to avoid repeating the mistakes of the interwar years, Allied economic policy makers met at Bretton Woods in 1944 to forge a new international monetary system for the postwar world. The exchange-rate regime that emerged from this conference had at its center the U.S. dollar. All other currencies had fixed exchange rates against the dollar, which itself had a fixed value in terms of gold. An International Monetary Fund was set up to oversee the system and facilitate its functioning by lending to countries with temporary balance of payments problems.

We are able to analyze some of the issues concerning internal and external balance by plotting a schedule for each in a graph with the exchange rate on the vertical axis and a measure of fiscal policy on the horizontal axis. The negative slope of the internal balance line (II) shows that the contractionary effects of a revaluation of the currency must be offset by the stimulative effects of a fiscal expansion to keep employment and prices stable. The external balance line (XX) has a positive slope since a devaluation, which would increase the balance of payments surplus, must be offset by greater fiscal stimulus to maintain balance of payments equilibrium. The intersection of the II and XX line represents overall balance. Any other point in the graph represents some type of "economic discomfort", and any point not on either line represents both internal and external imbalance.

A government may attempt to move back to balance through some combination of expenditure-switching and expenditure-changing policies. Expenditure-switching policies, such as a devaluation, affect consumption and production choices between domestic and foreign goods. These policies are reflected by vertical movements in the II-XX graph. Expenditure changing-policies affect the overall level of expenditures, and are depicted as horizontal movements in the II-XX graph. It is easy to see that, unless an economy is directly above or below the overall balance point, expenditure-changing policies are required and, unless it is directly to the left or to the right of the balance point, expenditure-switching policies are required.

The Bretton Woods system, with its emphasis on infrequent adjustment of fixed parities, restricted the use of expenditure-switching policies. Increases in U.S. monetary growth to finance fiscal expenditures after the mid-1960s led to a loss of confidence in the dollar and the termination of the dollar's convertibility into gold. The analysis presented in the text demonstrates how the Bretton Woods system forced countries to "import" inflation from the U.S. and shows that the breakdown of the system occurred when countries were no longer willing to accept this burden.

KEY TERMS

Define the following key terms.

1. Internal Balance _____
_____
_____
_____.

2. External Balance_____
_____
_____
_____.

3. Balance of payments equilibrium_____

_____

_____

_____.

4. Price-specie-flow mechanism _____

_____

_____

_____.

5. Bretton Woods agreement _____

_____

_____

_____.

6. Expenditure-changing policy _____

_____

_____

_____.

7. Expenditure-switching policy _____

_____

_____

_____.

REVIEW QUESTIONS

1.   In the late 1890s, gold was discovered in Alaska. During this time, the United States
      was a member of the international gold standard.

   a. Use the price-specie-flow analysis to show how the discovery of gold in Alaska affected
      the United States' balance of payments, price level, and money supply.

      _____

      _____

      _____.

b. Do you expect any permanent effects on the United States balance of payments or real money balances because of the discovery of Alaskan gold?

_____

_____

_____.

2. a. How is the money supply of a country which is a member of a gold-standard affected if it has a current account deficit and it follows the "rules of the game" described in the chapter?

_____

_____

_____.

b. How may a country avoid the effect on its money supply described in part (a)? What does this imply for its adherence to the "rules of the game?"

_____

_____

_____.

c. In a study of the gold standard period, Professor Alberto Giovannini of Columbia University found that there was a significant link between gold inflows and changes in the domestic interest rate for Germany between 1892 and 1907, and for France between 1900 and 1907. There is no significant link between gold inflows and the domestic interest rate, however, for the United Kingdom between 1889 and 1907. If we consider the domestic interest rate as a target that authorities may wish to influence, what do these results imply for the adherence to the rules of the game for these three countries? (Alberto Giovannini, "How do fixed-exchange-rate regimes work? Evidence from the gold standard, Bretton Woods and the EMS," in Marcus Miller, Barry Eichengreen and Richard Portes, eds. *Blueprints for Exchange Rate Management*, Academic Press Inc., San Diego, CA, c.1989)

_____

_____

_____.

d. Relate your answer to part (c) to the issue of asymmetry of the gold standard.

_____

_____

_____.

3. The country of Midas, which is on the gold standard, enjoys both internal and external balance. In the two diagrams below, this is reflected by an initial position for the economy at point a where there the II and XX schedules intersect.

a. Suppose that there is a change of tastes among people in Midas' main export market towards goods from countries other than Midas. In the diagram below show how this affects internal and external balance in Midas.

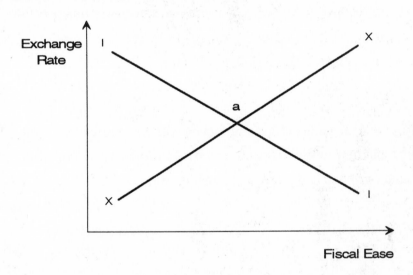

b. Midas economists, reasoning that the change in tastes for Midas exports is an "external" event, decide that their policy response to this should involve only their "external" policy tool, the exchange rate. Do you agree with their assessment?

_____

_____

_____.

c. Now suppose that, again beginning at point a, there is a sudden increase in the number of workers looking for jobs in Midas because the army of Midas is demobilized due to the removal of the threat from a neighboring country with the change of leadership in that country. In the diagram on the next page show how this event affects internal and external balance.

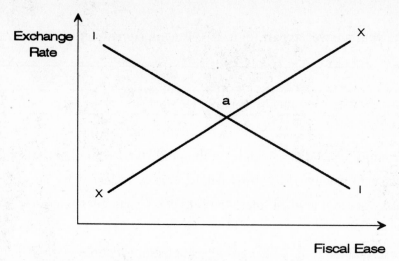

d. Midas officials decide to cut taxes since less revenue is required by the government when the army is reduced in size. Will this tax cut restore internal and external balance? Show the effects of the tax cut in the diagram to answer this question.

_____

_____

_____.

4. a. Suppose that the demand for real money balances grows by $1 for each $1 rise in real income and that money demand falls by $2 for each 1% rise in the interest rate. Use this relationship to complete the following chart;

Real Money Demand	Income	Interest Rates
$100	$120	10%
$100	$122	%
$100	$	13%
$	$130	10%
$	$135	10%

b. In a pure gold standard, the money supply of each member is equal to the gold holdings of its central bank. Under the assumptions in part (a), discuss the effects of a rate of growth of world gold stocks of 2% per year on the following;

i. Income, if the price level and interest rates are constant.

_____

_____.

ii. The price level, if income and interest rates are constant.

_____

_____.

iii. The interest rate, if inflation is 2% per year and income is constant.

_____

_____.

iv. The interest rate if there is no inflation and if income grows at 2% per year.

_____

_____.

c. Explain how a reserve-currency system, like Bretton Woods, allowed world liquidity to expand faster than the rate of growth of world gold stocks with reference to the stylized balance sheets of the United States and Germany below.

_____

_____

_____

_____.

Balance Sheet of U.S. Central Bank   Balance Sheet of German Bundesbank
(changes in billions U.S. $)   (changes in billions DM)

Assets	Liabilities	Assets	Liabilities
U.S. $ Supply	Dollar Money	E x (US$ Assets)	German Money Supply
Gold			

d. Discuss the "confidence problem" whereby the ability of the Federal Reserve to maintain a gold price of $35 per ounce is threatened by an increase in dollars at a rate that exceeds the increase in the world gold stock.

_____

_____

_____

_____.

e. Use your answers to parts (a) to (c) to discuss the two-horned dilemma of a reserve currency system; maintaining liquidity while maintaining confidence in the reserve currency.

_____

_____

_____

_____.

5. Below are stylized balance sheets for the central banks of the United States and of Canada during the Bretton Woods era. The assets of the United States central bank consist of U.S. dollar-denominated assets while the assets of the central bank of Canada consist of U.S. dollar-denominated assets and Canadian dollar-denominated assets.

Balance Sheet of U.S.Central Bank
(changes in billions U.S. $)

Assets	Liabilities
U.S. Dollar Assets	U.S. Money Supply

Balance Sheet of Canadian Central Bank
(changes in billions Canadian $)

Assets	Liabilities
U.S. Dollar Assets	Canadian Money Supply
Can. Dollar Assets	

a. Suppose that the United States increases its money supply. Given that exchange rates are fixed, what would happen to the relative attractiveness of United States versus Canadian bonds?

_____

_____

_____.

b. If people in Canada and in the United States attempt to alter their asset holdings in response to the change in relative bond returns, what would be the consequence for the US$/C$ exchange rate?

_____

_____

_____.

c. Since the United States central bank does not hold any Canadian-dollar denominated assets, the Canadian central bank must act to preserve the US$/C$ exchange rate. How would it do this, and what would the effect of this be on the Canadian money supply?

_____

_____

_____.

d. Suppose the Canadian central bank attempted an open market operation to increase its money supply. What would the effect of this be on its holdings of US dollar assets, on Canadian dollar assets, and on the money supply? Would there be an effect on the U.S. money supply?

_____

_____

_____.

ANSWERS TO ODD-NUMBERED PROBLEMS IN THE TEXT

1. a. Since it takes considerable investment to develop uranium mines, you would want a larger current account deficit to allow your country to finance some of the investment with foreign savings.

   b. A permanent increase in the world price of copper would cause a current account surplus if the price rise leads you to invest more in copper mining. If there are no investment effects, you would not change your external balance target because it would be optimal to simply spend your additional income.

   c. A temporary increase in the world price of copper would cause a current account surplus. You would want to smooth out your country's consumption by saving some of its temporarily higher income.

   d. A temporary rise in the world price of oil would cause a current account deficit if you were an importer of oil, but a surplus if you were an exporter of oil.

3. Changes in parities reflected both initial misalignments and balance of payments crises. Attempts to return to the parities of the prewar period after the war ignored the changes in underlying economic fundamentals that the war caused. This made some exchange rates less than fully credible and encouraged balance of payments crises.

   Central bank commitments to the gold parities were also less than credible after the wartime suspension of the gold standard, and as a result of the increasing concern of governments with internal economic conditions.

5.   The increase in domestic prices makes home exports less attractive and causes a current account deficit. This diminishes the money supply and causes contractionary pressures in the economy which serve to mitigate and ultimately reverse wage demands and price increases.

7.   An increase in the world interest rate leads to a fall in a central bank's holdings of foreign reserves as domestic residents trade in their cash for foreign bonds. This leads to a decline in the home country's money supply. The central bank of a "small" country cannot offset these effects since it cannot alter the world interest rate. An attempt to sterilize the reserve loss through open market purchases would fail unless bonds are imperfect substitutes.

CHAPTER 20

Macroeconomic Policy and Coordination under Floating Exchange Rates

CHAPTER ORGANIZATION

KEY THEMES

The floating exchange rate system in place since 1973 was not, in contrast with the Bretton Woods system, well planned before it began. Instead, it has developed over time and in response to the various events with which the world economy has had to contend. Disillusion with economic performance over the past 20 years has fueled recurrent demands for alternative international monetary arrangements. This chapter sets forth the case for and against floating exchange rates and considers the evidence concerning the performance of the international exchange-rate system since 1973.

The chapter begins with some theoretical arguments for and against floating exchange rates, arguments that frame the discussion for the entire chapter. Proponents of a floating exchange rate regime cite as its advantages the autonomy it gives to monetary policy, the symmetry of adjustment under floating, and the automatic stabilization which floating rates provide when aggregate-demand shocks occur. Critics fault floating rates on the grounds that they do not impose enough discipline on governments or promote economic policy coordination; because of alleged detrimental effects on international trade and investment; and because floating exchange rates may be susceptible to harmful destabilizing speculation. The DD-AA model can be used to demonstrate that money-market shocks are less disruptive to output under a fixed exchange-rate regime than under a floating regime while output-market shocks are less disruptive to output under a floating exchange rate regime.

This result is important in considering the relative attractiveness of floating exchange rates in face of the first oil shock in 1973. This shock led to "stagflation," simultaneous recession and inflation. Industrial countries chose expansionary macro policies as a response and recovery from the recession of 1974 was underway in most of these countries by the first half of 1975. It is unlikely that a fixed-exchange-rate system, which would have demanded less expansionary response from countries, would have survived unless there were widespread realignments which might have caused destabilizing speculative attacks on currencies. The success with which the floating-exchange-rate regime allowed countries to adjust to the first oil shock prompted a call by the leaders of the main industrial countries for the IMF to formally recognize the new arrangement. The IMF directors heeded this by amending the

Fund's Articles of Agreement to recognize the new reality of floating rates.

Floating exchange rates enabled countries to pursue divergent expansionary policies after the first oil shock. This advantage of floating exchange rates proved to be a disadvantage as the recovery of 1974-1975 turned into the slowdown of 1976. American policies more expansionary than those pursued by Germany and Japan weakened the dollar, pushed the U.S. current account into deficit, and contributed to a resurgence of inflation in the U.S. The second oil shock promoted fears of higher inflation, leading to restrictive monetary policies that plunged the world economy, in 1981, into the deepest recession since the Great Depression.

This chapter develops a two-country model to examine the global effects of fiscal and monetary policy in the 1980s. This model explicitly incorporates feedback effects from policy in one economy to economic performance in the other. The intuitive explanation for the positive slope of the HH and FF schedules presented in the text notes that an increase in output in one country raises output in the other through trade effects. A fiscal expansion in either country increases output in both countries, shifting both curves out. A monetary expansion in the domestic country, however, raises domestic output but, by making the foreign currency more expensive, lowers foreign output. In the text, the two-country model is used to analyze the effects of U.S. monetary and fiscal policy after 1980, particularly the Volcker disinflation and the Reagan fiscal expansion. The impact of the resulting dollar appreciation on world current accounts and on protectionist sentiment in the U.S. are also discussed.

In the face of growing protectionist pressure in the United States, economic officials of the Group of Five (G-5) countries met at the Plaza Hotel in New York in September 1985 where they agreed to jointly intervene in the foreign-exchange market to bring about a dollar depreciation. This marked a reversal from the United States' laissez-faire approach to dollar management in the first half of the 1980s. The dollar depreciated throughout 1986. In February 1987, at a meeting at the Louvre, finance ministers and central bankers from the G-5 countries plus Canada set up (unpublished) target zones to stabilize exchange rates around their then-current level. Currencies stabilized for several months thereafter, but this period of relative calm ended with the October 1987 stock market crash which initiated in a period of further dollar depreciation.

Conclusions concerning the advantages of floating exchange rates are not unambiguous. The insulation of economies from inflation, while important in the long run, may not hold in the short run. The exchange rate's role as a macroeconomic target also reduces the autonomy central banks actually enjoy under floating rates. Evidence does not support the "vicious circle" theory that, in the absence of accommodating monetary policy, currency depreciation leads to inflation, leading to further depreciation, and so on. Nor is there convincing evidence that floating rates have hindered international trade and investment. Lack of policy coordination has been a particularly disappointing feature of the system, but this problem is not unique to floating rates.

A lesson that emerges from this chapter is that no exchange rate system works well when countries act on the basis of narrowly- perceived self interest. The chapter appendix illustrates this point, using a simple game-theoretic example to show how the beggar-thy-neighbor effects of monetary restriction can lead to uncoordinated macroeconomic policies that make two countries worse off than they would be if they cooperated.

KEY TERMS

Define the following key terms.

1. Destabilizing speculation _____

_____

_____

_____.

2. Plaza accord _____

_____

_____

_____.

3. Symmetry (of an exchange rate system) _____

_____

_____

_____.

4. Automatic stabilizer _____

_____

_____

_____.

REVIEW QUESTIONS

1. The argument is made that floating exchange rates do a better job of stabilizing output in the short run when the economic events occurring in an economy are the type that affect the DD curve, such as shifts in investment demand, while fixed rates perform better when the shocks are the type that affect the AA curve, such as shifts in money demand.

   a. Use the diagram below to demonstrate how the variability in investment demand would translate to variability in output around Y under a fixed and a floating exchange rate system (for a floating exchange rate system, assume the monetary authorities follow a rule of a constant money supply).

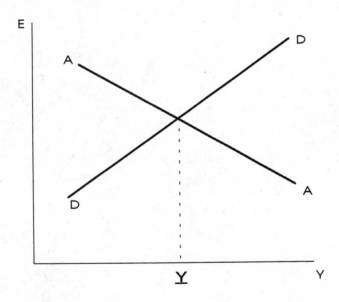

   b. Use the diagram below to demonstrate how the variability in money demand would translate to variability in output around Y under a fixed and a floating exchange rate system (again assume that, under the floating exchange rate system, assume the monetary authorities follow a constant money supply rule).

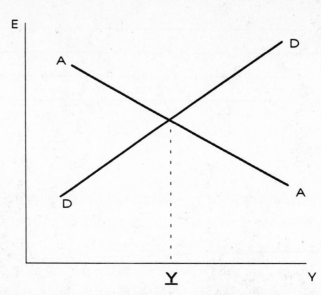

c. Refer to the diagrams above to explain how your conclusions concerning the desirability of different exchange rate regimes under different circumstances may change if governments are concerned about the short-run variability of the real exchange rate as well as output.

_____

_____

_____.

2. The two-country analysis developed in the chapter enables us to understand the feedback effects of policies in one country on output in another country. Use the diagrams below to answer the following questions.

a. What is the effect of a monetary expansion in Home on output in Home and in Foreign?

_____

_____

_____.

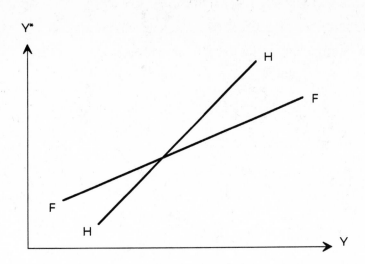

b. What is the effect of monetary expansions of equal size in both Home and Foreign on output in each country?

_____

_____

_____.

c. What is the effect of a fiscal expansion in Home on output in Home and in Foreign?

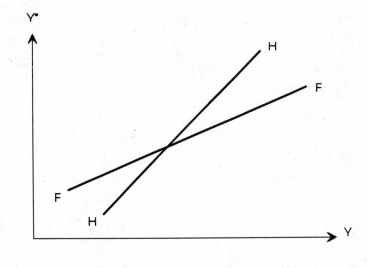

_____

_____

_____.

d. What is the effect of a fiscal expansion in Home and, at the same time, a fiscal expansion in Foreign, on output in each country?

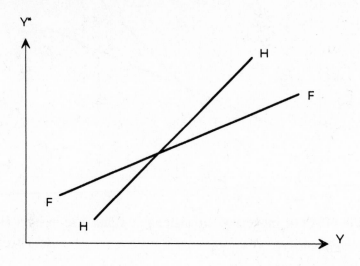

_____

_____

_____.

3.   With the problem of growing external imbalances serving as a backdrop, the finance ministers and monetary authorities of the United States, the United Kingdom, Germany, Japan and France met at the Plaza Hotel over the weekend of September 21 - 22, 1985. The communique issued on September 22 was widely interpreted as calling for a depreciation of the dollar.

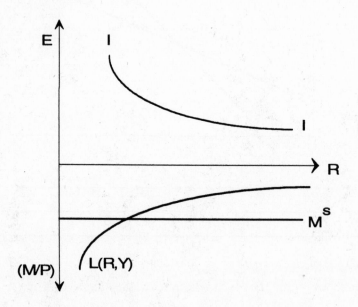

a. Use the money market / interest parity diagram on the preceding page to show the effect of this communique on the value of the $/DM exchange rate on Monday, September 23.

b. The motivation for the Plaza meeting was the large current account deficit in the United States and the fear that protectionist measures would be enacted. Research has found that announcements of larger than expected current accounts had an immediate, significant effect on the exchange rate after the Plaza meeting, but not before the meeting. Use the diagram below to explain why we may have observed this difference before and after the Plaza meeting. (hint: Remember that the United States had taken a "hands-off" approach to exchange rate management before the Plaza meeting. If monetary authorities were concerned with the current account, and were willing to intervene, what action would they take in response to a larger-than-expected current account deficit?)

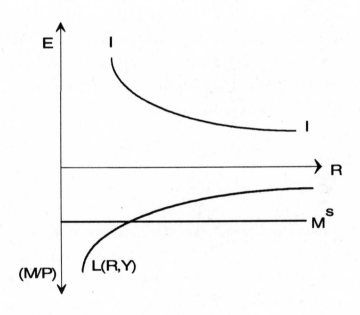

_____
_____
_____.

4.   On July 2, 1990 the monetary systems of West Germany and East Germany were unified. East Germans were able to exchange up to 4,000 Ost-marks (the former East German currency) for Deutschemarks at the rate of one Ost-mark to one

Deutschemark. For amounts beyond that, each Deutschemark cost two Ost-marks. Wages and pensions denominated in Ost-marks were converted at a one-to-one rate. There was extensive debate before unification concerning the proper exchange rate between West German Deutschemarks and East German Ost-marks. The black market rate for Ost-marks before discussion of monetary union was between five and seven Ost-marks for one Deutschemark.

a. Discuss how the rate of conversion of Ost-marks into Deutschemarks affects the money supply in a unified Germany. Compare the effects on the money supply of conversion at the black market rate with conversion at a one-to-one rate. Do you think that an excessive increase in the money supply would fuel continuing German inflation?

_____

_____

_____

_____.

b. Discuss how the rate of conversion of Ost-marks into Deutschemarks affects the relative wages in East and West Germany. What are the likely effects of choosing a one-to-one conversion rate, rather than a five-to-one conversion rate, on the viability of East German firms in the short run? In the long run?

_____

_____

_____.

c. The average wage in East Germany before unification was about 1,100 Ost-marks, and the average wage in West Germany was about 3,300 Deutschemarks. What is the likely effect of the removal of intra-German barriers to labor mobility on emigration between East and West Germany, and on wages throughout the country?

_____

_____

_____.

1.   A rise in the foreign price level leads to a real domestic currency depreciation for a given domestic price level and nominal exchange rate; thus, as shown in the following diagram, the output market curve shifts from DD to D'D' moving the equilibrium from point 0 to point 1. This shift causes an appreciation of the home currency and a rise in home output. If the expected future exchange rate falls in proportion to the rise in P*, then the asset market curve shifts down as well, from AA to A'A' with the equilibrium at point 2. Notice that the economy remains in equilibrium in this case, at the initial output level, if the current exchange rate also falls in proportion to the rise in P*. Why? The goods market is in equilibrium because the real exchange rate has not changed; the foreign-exchange market is in equilibrium if the domestic interest rate does not change (there has been no change in the expected rate of future currency depreciation); and with output and the interest rate the same, the money market is still in equilibrium. The economy thus remains in internal and external balance if these conditions held initially.

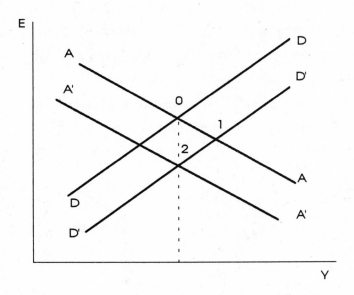

3.   The effect of a permanent rise in the foreign nominal interest rate depends upon whether that rise is due to an increase in inflationary expectations abroad or a rise in the foreign real interest rate. If the foreign real interest rate rises because of monetary contraction abroad, say, there is a long-run depreciation of the domestic currency. The expansionary effect on home output is thus greater than in the transitory case. If the foreign nominal interest rate rises only because foreign inflationary expectations rise, however, the expectations effect goes the other way and the long-run expected price of

foreign currency falls, shifting AA to the left. Domestic output need not rise in this case. Under a fixed exchange rate there is still no short run effect on the economy in the DD-AA model, but as P* starts to rise the home country will have to import foreign inflation. Under a floating rate the home economy can be completely insulated from the subsequent foreign inflation.

5.   We can include the aspect of imperfect asset substitutability in the DD-AA model by recognizing that the AA schedule now must equate M/P = L(R* + expected depreciation + risk premium,Y). An increase in the risk premium shifts out the AA curve, leading to an currency depreciation and an increase in output. Output will not change under a fixed-exchange-rate regime: since the exchange rate parity must be preserved, there will be no depreciation and no effect on output.

7.   In Chapter 19 there is an analysis of internal and external balance for fixed exchange rates. It is possible to construct a corresponding diagram for floating exchange rates. In the following diagram, the vertical axis measures expansion of the money supply and the horizontal axis measures fiscal ease. The internal balance curve II has a negative slope since monetary restraint must be met by greater fiscal expansion to preserve internal balance. The external balance curve XX has a positive slope since monetary expansion, which depreciates the exchange rate and improves the current account, must be matched by fiscal expansion to preserve external balance.

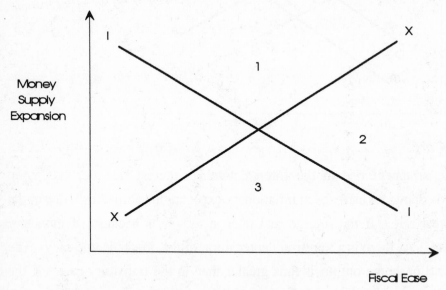

The "four zones of economic discomfort" are :
Zone 1 -- overemployment and excessive current account surplus;

Zone 2 -- overemployment and current account deficit;

Zone 3 -- underemployment and current account deficit;

Zone 4 -- underemployment and current account surplus.

For more details, see the 1985 Brookings paper by Obstfeld in listed in Further Reading.

9.   Fiscal expansion in Germany and Japan would have appreciated the currencies of those countries and diminished the bilateral U.S. trade deficits with them, as desired by American officials. On the other hand, monetary expansion in these countries would have worsened the U.S. current account since the dollar would have appreciated relative to the deutschemark and the yen. Our two country models suggests that U.S. output would have fallen as a result. These effects would differ, of course, if the United States altered its policies in response to policy changes in Germany or Japan. For example, if the United States expanded its money supply with the expansion in either Germany or Japan there would be no bilateral effects. If the United States contracted fiscal policy as Germany or Japan expanded fiscal policy there would less of an effect on output in each country.

11.   One can construct a matrix analogous to figure 21A-1 in the text to show the change in inflation and the change in exports for each country in response to monetary policy choices by that country and by the other country. Export growth in a country will be greater, but inflation will be higher, if that country undertakes a more expansionary monetary policy given the other country's policy choice. But there is a beggar-thy-neighbor effect because one country's greater export growth implies lower export growth for the other country. Without policy coordination, the two countries will adopt over-expansionary monetary policies to improve their competitive positions, but these policies will offset eachother and simply result in higher inflation everywhere. With coordination, the countries will realize that they can both enjoy lower inflation if they agree not to engage in competitive currency depreciation.

CHAPTER 21

Optimum Currency Areas and the European Experience

CHAPTER ORGANIZATION

KEY THEMES

The attempt to establish a common European currency and the debate over its possible benefits and costs is one of the key economic topics of the early 1990s. As the discussion in this chapter points out, European monetary integration has been an ongoing process. Fixed exchange rates in Europe were a by-product of the Bretton Woods system. When strains began to appear in the Bretton Woods system concerns arose about the effects of widely-fluctuating exchange rates between European countries. Sources of concern included the extent of intra-European trade and some institutional aspects of the European Community especially the Monetary Compensation Amount of the Common Agricultural Policy. The 1971 Werner report called for the eventual goal of fixed exchange rates in Europe.

The first attempt at a post-Bretton Woods fixed exchange rate system in Europe was the "Snake." This effort was limited in its membership. The European Monetary System (E.M.S.), established in 1979, has been more successful. The original member countries of the E.M.S. included Germany, France, Italy, Belgium, Denmark, Luxembourg, the Netherlands and Ireland. In recent years, the roll of membership grew to include Spain, Great Britain and Portugal. The E.M.S. fixes exchange rates around a central parity. Most currencies are allowed to fluctuate above or below their central rate by 2.25 percent although the original band for the Italian lira and the bands for the Spanish peseta and the Portuguese escudo allowed for fluctuations of 6 percent in either direction from the central parity. At the beginning of August 1993 the currency bands were widened to 15 percent on either side of the central parities.

By the end of the 1980s the E.M.S. seemed to be an increasingly stable exchange rate system. Inflation rate differentials across member countries had been reduced and controls on the movement of financial capital had been largely removed. Also, while realignments had been a frequent occurrence in the early years of the E.M.S. (there were 10 realignments between the beginning of the E.M.S. and 1986) the only realignment between 1986 and 1992 was in 1990 when the lira was devalued against the Deutsche mark in order to facilitate its move to a 2.25 percent band from a 6 percent band.

The success of the E.M.S. in the late 1980s led to calls for a further tightening of the exchange rate system with the eventual establishment of a single European currency. The single currency was also seen as an important part of the E.C. 1992 initiative which called for the free flow within Europe of labor, capital, goods and services. As the text points out, a common currency imposes costs as well as benefits. The theory of optimum currency areas provides a way to frame an analysis of the benefits and costs of a single currency. The benefits of a common currency are the monetary efficiency gains realized when trade and payments are not subject to devaluation risk. These benefits rise with an increase in the amount of trade or factor flows, that is with the extent of economic integration. A common currency also forces countries to give up their independence with regards to monetary policy (at least those countries which are not at the "center" of the system). This may lead to greater macroeconomic instability, although the instability is reduced the more integrated the country is with the other members of the common currency area. The analyses of the benefits and costs of membership in a common currency area are presented in the text chapter as the GG and LL schedules, respectively.

The GG-LL framework is applied to the question of whether Europe is an optimum currency area. An illuminating way to frame the question is to compare the United States to Europe. The evidence that Europe is an optimum currency area is much weaker than the evidence supporting the notion that the United States is an optimum currency area. Trade among regions in the United States is much higher than trade among European countries. Labor is much more mobile within the United States than within Europe. Federal transfers and changes in federal tax payments provide a much bigger cushion region-specific shocks in the United States than do analogous E.C. revenues and expenditures.

A roadmap for the final drive towards a single European currency was provided by the Maastricht Treaty which was signed at the end of 1991. Subsequent events, however, disrupted the course envisioned by this treaty. In the summer of 1992 Danish voters narrowly rejected the Maastricht Treaty. In September 1992 speculative pressures caused the Finnish markka, which had been shadowing the Deutschemark, to be devalued. Swedish authorities raised overnight interest rates to an annual rate of 500 percent in an attempt to prevent the devaluation of the krona. The Italian lira was devalued over the weekend of September 12-13. The following Wednesday, dubbed "Black Wednesday," the pound and the lira were removed from the E.M.S. while Spanish authorities devalued the peseta and re-imposed capital controls. The French franc was subject to speculative pressures throughout the autumn. After the textbook went to press, the currency bands were widened to 15 percent from 2.25 percent in response to speculative pressures in July and August 1993. The likelihood of a single European currency by the end of the century is much lower at present than before the events of 1992.

An appendix to the chapter uses the IS-LM model to demonstrate how a boom in Germany leads to a slump in Britain. The increase in German aggregate demand raises German interest rates. British monetary authorities are forced to decrease British money supply in order to raise the British interest rate and preserve the pound-Deutsche mark exchange rate. The increase in the British interest rate, however, reduces aggregate demand in Britain and causes a slump there.

KEY TERMS

Define the following key terms:

1. Optimum currency area_____
_____
_____
_____.

2. European Monetary Union_____
_____
_____
_____.

3. Currency grid_____
_____
_____
_____.

4. Monetary efficiency gain_____
_____
_____
_____.

5. Economic stability loss_____
_____
_____
_____.

6. Credibility theory of the EMS_____
_____
_____
_____.

7. Maastricht Treaty_____
_____
_____
_____.

REVIEW QUESTIONS

1.   One often-cited success of the European Monetary System is the convergence in inflation rates among its members since the EMS began in 1989. Below are the annual CPI inflation rates for a number of the EMS countries. Plot these rates on the graph and then answer the questions that follow.

Year	1979	1980	1981	1982	1983	1984	1985	1986	1987	1988
France	10.8	13.3	13.4	11.8	9.6	7.4	5.8	2.5	3.3	2.7
Germany	4.1	5.4	6.3	5.3	3.3	2.4	2.2	-0.2	0.3	1.3
Italy	14.8	21.3	19.5	16.5	14.6	10.8	9.2	5.9	4.7	5.0
Ireland	13.2	18.2	20.4	17.1	10.5	8.6	5.4	3.8	3.1	2.1

a. What happens to the inflation rates in each country over the 1980s? If you were to pick a country as the one which the others followed, which would it be, based upon the data?

_____
_____
_____.

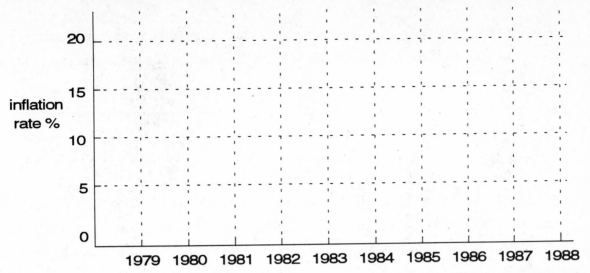

b. Explain how the relationship of the data to the argument that the EMS is an asymmetric system. Which of the four countries listed above serves as the center?

_____

_____

_____.

c. Below are data for inflation rates in the United States and the United Kingdom, which were not members of the EMS in the 1980s. In the graph below, plot these inflation rates, as well as the inflation rate for the EMS's center country.

Year	1979	1980	1981	1982	1983	1984	1985	1986	1987	1988
U.K.	13.4	18.0	11.9	8.6	4.6	5.1	6.1	3.4	4.2	4.8
U.S.	11.3	13.5	10.4	6.2	3.2	4.3	3.6	1.9	3.7	4.0

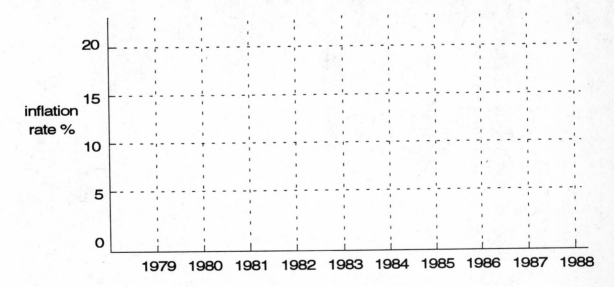

d. Discuss how the data for the United Kingdom and the United States may offer evidence for an alternative to the hypothesis that inflation convergence in Europe was due to the EMS.

_____

_____

_____.

2.   The average value of the European Currency Unit (ECU) in 1979 was 2.51 Deutsche marks, 5.83 French francs and 1139 Italian lira. In 1985, after a number of realignments, the ECU was worth 2.23 Deutsche marks, 6.80 French francs and 1431 Italian lira.

a. Fill in the following table:

	1979	1985
DM/ lira	_____	_____
DM/ franc	_____	_____
franc/ lira	_____	_____

b. Fill in the bilateral real exchange rates among the three countries in the following table using the data above and the following data on the CPIs in France, Germany and Italy. Also calculate what the real exchange rates in 1985 would have been if there had never been any realignments and the nominal exchange rates in 1985 were the same as those that were in place in 1979.

CPI in:

Year	France	Germany	Italy
1979	100	100	100
985	179	128	233

Bilateral Real Exchange Rates:

	1979	Actual 1985	If No Realignment
DM/ lira	100	_____	_____
DM/ franc	100	_____	_____
franc/ lira	100	_____	_____

c. How do your calculations demonstrate the need for realignments in the early years of the EMS?

_____

_____

_____.

3.　At the end of August 1992 the pound was worth 2.8 Deutsche marks. Strains in the EMS were evident at that time.

a. Suppose that there was a 25 percent chance that the pound would be devalued within the year to 2.6 Deutsche marks and an 75 percent chance that the DM/pound exchange rate would be maintained. What was the expected value of the DM/pound exchange rate in August 1993?

_____

b. What was the difference between one-year interest rates on pound deposits and DM deposits at that time?

_____

c. In early September 1992 comments by the Helmut Schlesinger, the head of the German Bundesbank, made it clear that German policy was less likely to ease. This meant that Britain, which was already suffering from high unemployment, could not expect much in the way of German monetary expansion. The cost of staying in the EMS therefore rose for Britain. Suppose that in the wake of Schlesinger's comments the likelihood of Britain staying in the EMS (at 2.8 DM/pound) fell to 50 percent while the likelihood of the devaluation of the pound to 2.6 Deutsche marks by August 1993 rose to 50 percent. What was the new expected value of the DM/pound exchange rate in August 1993?

_____.

d. What is the new spot DM/pound rate if the probability of Britain leaving the EMS (and the exchange rate going to 2.6 DM/Pound) rose to 50 % and if the interest rate differential was 2 % (with the pound-denominated securities paying the higher rate)?

_____.

4. Suppose that the voters of Quebec are to decide whether to keep the Canadian dollar as their currency or instead to establish a new currency called the Quebec franc. The Quebec franc would float against the Canadian dollar. Determine whether each of the following factors makes the establishment of the Quebec franc more or less economically desirable from the point of view of citizens of Quebec.

a. The dominant language and culture of Quebec differs from that of the rest of Canada. This makes the establishment of the Quebec franc (more / less) desirable because

_____
_____
_____.

b. Most of Quebec's trade is with the province of Ontario. This makes the establishment of the Quebec franc (more / less) desirable because

_____
_____
_____.

c. Most of Quebec's income is derived from services and manufacturing while the economies of western Canada and the maritime provinces in the east are dominated by agriculture and fishing. This makes the establishment of the Quebec franc (more / less) desirable because

_____
_____
_____.

d. The extent of fiscal transfers from the central government to the provincial governments is smaller than the analogous transfers between federal and state governments in the United States. This makes the establishment of the Quebec franc (more / less) desirable because

_____
_____
_____.

5. There is debate within Europe about widening the membership of the E.M.S. Suppose the two countries of Scandia and Cyrillica each wanted to become members of the E.M.S. Use the GG-LL analysis developed in the text to determine how each of the following factors affects the comparative net benefits to Scandia and Cyrillica of E.M.S. membership.

a. The industrial structure of Scandia is much more similar to that of Germany and France than is the industrial structure of Cyrillica.

b. A large opposition party in Cyrillica is against E.M.S. membership while there is near unanimity in Scandia in its commitment to be a member of the E.M.S.

c. Citizens of Scandia hold a greater proportion of their portfolio in E.M.S. investments than do citizens of Cyrillica.

d. Cyrillica produces a set of goods very different from those produced in the E.M.S., while Scandia produces a more similar set of goods; therefore, there is a greater potential for trade between the E.M.S. countries and Cyrillica than between the E.M.S. countries and Scandia.

ANSWERS TO ODD-NUMBERED PROBLEMS IN THE TEXT

1. The stability of the EMS depends upon the ability of member countries' central banks to defend their currencies. The level of foreign currency reserves to which a central bank has access affects its ability to defend its currency; the larger the stock of reserves, the better positioned a central bank to defend its currency. Credits from the central bank of a strong-currency country can help a weak-currency central bank defend its currency by putting at its disposal more reserves when its currency is threatened. Participants in the foreign exchange market may be less apt to speculate against a weak currency if they know there are ample reserves in place to defend it.

3. A 3 percent difference on the annual rate of a five-year bond implies a difference over five years of $1.03^5 = 1.159$ (that is 15.9 percent). This means that the predicted change in the lira/DM exchange rate over 5 years is far above the amount that would be consistent with the maintenance of the EMS bands. Thus, there is little long-term credibility for the maintenance of the EMS band with these interest differentials on five-year bonds.

5. A favorable shift in demand for a country's goods appreciates that country's real exchange rate. A favorable shift in the world demand for non-Finnish EMS exports appreciates all EMS currencies (including the Finnish markka) against non-EMS currencies. This adversely affects Finnish output. The adverse output effect for Finland is smaller the greater the proportion of trade between Finland and other EMS countries (and therefore the smaller the proportion of trade between Finland and non-EMS countries).

7. a. While in the ERM, British monetary authorities were obliged to maintain nominal interest rates at a level commensurate with keeping the pound in the currency band. If this obligation were removed, British monetary authorities could run an expansionary policy to stimulate the economy. This would cause the pound to depreciate vis-a-vis the DM and other currencies.

    b. Writers at the *Economist* believe that expected future inflation will rise in Britain if it leaves the EMS which will cause nominal interest rates to rise through the Fisher effect.

    c. British policymakers may have gained credibility as being strongly committed to fight inflation and to maintain the pound's value through Britain's membership in the ERM since they were willing to allow the British economy to go through a protracted slump without resorting to a monetary expansion which would have jeopardized their membership in the ERM.

    d. A high level of British interest rates relative to German interest rates would suggest high future inflation in Britain relative to that in Germany by the Fisher relationship. Higher British interest rates may also result from a relatively higher money demand in Britain (perhaps due to relatively higher British output) or relatively lower money supply growth in Britain than in Germany.

    e. British interest rates may have been higher than German interest rates if British output were relatively higher. The smaller gap at the time of the writing of the article cited may reflect relatively poor British output growth over the past two years. Also, German real interest rates may have risen because of the increased demand for capital for investing in eastern Germany after re-unification.

9. A single labor market would facilitate the response of member countries to country-specific shocks. Suppose there is a fall in the demand for French goods which results in higher unemployment in France. If French workers could easily migrate to other countries where opportunities for employment were better the effect of the reduction in demand is mitigated. If workers could not move, however, there is a greater incentive

to devalue the franc to make workers more competitive with respect to workers in other countries. Realignments within the EMS, or even the threat of realignments, disrupt the smooth operation of the system.

CHAPTER 22

The Global Capital Market: Performance and Policy Problems

CHAPTER ORGANIZATION

KEY THEMES

The international capital market, involving Eurocurrencies, offshore bond and equity trading, and International Banking Facilities, may seem at first as one of the more esoteric and enigmatic topics covered in this course. Much of the apparent mystery of the international capital market is (hopefully) dispelled in this chapter. This chapter also demonstrates that issues in this area are directly related to other issues already discussed in the course including macroeconomic stability, the role of government intervention, and the gains from trade.

Using the same logic that we applied to show the gains from trade in goods or the gains from intertemporal trade, we can see how the international exchanges of assets with different risk characteristics can make both parties to a transaction better off. International portfolio diversification allows people to reduce the variability of their wealth. When people are risk-averse, this diversification improves welfare. An important function of the international capital market is to facilitate such welfare-enhancing exchanges of both debt instruments, such as bonds, and equity instruments, such as stocks.

Offshore banking activity is at the center of the international capital market. Central to offshore banking are Eurocurrencies, which are bank deposits in one country that are denominated in terms of another country's currency. Relatively lax regulation of Eurocurrency deposits compared with onshore deposits allows banks to pay relatively high returns on Eurocurrency deposits. This has fostered the rapid growth of offshore banking. Growth has also been spurred, however, by political factors, such as the reluctance of Arab OPEC members to place surplus funds in American banks after the first oil shock.

The rapid growth of offshore banking has raised fears concerning the effects of Eurocurrencies on the pool of world liquidity and on monetary control. The text shows that most of these fears are groundless. For example, Eurodollars cannot come "flooding back" into the U.S. since they are already here. While the development of a Eurocurrency market will not affect a country's monetary base, it may have an impact on monetary control through its effect on the money multiplier. This is not a unique characteristic of Eurocurrency markets since domestic financial innovation also affects the money multiplier. (Recall that the money multiplier shows how much a country's money supply rises with an increase in its monetary base. This number is greater than one due to fractional reserve banking. You may want to review the concept of the money multiplier by looking at a Principles of Economics or

Intermediate Macroeconomics textbook).

There are legitimate concerns about the Eurocurrency markets. Industrialized countries are involved in an effort to coordinate their bank supervision practices to enhance the stability of the global financial system. Common supervisory standards set by the Basle Committee are to be phased in by 1992. Potential problems remain, however, especially regarding the clarification of the division of lender-of-last-resort responsibilities among countries and the increasingly large role of nonbank financial firms which makes it harder for regulators to oversee global financial flows.

The evidence on the functioning of the international capital market is mixed. International portfolio diversification appears to be limited in reality. Studies in the mid-1980s cited the lack of intertemporal trade, as evidenced by small current account imbalances, as evidence of the failure of the international capital market. The large external imbalances since then, however, have cast doubt on the initial conclusions. Studies of the relationship between onshore and offshore interest rates on the same currency also tend to support the view of well-integrated international capital markets. The developing country debt crisis represents a dramatic failure of the world capital market to funnel world savings to potentially productive uses, a topic taken up again in the next chapter.

The recent performance of one component of the international capital market, the foreign exchange market, has been the focus of public debate. Government intervention might be uncalled for if exchange-rate volatility reflects market fundamentals, but may be justified if the international capital market is an inefficient, speculative market drifting without the anchor of underlying fundamentals. The performance of the foreign exchange markets has been studied through tests of interest parity, tests based on forecast errors, attempts to model risk premiums, and tests for excess volatility. Research in this area presents mixed results that are difficult to interpret, and there is still much to be done.

KEY TERMS

Define the following key terms.

1. Risk aversion _____

_____

_____

2. Portfolio diversification _____
_____
_____
_____.

3. Eurocurrencies _____
_____
_____
_____.

4. Lender of last resort _____
_____
_____
_____.

5. Offshore banking _____
_____
_____
_____.

6. Debt instrument _____
_____
_____
_____.

7. Equity instrument _____
_____
_____
_____.

1.   Below are the balance sheets of three banks; the Baybanks (in Massachusetts), First New Jersey Bank, and Barclays Bank (London). A customer of Baybanks in Massachusetts writes a check for $5,000 to Harrod's Department store in London which deposits this money in a Eurodollar account at Barclays.

   a. Fill in the balance sheets below to show how a deposit by Barclays in its account in the First New Jersey bank leaves the United States monetary base unaffected.

Balance Sheet of Baybank		Balance Sheet of 1st N.J. Bank		Balance Sheet of Barclays	
Assets	Liabilities	Assets	Liabilities	Assets	Liabilities
_____	_____	_____	_____	_____	_____

We see that the monetary base of the United States is unaffected because

_____

_____

_____.

The amount of Eurocurrency deposits created by this process are _____.

   b. Now suppose that Barclays lends out $4,000 of its dollar reserves to a British citizen who purchases an American-made personal computer. Demonstrate the manner in which the balance sheet of Barclays bank changes as a result of this loan.

Balance Sheet of Barclays

Assets	Liabilities	The amount of Eurocurrency deposits changes
_____	_____	by _____.

   c. The United States company that sold the personal computer to the British resident is located in Massachusetts and has an account at Baybank. Use the two balance sheets below to demonstrate the effect on the United States monetary base of the change in

Eurocurrency deposits due to the transaction discussed in part (b).

Balance Sheet of Baybank   Balance Sheet of 1st N.J. Bank

Assets   Liabilities   Assets   Liabilities
_____   _____   _____   _____

The United States' monetary base changes, as a consequence of the change in the Eurodollar deposits, by _____ because _____

_____

_____.

2.   Analyze the revenues and costs of an onshore U.S. bank and a Eurobank to determine the spread between the interest rate on deposits offered by the two banks. In each of the following cases, assume that the bank has $100 of deposits and that the Eurobank does not face any reserve requirements. Also assume that banks operate in a perfectly competitive market so their revenues equal their costs, and that each bank faces the same annual operating costs per $100 of deposits.

a. The onshore bank faces a reserve requirement of 10% and each bank has an annual operating cost of $1 per $100 of deposits. Also, each bank receives 10% interest on loans it makes.

   U.S. Onshore Bank: Revenues = 10% x $_____ = $_____.
                       Costs = $1 + _____% x $_____ = $_____.

   Offshore Eurobank: Revenues = 10% x $_____ = $_____.
                       Costs = $1 + _____% x $_____ = $_____.

   Spread   =   _____%   -   _____% = _____%
                offered on   - offered on
                Eurobank deposits   Onshore deposits

b. The onshore bank faces a reserve requirement of 20% and each bank has an annual operating cost of $1 per $100 of deposits. Each bank receives 10% interest on loans it makes.

U.S. Onshore Bank: Revenues = 10% x $_____ = $_____.

Costs = $1 + _____% x $_____ = $_____.

Offshore Eurobank: Revenues = 10% x $_____ = $_____.

Costs = $1 + _____% x $_____ = $_____.

Spread = _____%   - _____% = _____%

offered on   -   offered on

Eurobank deposits   Onshore deposits

c. The onshore bank faces a reserve requirement of 10% and each bank has an annual operating cost of $1 per $100 of deposits. Each bank receives 20% interest on loans it makes.

U.S. Onshore Bank: Revenues = 10% x $_____ = $_____.

Costs = $1 + _____% x $_____ = $_____.

Offshore Eurobank: Revenues = 10% x $_____ = $_____.

Costs = $1 + _____% x $_____ = $_____.

Spread = _____%   - _____% = _____%

offered on   -   offered on

Eurobank deposits   Onshore deposits

d. The onshore bank faces a reserve requirement of 10% and each bank has an annual operating cost of $2 per $100 of deposits. Each bank receives 10% interest on loans it makes.

U.S. Onshore Bank: Revenues = 10% x $_____ = $_____.

Costs = $1 + _____% x $_____ = $_____.

Offshore Eurobank: Revenues = 10% x $_____ = $_____.

Costs = $1 + _____% x $_____ = $_____.

Spread = _____%   - _____% = _____%

offered on   -   offered on

Eurobank deposits   Onshore deposits

248

3.   Suppose that you have three assets available for purchase in early May, and each asset pays a return at the end of the summer. The return on two of the three assets depend upon whether it is a rainy or a dry summer. The return on the third asset does not depend upon the weather. There is a 50% chance that the summer will be rainy and a 50% chance that it will be dry.

	Payment if it is	
Asset	A Rainy Summer	A Dry Summer
A. Share in an Umbrella Store	$ 8	$ 4
B. Share in a Sunglasses Store	$ 4	$ 6
C. Share in a Steel Mill	$ 5	$ 5

Suppose that your utility, U, is equal to the expected return, ER, minus some number times the volatility of returns;

$$U = (ER) - B \times (\text{Volatility of Returns})$$

where the expected return, ER is the average of the two possible outcomes, and the volatility of returns (VR) is measured as follows;

$$VR = 0.5 \times [(\text{return if rainy}) - (ER)]^2 + [(\text{return if dry}) - (ER)]^2$$

If B = 0 then you are risk-neutral. If you are risk-averse then B equals some positive number (say B = 1 if you are risk-averse).

a. Complete the following table;

			Risk-Neutral	Risk-Averse
Asset	Expected Return	Volatility of Return	Utility $(B = 0)$	Utility $(B = 1)$
A. Share in an Umbrella Store	_____	_____	_____	_____
B. Share in a Sunglasses Store	_____	_____	_____	_____
C. Share in a Steel Mill	_____	_____	_____	_____

b. Suppose all three assets cost the same. If you could purchase only one type of asset, which one would it be if you were risk-neutral? Which asset would you pick if you were risk-averse?

_____

_____

_____.

c. Suppose now that you can either pick either one type of asset, or one of the following three combinations;

I -- half of your assets are in steel mills and half are in umbrella stores.

II -- half in steel mills and half in sunglasses stores.

III-- half in umbrella stores and half in sunglasses stores.

Complete the following table;

			Risk-Neutral	Risk-Averse
Asset Combination	Expected Return	Volatility of Return	Utility $(B = 0)$	Utility $(B = 1)$
I	_____	_____	_____	_____
II	_____	_____	_____	_____
III	_____	_____	_____	_____

d. Which asset combination provides you with the highest utility if you are risk-neutral? Which if you are risk-averse?

_____

_____

_____.

4.   One way researchers have tested for efficiency in the foreign exchange market has been to use statistical techniques to find the values of a and b in the following equation;

$$((E_{t+1} - E_t)/E_t) = a + b ((F_{t+1} - E_t)/E_t) + u_t$$

where E_{t+1} is the exchange rate in period t+1, E_t is the exchange rate in period t, F_{t+1} is the forward exchange rate in period t for delivery of foreign exchange in period t+1, a and b are numbers that will be estimated through statistical techniques, and u_t is a random error term since the equation does not fit the data exactly.

a. Suppose that the forward exchange rate accurately measures people's expectations about the actual future value of the exchange rate and that, on average, people guess this value correctly. If foreign exchange markets are efficient, what values will a and b have?

_____

_____

_____.

b. If we expect to find a constant risk premium what values would you expect to find for a and b?

_____

_____

_____.

c. Much of the empirical research on this topic has found that b is less than one. What does this imply for the risk premium if the forward exchange rate is a good predictor of the actual future value of the spot rate?

_____

_____

_____.

d. An alternative explanation for the finding of a value for b that is less than one is that people's expectations of the future value of the exchange rate are not well-represented by the forward rate. If b is less than one, do people think that the exchange rate is more volatile or less volatile than it actually is?

_____

_____

_____.

ANSWERS TO ODD-NUMBERED TEXTBOOK PROBLEMS

1. The better diversified portfolio is the one that contains stock in the dental company and the dairy company. Good years for the candy company may be correlated with good years for the dental company, and conversely. The return from a portfolio consisting of these stocks would be more volatile than the return from a portfolio consisting of the dental and dairy company stocks.

3. The main reason is political risk--as discussed in the appendix to Chapter 14.

5. A $100 Eurobank deposit can be loaned out to earn $15 at an interest rate of 15%; after covering the operating cost of $1, Eurobanks can offer a return of $14 (or 14%). When domestic banks receive a $100 deposit they must hold $10 in reserves. The banks earn $13.50 on the $90 which is lent. Subtracting the $1 cost, we see that these banks earn $12.50 from the $100 deposit and can offer a return of 12.5%. The difference between the rate offered by Eurobanks and by domestic banks is 1.5%; in the example provided in the text, when the loan rate was 10%, the difference was 1%.

7. There will be no effect on the balance of payments for either the U.S. or the U.K. since the dollar claim has shifted from one foreign agent (the London bank) to another (the English resident). Likewise, there is no effect on the monetary base in the U.S. or Britain. The only change is in the supply of Eurodollars, which has decreased by $10,000 (other things equal).

9. Tighter regulation of U.S. banks increased their costs of operation and made them less competitive relative to banks which were not as tightly regulated. This made it harder for U.S. banks to compete with foreign banks, and led to a decline in U.S. banking in those markets where there was direct, unregulated foreign competition.

CHAPTER 23

Developing Countries: Debt, Stabilization, and Reform

CHAPTER ORGANIZATION

KEY THEMES

The problems facing developing countries are among the most challenging and important economic issues of the day. This chapter provides the theoretical and historical background you need to understand the macroeconomic characteristics of developing countries, the problems these countries face, and some proposed solutions to these problems. Foremost among these problems is the issue of the repayment of large debts that many developing countries undertook in the 1970s and early 1980s. Much of this debt, whether originally extended to governments or to private citizens, is guaranteed by governments and is thus termed sovereign debt. In this chapter we examine the issues related to sovereign debt default decisions, and we analyze market-based debt reduction schemes. The chapter also presents a history of developing-country borrowing from before World War I to the present, with a special emphasis on the post-1982 problems and recently-proposed solutions.

The chapter begins by discussing how the economies of developing countries differ from industrial economies. The scope of the problems facing developing countries is dramatically demonstrated by the wide differences in per capita income and life expectancy across different classes of countries. There are important structural differences between developing economies and industrial economies. The economies of developing countries are typically not well diversified, with a small number of commodities providing the bulk of exports. These commodities, which may be natural resources or agricultural products, have extremely variable prices. Economies of developing countries typically lack developed financial markets. Governments in developing countries have a pervasive role in the economy, setting many prices, including the price of foreign exchange, and limiting transactions in a wide variety of markets. These governments often finance their budget deficits through seigniorage.

Seigniorage revenues are obtained by a government when it prints money. Seigniorage serves as a tax on money holdings since inflation, which accompanies money creation, erodes the value of nominal balances. The real revenue from seigniorage equals the money growth rate (which, in the long run, equals the inflation rate) times the real balances held by the public. The amount of seigniorage governments collect does not grow one-for-one with the rate of monetary expansion, however, because an increase in the "tax rate" (that is, the rate of inflation) is accompanied by a reduction in the "tax base" (that is, the amount of real balances in the economy). Higher monetary growth leads to higher expected future inflation and (through the Fisher effect) to higher nominal interest rates. An increase in the nominal interest rate reduces the real balances people are willing to hold, leading to a fall in real seigniorage.

In principle, developing countries (and the banks lending to them) should enjoy large gains from intertemporal trade. Developing countries, with their rich investment opportunities relative to domestic saving, can build up their capital stocks through borrowing. They can then repay interest and principal out of the future output the capital generates. Developing-country borrowing can take the form of equity finance, direct foreign investment, or debt finance, including bond finance, bank loans, and official lending.

European lending to developing countries was important before World War I. Lending diminished to a trickle, however, after many developing countries defaulted at the outset of the Great Depression. From the end of World War II until the early 1970s, developing-country external finance was composed mostly of official lending, short-term trade credits, and direct foreign investment. Banks became more involved in lending to developing countries after the early 1970s when a number of factors--including the need to recycle OPEC surpluses--sparked a boom in the development of the international capital market (the subject of Chapter 20). Bank loans became the major source of external finance for many Latin American countries.

The current crisis began in the early 1980s. The pool of OPEC funds available after the second oil shock disappeared in 1981 but developing-country borrowing remained high.

Disinflation policies in industrial countries made debt servicing more difficult for several reasons. Loans had floating interest rates, so past loans became more expensive when interest rates rose. Dollar appreciation also increased real repayment costs. The 1981 recession shrunk developing-country export markets and depressed terms of trade. The discussion of Mexico demonstrates the crisis faced by a country which fits many of the stylized facts about the structure of developing countries discussed earlier in the chapter.

Defaults were not uncommon during the period of substantial capital flows before World War I. There have been fears of default during the current crisis, though open debt repudiation has not yet occurred. We can understand the factors going into a decision about sovereign default by considering the costs and benefits of this action from the debtor's point of view. An important component of this decision is the real resource transfer received by a debtor. Data on the real resource transfer to developing countries during the 1980s shows how there has been a mushrooming reverse transfer from debtors to creditors after 1982.

Much of the management of the debt crisis is an attempt to mediate the conflict over the resource transfer between commercial banks and developing countries. There have been several phases of the debt crisis since it first began. The first phase, from 1982 to 1985, was marked by concerted lending. Concerted lending was a response to the problem of banks attempting to "free-ride" on the lending of other banks; that is, any one bank hopes that other banks will provide fresh loans. If this occurs, countries are better able to service their debt while the bank which did not provide any new lending has not increased its portfolio of risky loans. The problem here is that each bank faces the same situation, so no bank will make any new loans. The second phase of the debt crisis, from 1985 until 1989, consisted of an attempt to "muddle through" the problem in the hope that debt-ridden countries would grow out of their problem. The persistence of the problem led to a new initiative, the Brady Plan, in March 1989. Central to the Brady Plan are market-based debt reduction schemes. Market-based debt reduction is an attempt to exploit the discount available on debt in secondary markets. Countries that undertake market-based debt reduction, however, are likely to gain less than they spend.

In recent years there has been renewed capital inflows to a number of developing countries. This has occurred against the backdrop of the Brady plan but, probably more importantly, lower United States interest rates and, perhaps most importantly, liberalization and stabilization in several developing countries, especially in Latin America. But access to world capital markets remains elusive for many other developing countries in other parts of Latin

America and in much of Africa. Also, the former communist countries of Eastern Europe will need capital to grow; a topic taken up in the next chapter.

KEY TERMS

Define the following key terms.

1. Seigniorage _____

_____

_____

_____.

2. Sovereign default _____

_____

_____

_____.

3. Concerted lending _____

_____

_____

_____.

4. Debt relief _____

_____

_____

_____.

5. Market-based debt reduction _____

_____

_____

_____.

6. Privatization _____

_____

_____

_____.

REVIEW QUESTIONS

1. The following table reports inflation rates and seigniorage as a percentage of GNP, for a number of countries for 1987 (these data are from the 1989 *World Development Report* published by the World Bank).

Country	Seigniorage	Inflation
Argentina	4.0	174.8
Ghana	2.0	34.2
Mexico	3.7	159.2
Nigeria	0.9	9.6
Peru	4.8	114.5
Philippines	0.6	7.5
Turkey	2.8	55.1
Zaire	4.2	106.5

a. Plot the seigniorage and inflation data on the following graph;

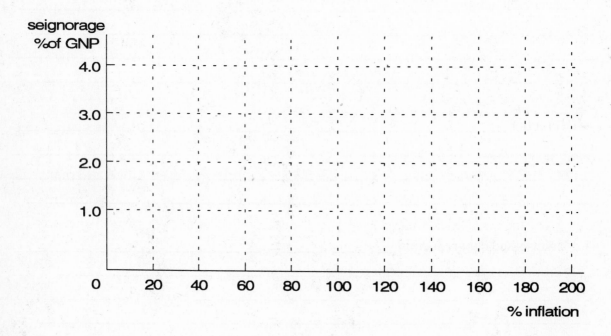

b. If seigniorage rose one-for-one with inflation, how would the graph appear? Does the graph in fact seem to reproduce a one-for-one relationship? What may be a reason for this?

_____

_____

_____.

2. Often, the official fixed exchange rate in many developing countries differs from the exchange rate that would prevail if the government allowed its currency to float freely. In light of this, black markets for foreign exchange flourish in many developing countries.

a. Would you expect the black market exchange rate to be more appreciated or more depreciated than the official rate?

_____

_____

_____.

b. What are some political ramifications of aligning the official exchange rate with the black market rate, a policy move often prescribed for developing countries?

_____

_____

_____.

c. Suppose exporters must surrender the foreign currency they earn to the government at the official exchange rate. Explain why this represents a type of tax on exports and why the black market premium, that is the difference between the black market and the official exchange rate, represents the size of the tax.

_____

_____

_____.

3. Problem 6 in the textbook concerns the experience of the Latin American "Southern Cone" countries of Argentina, Chile and Uruguay in the late 1970s. The governments of these countries instituted a crawling-peg exchange rate during this period whereby the rate of devaluation of their currencies was to proceed according to a preannounced

rate, eventually falling to zero. People in these countries expected, however, that governments would abandon the crawling peg and carry out a large surprise devaluation. What would the effect of this belief be on capital flight in these countries?

_____

_____

_____

_____

_____

_____.

4. Discuss how each of the following affect the likelihood of sovereign default;

a. A debtor country government repatriates its assets, which had been held in a bank in an industrialized country.

_____

_____

_____.

b. A worldwide disinflationary policy increases the interest rate on the sovereign debt.

_____

_____

_____.

c. Debt-ridden countries establish a wide network of barter arrangements with for their export and import markets.

_____

_____

_____.

d. Commercial banks refuse to lend any fresh funds to debt-ridden countries and do not intend to do so in the future.

_____

_____

_____.

ANSWERS TO ODD-NUMBERED TEXTBOOK PROBLEMS

1. The amount of seigniorage governments collect does not grow monotonically with the rate of monetary expansion. The real revenue from seigniorage equals the money growth rate times the real balances held by the public. But higher monetary growth leads to higher expected future inflation and (through the Fisher effect) to higher nominal interest rates. To the extent that higher monetary growth raises the nominal interest rate and reduces the real balances people are willing to hold, it leads to a fall in real seigniorage. Across long-run equilibriums in which the nominal interest equals a constant real interest rate plus the monetary growth rate, a rise in the latter raises real seigniorage revenue only if the elasticity of real money demand with respect to the expected inflation rate is greater than -1. Economists believe that at very high inflation rates this elasticity becomes quite large in absolute value.

3. Although Brazil's inflation rate averaged 147% between 1980 and 1985, its seigniorage revenues, as a percentage of output, were less than half the seigniorage revenues of Sierra Leone, which had an average inflation rate of 43%. Since seigniorage is the product of inflation and real balances held by the public, the difference in seigniorage revenues reflects lower holdings of real balances in Brazil than in Sierra Leone. In the face of higher inflation, Brazilians find it more advantageous than residents of Sierra Leone to economize on their money holdings. This may be reflected in a financial structure in which money need not be held for very long to make transactions due to innovations such as automatic teller machines.

5. Under interest parity, the nominal interest rate of the country with the crawling peg will exceed the foreign interest rate by 10% since expected currency depreciation (equal to 10%) must equal the interest differential.

7. Capital flight exacerbates debt problems because the government is left holding a greater external debt itself but may be unable to identify and tax the people who bought the central-bank reserves that are the counterpart of the debt, and now hold the money in foreign bank accounts. To service its higher debt, therefore, the government must tax those who did not benefit from the opportunity to move funds out of the country. There is thus a change in the domestic income distribution in favor of people who are likely to be quite well-off already. Such a regressive change may trigger political problems.

9. By making the economy more open to trade and to trade disruption, liberalization is likely to enhance an Developing Country's ability to borrow abroad. In effect, the penalty for default is increased. In addition, of course, a higher export level reassures prospective lenders about the country's ability to service its debts in the future.

11. This is an open-ended question. Banks entered loan agreements willingly, even though this was often inadvisable. In a competitive economy, firms which make bad business decisions suffer the consequences of these decisions. Perhaps banks should not be treated differently than other firms. Banks, however, hold a special place in the economy in terms of the money stock and monetary control. Bank failures may have dire consequences. There is also the problem of overborrowing in the future if debt forgiveness is seen as one alternative for debtors -- a moral hazard problem.

CHAPTER 24

International Economic Problems of Former Communist Countries

CHAPTER ORGANIZATION

Trade in Eastern Europe Before 1989
>   CMEA Trade Under Communism
>   The Management of Trade within the Soviet Union
>   The Management of Trade among CMEA Nations

The Adjustment Problem in Eastern Europe
>   The Decline in Intra-CMEA Exports
>   The Terms-of -Trade Shock
>   How Severe was the Shock?
>   Policy Options
>   The Case for Policy Coordination

The Coordination Problem in the Soviet Union
>   Price Controls, Central Planning, and Interregional Trade

Monetary Problems within the Former Soviet Union

Prospects for the Former Communist Countries

KEY THEMES

The fall of Communism has raised many important adjustment and trade problems in Eastern Europe and the former Soviet Union. In this final chapter, following a brief overview of the earlier trade relationships that existed between countries within this region, the macroeconomic and microeconomic implications of the breakup are discussed. The chapter concentrates mainly on the international economic implications.

Viewed as a unit, although the Council for Mutual Economic Assistance (the C.M.E.A) countries which contained the Soviet-bloc nations were largely shut off from the rest of the world, countries within the C.M.E.A. were highly interdependent. This interdependence did not evolve over time as a product of market trading relations. Instead, a policy of intensive regional specialization was maintained and trade flows were decided as part of a coordinated central planning process or negotiated through inter-governmental barter agreements. The implementation of such an extensive the system of planning was both very complex and highly inefficient. Resources were not used or pricing in relation to scarcity values and the goods that ultimately were produced often were of low quality. Since trade in these goods was by directive or inter-governmental agreements, the effective relative prices on intercountry goods trade generally were very different from those observed in world markets. This means that integration of these countries into the world economy also implied a large relative price shock.

With the breakup of the Soviet Union and the collapse of communism, countries faced major problems of economic adjustment and reorientation, as well as a loss of coordination or centralized control prior to the establishment of a functioning market system. Intra-C.M.E.A. trade collapsed, and due to the export-multiplier effect, so did output throughout Eastern Europe. Another important reason for the sharp output contractions in Eastern Europe was the massive terms-of-trade shock that occurred as trade within the former Soviet bloc moved toward world prices. Combined, these enormous shocks have contributed to deep recessions and social turmoil. The chapter discusses a variety of policy options that could have been pursued in response to these shocks. While many windows of opportunity have been lost, and while the situation remains bleak, it is not hopeless.

Given the collapse of the coordinated system of central planning and the new autonomy of enterprises in the former Soviet Union, a significant second best problem arose: remaining price controls and the absence of clear property rights meant that the incentives faced by enterprise managers were highly distorted. The economic situation became worse off rather than better. Attracting domestic and foreign capital, privatizing and restructuring industry, and improving the laws on property ownership are utmost priorities. Growth and restructuring are necessary for economic recovery. A stable macroeconomic and policy environment also remains a top priority for creating an environment in which the investment and growth will take place.

Another new set of problems among the former Soviet republics involve monetary relations. Most of the republics have large budget deficits and limited ability to finance these through borrowing on the open market. When the ruble zone was fully in place, only the central bank of Russia had the ability to print cash rubles. This implied that Russia was able to extract seignorage rents from the other countries. It also meant that Russia could interfere with the different reform trajectories pursued by other countries in the ruble zone. The incentives to depart from the zone were strong. First, if the countries had independent currencies they could capture the seignorage rents themselves. This, along with the symbolic importance of sovereign currencies, added to the pressure for new currency introduction observed at the end of 1992 and into 1993. The drawbacks to currency independence include the limited experience of many of the former republics with central banking procedures and monetary policy formation. Also, there remains the potential problem of excessive monetization of government deficits by weak newly formed governments.

KEY TERMS

Define the following key terms.

1. Centrally planned economies _____
_____
_____
_____.

2. C.M.E.A. _____
_____
_____
_____.

3. Ruble zone _____
_____
_____
_____.

4. Property rights_____
_____
_____
_____.

5. Adjustment problem_____
_____
_____
_____.

6. Coordination problem _____

_____

_____

_____ .

REVIEW QUESTIONS

1. Suppose a country receives a sharp negative terms-of-trade shock.

    a. What are the implications for real output of the country if it is unable to reallocate factors of production to an alternative production mix?

    _____

    _____

    _____ .

    b. What types of costs are involved in reallocating factors of production in an economy in response to a large relative price shocks?

    _____

    _____

    _____ .

    c. If the experiences of the industrialized countries provide any lessons, how many years do you think it would take for the adjustment problem to be resolved in the former Communist countries?

    _____

    _____

    _____ .

2. Suppose Country A is a heavy raw materials producer and its trading partner, Country B, specializes in manufacturing production, which relies strongly on raw materials as an input into production. Through bilateral trade agreements raw materials are traded for manufactured goods, but the raw materials are underpriced relative to prices observed outside of the trade between these countries.

a. Which country would experience an improvement (worsening) in its terms of trade when trade opens to world markets? Why?

_____

_____

_____.

b. What would happen to trade between Country A and Country B in the absence of bilateral trade agreements? How would trade between each country and the rest of the world change?

_____

_____

_____.

c. Why would Country A ever agree to receive lower than world market prices on its raw materials exports?

_____

_____

_____

_____.

3. a. What are the expected implications for Western industrialized countries of the increased openness of the former communist countries to trade with world markets?

_____

_____

_____

_____

_____.

b. What are the expected implications for Western industrialized countries of reduced border controls and increased labor migration from the former communist countries to world markets?

_____

_____

_____

_____.

4. By the Summer of 1993 the ruble zone had largely disintegrated. Many of the non-Russian republics of the former Soviet Union now have the ability to print their own currencies and use these countries for monetizing their budget deficits. However, departure from the ruble zone also has meant the elimination of some of the implicit transfers from Russia to these countries through the distorted system of pricing on inter-republican trade. Discuss the implications of these developments for Russia and the countries with independent currencies.

_____

_____

_____

_____

_____

_____

_____

ANSWERS TO ODD-NUMBERED TEXTBOOK PROBLEMS

1. Initially both countries specialize in tractor production, with real wages identical across countries. If each country specializes in tractor production, each produces 200,000 tractors, yielding a total income of $6 billion With the price of buses and tractors at $30,000, and 5 units of labor (workers) per tractor, the worker receives $6000 (compared with $5000 for bus production in Hungary or $3750 for bus production in Poland). If half of each country's income is spent on tractors and the other half on buses, 100,000 buses are imported and 100,000 tractors are exported. Since combined GDP of the region is $12 billion and combined exports are $6 billion, exports account for half of each country's GDP and half of the income of the region.

3. Before 1991 manufactured goods from Finland had a privileged place in Soviet markets. However, now trade from other countries compete more with Finnish goods and demand for the Finnish goods has declined. Finland also must pay world market prices for its raw material purchases from the former Soviet Union. The trade volume shock and the terms-of-trade shock have led to recession and the devaluation of the markka. Finland must reallocate its factors of production in response to the new terms-of-trade and demand conditions, and such reallocations are costly for any country. However, Finland differs from the Eastern European nations by already having the

constitutional, legal, monetary and distributional channels that are necessary for facilitating such adjustment.

5.   Low transport costs provide lower incentives to locate production facilities near centers of product demand. As large plant construction is encouraged regardless of whether the plants have production techniques characterized by diminishing returns to scale or increasing returns to scale. The diminishing returns (increasing marginal cost) plants are larger than they otherwise would be since the transport component of total marginal costs is smaller. The increasing returns plant expands by the same logic. Both expand beyond efficient scale, although this expansion is much more of an issue for the diminishing returns (or even constant marginal cost) plants.

7.   Russia's central bank has been extracting seignorage rents from the other countries in the ruble zone. In addition to this form of transfer from the former republics to Russia (which also should not be viewed isolation from the many transfers that had flowed from Russia to these other countries), the control over cash shipments by Russia also interferes with the ability of the other countries to pay wages (since this is done using cash), to monetize their own budget deficits, and to pursue independent reform strategies. The latter point is important because reform strategies with distinct speeds also have distinct inflationary consequences. This, in turn, places asymmetric constraints on a country's ability to pay nominal wages that will have a desired amount of purchasing power.

STUDY GUIDE REVIEW QUESTION SOLUTIONS

ANSWERS TO REVIEW QUESTIONS OF CHAPTER 2

1. a. Home is more efficient and has an absolute advantage in the production of butter, while Foreign has an absolute advantage in the production of cloth.

   b. Given the unit labor requirements of the problem, Home can trade off 5 units of butter for 1 unit of cloth when both goods are produced domestically. If, instead, Home trades 5 units of butter for 3 units of cloth with Foreign, Home gains 2 units of cloth or saves 2 labor hours. Likewise, the 5 units of butter which Foreign receives when it trades with Home would have required 5 labor hours to produce. These same 5 labor hours can be used to produce 15 units of cloth. Through trade Foreign has a net gain of 12 units of cloth.

   c. If Home trades 5 units of butter for 6 units of cloth with Foreign, Home gains 5 units of cloth. Since 5 units of butter is equivalent to 15 units of cloth in Foreign and Foreign only sacrifices 6 units of cloth for 5 units of butter, Foreign gains 9 units of cloth.

2. a. The graphical representation of the Home and Foreign production possibility frontiers are:

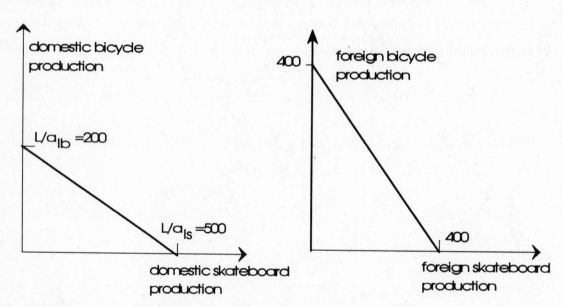

   b. Home: $p_b/p_s = a_{Lb}/a_{Ls} = 5/2 = 2.5$
      Foreign: $p_b^*/p_s^* = a_{Lb}^*/a_{Ls}^* = 3/3 = 1$

c. In the absence of trade, Home and Foreign consumption possibilities are limited along their respective production possibilities frontiers, as in part a. With trade, however, each economy can consume a bundle of bicycles and skateboards which is greater than what it alone can produce. Specifically, with trade, Home consumption possibilities expand from AB to TB while foreign consumption possibilities expand from A^*B^* to A^*T^*.

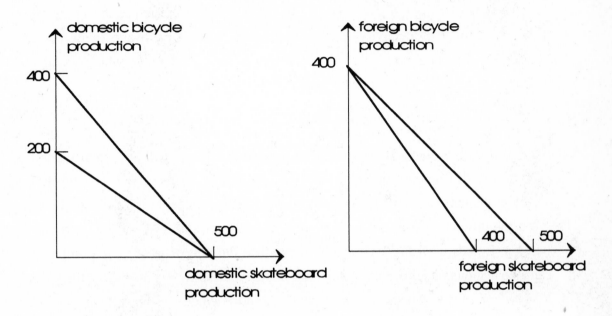

3. a. Home has a relative productivity advantage in Tennis Rackets.

   b. Home opportunity cost equals $a_{LR}/a_{LB} = 2/6 = 1/3$. Foreign opportunity cost equals $a_{LR}^*/a_{LB}^* = 4/1 = 4$.

   c. The world equilibrium price of rackets to bats will lie between the two autarky prices: $1/3 < (p_r/p_B)^W < 4$.

   d. Given $p_r/p_b = 2$, each country's production specialization can be determined by comparing the wages which workers earn in the tennis racket industry with those earned in the bat industry. The Home worker earns $p_r/a_{Lr} = 2/2 = 1$ producing rackets and $p_B/a_{LB} = 1/6$ producing bats. The workers will seek the highest wages and will move into the racket industry, leading to Home specialization in rackets. By an analogous argument you can show that the foreign country will specialize in bat production.

   e. In autarky, an hour of Foreign labor can produce 1 bat or 1/4 tennis racket. If Foreign labor chooses to produce 1 bat, this bat can be traded at $p_r/p_B = 2$ for 1/2 racket. This is twice as many rackets as it would receive if Foreign produced and consumed domestically. This demonstrates that foreign gains from trade.

4. a. Relative Home productivity advantage is given by a_{Li}^*/a_{Li}. Thus, its' greatest productivity advantage lies in production of good A at 12 (12/1) and its' worst advantage lies with good D at 2 (30/15). The reverse order is true for the foreign advantage.

b. Goods A and B will be produced at Home. Goods C and D will be produced in the Foreign country. To determine which country produces which goods, you must know the relative wage ratio (w/w^*). The Home will have a cost advantage in any good i for which its relative productivity (a_{Li}^*/a_{Li}) exceeds the relative wage (w_i/w_i^*). The Foreign country will have a cost advantage in any good i for which its relative productivity (a_{Li}^*/a_{Li}) is less than the relative wage (w_i/w_i^*).

c. The gains from trade can be seen by comparing the labor costs of producing the good directly in a country with the costs of producing another good and then engaging in trade. If the relative wage rate is 8, part b showed that Home will not produce goods C or D and would instead import them from Foreign. To produce one unit of good C requires 24 units of Foreign labor compared with only 4 units of Home labor. However, given the difference in wages of 8 to 1, it costs Home 4*8=32 versus 24*1=24 for Foreign. It ends up being least costly to produce the unit of good C in Foreign. You can also demonstrate this point using man-hours required for production of the goods.

d. If $w/w^*=6$, Home will still produce goods A and B while Foreign produces good D. Moreover, it is likely that good C (with $a_{Lc}^*/a_{Lc}=w/w^*=6$) will be produced in both countries.

e. The high transport costs for certain goods moved over large distances may lead countries to choose self-sufficiency in production in certain goods despite the country's lack of comparative advantage in those goods.

5. a. In the absence of trade, Home can produce 1 unit of butter with half of the labor hours required to produce 1 unit of cloth. This implies that in autarky the Home price of producing 1 unit of butter is expressed as $p_B/p_C=1/2$. In the absence of trade, Foreign requires twice as much labor to produce butter as cloth so that the pre-trade price is 2.

b. The pre-trade relative prices reflect the Home comparative advantage in butter and the Foreign comparative advantage in cloth.

c. The world relative price of butter in terms of cloth will fall somewhere between the two autarkic prices.

d. If $p_B/p_C=1$ with trade, Home gains by being able to import cloth from Foreign at a lower relative price than it would have if the cloth had been produced domestically.

Alternatively stated, Home can import 1 unit of cloth by giving up only 1 unit of butter if trade is allowed, whereas Home would have to give up 1 units of butter if it did not trade.

ANSWERS TO CHAPTER 3 REVIEW QUESTIONS

1. a. With an 8 percent decline in p_f, the food labor demand schedule shifts down and equilibrium moves from point 1 to point 2 on the figure below.

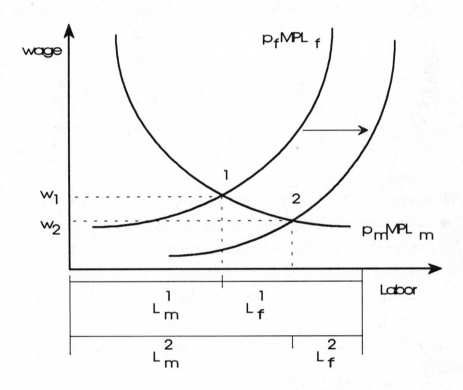

b. Wages fall from w_1 to w_2, but their decline is less than the fall in p_f. So, if p_f declines by 8 percent, wages decline by approximately 5 percent.

c. As the equilibrium allocation of workers shifts from point 1 to point 2 in the figure, labor shifts out of food production and into manufactures production. Likewise, the output of food declines while the output of the manufacturing sector increases. (This is shown graphically in d.)

d. The decline in p_f implies an increase in p_m/p_f. This shift in the relative price line (now steeper) causes the production point to move from point 1 to point 2 in the figure below. The output of food declines and the output of manufactured goods increases.

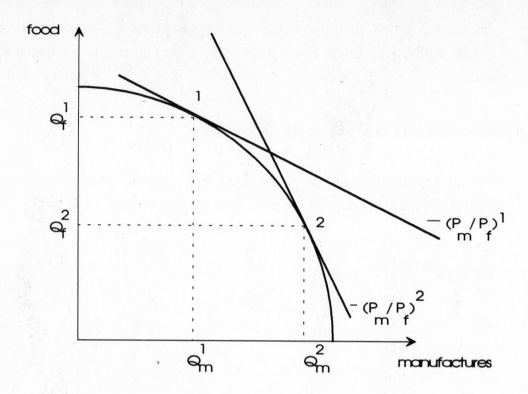

food

Q_f^1

Q_f^2

1

2

$-(P_m/P_f)^1$

$-(P_m/P_f)^2$

Q_m^1

Q_m^2

manufactures

e. The owners of capital "gain" because the real wage paid to their workers (w/p_m) falls in terms of the manufactured good. Landowners are made worse off because they must pay a higher real wage to workers and therefore receive lower profits.

f. Workers observe a decline in their nominal wage but this decline is less than the decline in the price of food. Their real wage in terms of manufactured goods falls while the real wage in terms of food rises. To determine whether the welfare of the workers has increased or decreased, one must examine the worker's consumption demands for the two products.

2. a. When both prices increase, each labor demand schedule shifts up. In this example, the upward shift in the manufactures labor demand curve is proportionately twice as great as the upward shift in the food sector. The new equilibrium is at a higher wage, with more labor in manufacturing and less in food production.

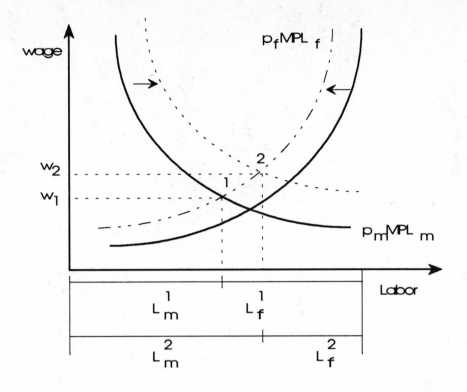

b. Wages increase by more than the rise in p_f but by less than the increase in p_m. This means that the real wage in terms of manufactures (w/p_m) declines while the real wage in term of food rises. The effect on workers is therefore ambiguous. Capital owners are better off and land owners are worse off.

c. The new equilibrium allocation of labor is characterized by an increase in workers in manufacturing exactly equal to the decrease in workers in food production. You can demonstrate the output effects by examining the effect of a change in relative prices on the production possibilities frontier. The new tangency of the price line with the PPF yields lower output in food and higher manufacturing output.

3. a. A decrease in land causes the MPL_f to decline (assuming that land is specific to the food sector). This shifts out the demand curve for labor, so that at every wage less workers are demanded in the food sector. Alternatively stated, each worker has a lower marginal product in food because he has less productive land at his disposal.

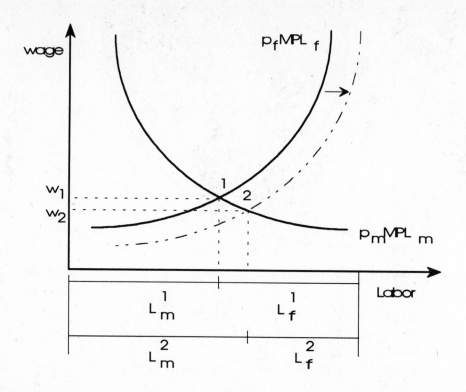

b. The graphical solution shows an intersection between p_fMPL_f and p_mMPL_m at a lower wage level, with labor drawn away from food into manufactures, which provided a higher wage to the marginal workers after the decline in arable land.

c. There are two reasons that food production declines. First, less workers are now in the food sector. Second, the remaining workers have less land with which to work .

4. a. D_f- $Q_f = (p_m/p_f)(Q_m - D_m)$ is the open economy budget constraint, where $(D_f - Q_f)$ equals food import volumes and $(Q_m- D_m)$ equals manufacturing export volumes. Substituting into this budget constraint yields $D_f = 400$. Since domestic residents demand 400 units of food, but only produce 100 domestically, they import 300 units of food from abroad.

b. See figure below.

c. If p_m/p_f rises to 4, the exporter of manufactured goods experiences gains and is able to import greater quantities. While the units of exports will remain the same (150 units) their value increases. Since the price of food imports is unchanged, the volume of food imports rises to 600. This is computed in two steps: first calculate D_f; second, subtract off Q_f to get import volumes.

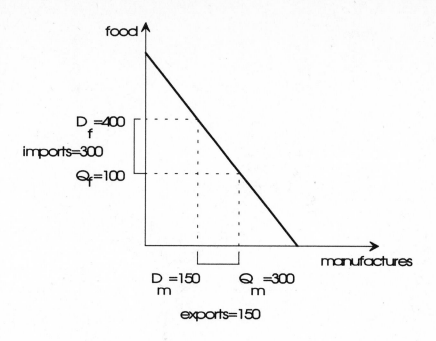

food

D_f =400

imports=300

Q_f=100

manufactures

D_m =150 Q_m =300

exports=150

d. If the price ratio falls to $p_m/p_f = 1$, the manufacturer is hurt. At this price D_f= 250, so that food imports equal 150 units. Manufacturing exports are also 150 units.

ANSWERS TO CHAPTER 4 REVIEW QUESTIONS

1. a. Wine production is labor intensive. Cheese production is land intensive.
    b. The following two constraints must be satisfied:
    $$a_{Lc}C + a_{Lw}W < L$$
    $$a_{tc}C + a_{tw}W < T$$
    The information provided is that a_{Lc}=4, a_{tc}=8, a_{Lw}=10, and a_{tw}=5. Also, L=400 and T=600. If C=50 + w=90 then the labor and land constraints are not satisfied. Since neither of these constraints are satisfied the equilibrium does not reflect a feasible production point.
    c. (see figure below)
    d. If L increases by 100, the LL constraint shifts upward, expanding the feasible production set.

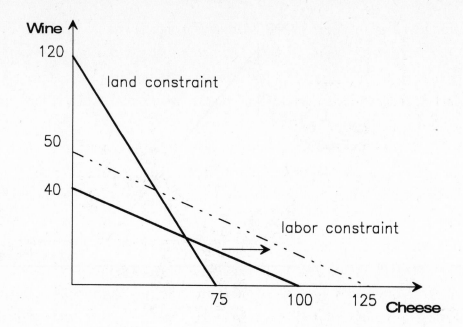

2 a.

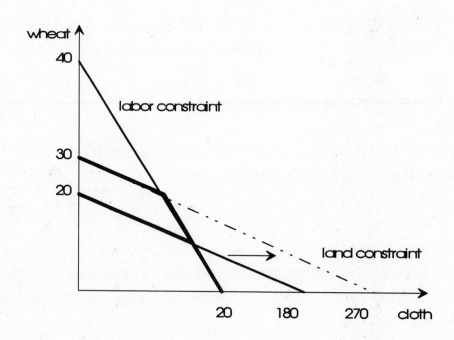

where L/a$_{Lw}$=120/3, L/a$_{Lc}$=120/20, T/a$_{tw}$=180/9, T/a$_{tc}$=180/1.

b. The TT line shifts up to yield a new production possibilities frontier where T/a$_{tw}$=270/9 and T/a$_{tc}$= 270/1. When the supply of land increases the TT constraint is relaxed and the production possibilities expand with a bias in favor of the land intensive good, wheat. This explains why an economy tends to be very effective at producing goods that are intensive in the factors which are relatively abundant at home.

3. a. The factor proportions theory predicts that countries tend to export goods whose

production is intensive in the relatively abundant factors of the economy. In this example, Foreign would be considered to be labor-abundant even though it has less labor than home. (Remember that abundance is defined in a relative sense.) Home is land abundant. Consequently, we can expect Home to export rice which Foreign exports televisions, the labor intensive good.

b. The "Leontief Paradox" calls into question the predictions of the factor-proportions theory. Leontief showed that United States exports were less capital intensive than United States imports, despite the observation that the United States is relatively capital intensive. Part of the explanation of this paradox is based on the definition of and measurement of the factors of production. There are differences within the category of labor (skilled versus unskilled workers) that suggest that aggregation into a single category of labor is misleading. There are other problems in the definition of capital, since it doesn't reflect the technology intensiveness of exports compared with imports.

c.

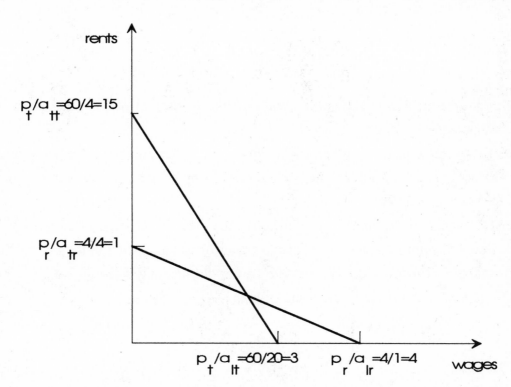

4. a. In a competitive economy, the price of any good is exactly equal to the cost of producing it. This means that the following constraints must hold:

$p_c = a_{Lc}w + a_{tc}r$

$p_w = a_{Lw}w + a_{tw}r$

However, plugging in to these constraint equations shows that prices are less than marginal costs for both goods. These prices would not exist in a competitive economy because the producers would be taking losses on each unit sold.

b.

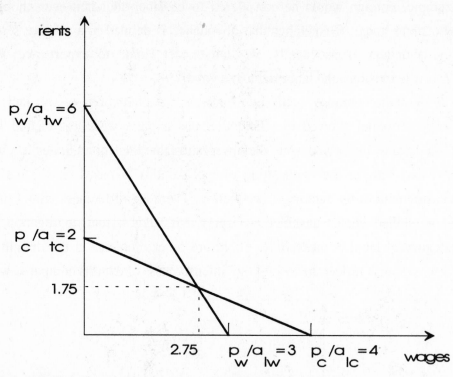

c. From the graph it is evident that rent on land equals 1.75 per unit and wages paid on labor equals 2.75 per unit.

d. The increase in the price of cheese shifts out the cheese price line so that the new equilibrium factor price point is characterized by a higher rental rate on land and a lower wage rate.

e. The increase in the rental rates on land caused by the increase in the price of cheese leads to an increase in the purchasing power of the landowner in terms of both cheese and wine. However, the laborer who derives income only from his wages will find his purchasing power reduced in terms of both wine and cheese.

1. a. At a new $p_c/p_w=6$, the isovalue line gets steeper. (initial v_1v_1 line rotates to v_2v_2).

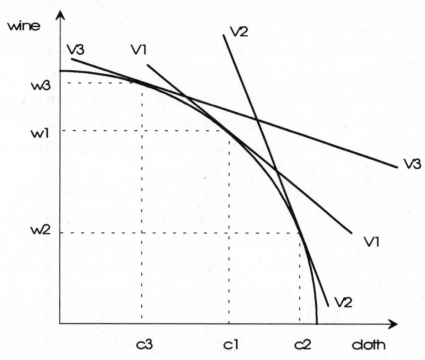

b. At the new equilibrium at point 2, the production shift is characterized by lower wine output and higher cheese output. The relative price of cheese has risen.

c. When the relative price of cheese declines, the isovalue line gets flatter. The production point shifts to 3 with the new isovalue line of v_3v_3. Output of cheese declines and output of wine rises.

d. The relative supply of cheese is positively related to its relative price.

2. a. Given the economy's PPF, a point such as A characterizes a country with consumption preferences which lead to an import of cheese and an export of wines. Since production occurs at point 1 output levels of wine and cheese are w_1 and c_1 respectively.. Consumption of wine and cheese occurs at w_a and c_a respectively. The value of wine exports is equal to the value of cheese imports.

b. The increase in the relative price of cheese shifts the isovalue line to v_2v_2 and moves the production mix to point 2, reflecting an increased production of cheese and a reduced production of wine. The consumption choice shifts from point A to point B.

c. This relative price movement had shifted the economy to a lower indifference curve, and has therefore made consumers worse off. Imports have become more expensive while exports have become less valuable.

d. The substitution effect is the shift in consumption demand patterns that would arise if production remained at point 1 but the relative prices of goods changed. leading to a tangency between the new isovalue curve and a lower indifference curve. When production adjusts so that the isovalue line is tangent to the PPF at higher cheese production and lower wine production, the additional changes in consumption demands reflect the income effect.

e. The decline in p_C/p_W shifts production toward wine production and away from cheese production. This is an improvement in the country's terms of trade which leads to a higher isovalue line and a consumption choice along a higher indifference curve.

3. a. At a point such as A the economy has reached its highest indifference curve along isovalue line v_1v_1. This describes an economy which exports cheese and imports wine.

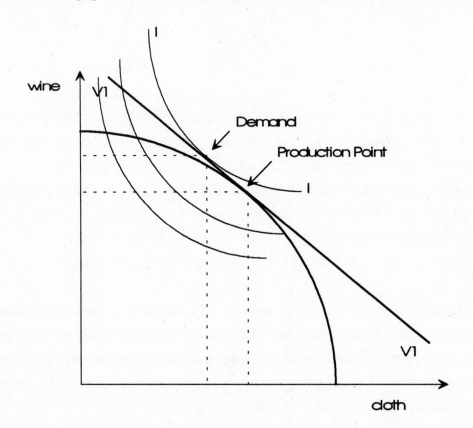

b. A decline in p_C/p_W causes the isovalue line to flatten out, yielding increased wine production and decreased cheese production.

c. The terms of trade have worsened, and the trading equilibrium reflects a tangency between the isovalue line and a lower indifference curve. The combination of income and substitution effects make the economy worse off.

d. An improvement (worsening) in an economy's terms of trade increases (reduces) its welfare.

4. a. With biased growth, production possibilities expand in favor of wine production, the land intensive good.

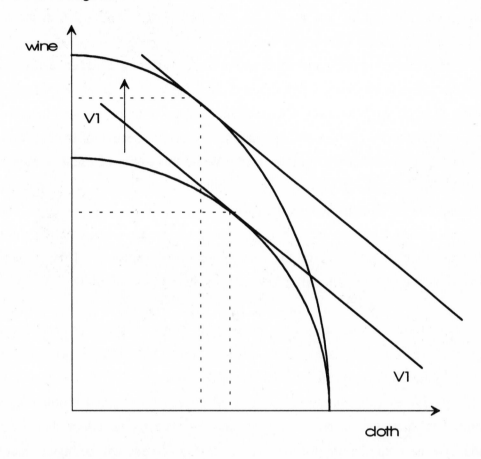

b. Both the specific factors and the factor proportions models show that an increase in a country's endowment of a factor of production will produce a biased expansion of production possibilities in favor of the good to which that factor is specific or which uses that factor relatively intensively.

c. If the relative price of cheese is unchanged following a biased production expansion in favor of wine, this implies that the new equilibrium is characterized by higher wine production and lower cheese production.

d. If the policy objective is to stabilize the production of cheese, despite biased growth in favor of wine, the relative price of cheese would have to increase. This might be accomplished through a distortionary subsidy to cheese production or a tax on wine production. Even with such a relative price increase, the new equilibrium is characterized by a higher relative output of wine after biased growth.

5. a. Holding the relative price of sneakers and beets constant, the new production point reflects increased production of sneakers and decreased production of beets. The good which experiences biased growth expands production. In doing so it draws some resources away from the low growth sector and leads to contraction in the output of the low growth good.

   b. The world relative supply curve shifts to the right, reflecting a higher relative supply of sneakers to beets at every p_s/p_b. This causes the relative price of sneakers to fall leading to an increase in the world equilibrium consumption of sneakers increases.

   c. Since sneakers are the export of this country, the relative decline of the export price is a worsening of this country's terms of trade. While this terms of trade worsening could bring about immiserizing growth, this possibility is a remote one. It is more likely that the welfare of this country will be improved.

   d. If biased growth occurs in the import competing sector, the terms of trade will improve following the leftward shift of the relative supply of sneakers. This terms of trade improvement due to growth will improve the welfare of the economy.

6. a. The relative price of wine to cheese facing both consumers and producers will be 25 percent higher than the relative price on world markets. The relative price of cheese will be comparatively lower at Home than in world markets.

   b. Home producers will contract production of cheese and expand production of wine. Home consumers will increase their demand for cheese and reduce their demand for wine. The new equilibrium price of cheese relative to wine will be higher than the pre-tariff price. The size of the shifts of the relative demand and supply curves must be determined before one can posit whether there is an overall expansion or contraction in the equilibrium quantity of cheese relative to wine and whether the relative price adjustment exceeds the 25 percent tariff.

   c. The Home terms of trade improves.

   d. The outcome depends on the large country assumption. Unlike a large country, a small country could not achieve substantial changes in world relative prices or quantities by imposing a tariff.

1. a. Using the equation for average cost, $AC=F/X + c$, where $F=20$, $c=2$, and $X=5,10,20,40$ yields respective average costs equal to 6,4,3,2.5.

  b. Average costs decline as output increases because the firms fixed costs are spread over larger output.

  c. Marginal cost is constant at 2, and average cost declines as reflected in part d. The Average cost curve does not cross the marginal cost curve.

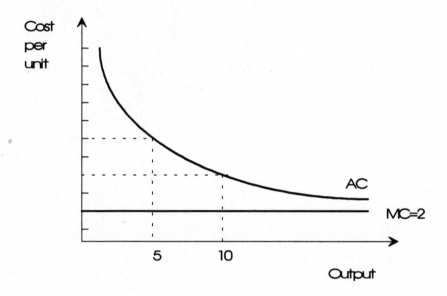

  d. As output gets large, average cost approaches marginal cost.

  e. All else equal, the more firms that there are in an industry, the higher the average cost. This is because the production by each firm declines, leading to less output per firm and higher average costs.

2. a. The CC curve is drawn from the equation $AC=n*F/S + c$, and the PP curve is drawn from the equation $P=c + 1/bn$, where $b=1/8000$. The following points should therefore be plotted for each curve:

n	PP	CC
1	8800	880
10	880	1600
20	480	2400
40	280	4000

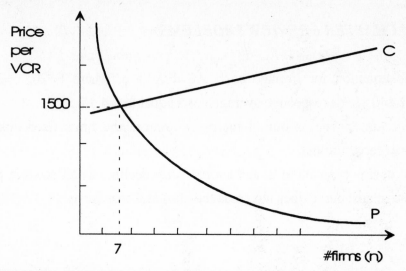

b. The downward sloping PP curve implies that as the number of firms in an industry increases, (and hence competition increases) the lower the price that each firm will charge. The upward sloping CC curve reflects the higher average cost facing each firm as output per firm falls with new industry entrants.

c. In the absence of trade, there will be approximately n=7 firms and a price of $1500.

d. At 7 firms, each firm will make zero profits since at n=7 P=AC.

e. To the left of the intersection of the PP and AC curves, P>AC which suggests that additional firms will enter the industry to capture excess profits.

3. a. Using the same equations as in problem 2, the points on the AC and PP curves are:

n	PP	CC
10	12000	10000
20	10000	12000
30	9333	14000
40	9000	16000

b. n=15, P=10,800, approximately.

c. To confirm the long run equilibrium you must show that 1) the pricing equation is satisfied (MR=MC) and 2) P=AC. For the first criteria, substitute in the actual values of demand parameters, marginal cost and the number of firms. Check whether this equals P=10800. This is approximately true at n=15. For the second criteria, substitute into the average cost equation, and check whether the AC equals price at n=15. Since this is approximately true, all monopoly profits

286

are eliminated by new entrants. The solution is that 15 firms will each produce 40,000 tractors at a price of $11,000 in the long run equilibrium.

4. a. Economies of scale describes the growth in output which is proportionately more than the increase in the use of inputs or factors of production. Economies of scale arise because division of labor and specialization become possible when the scale of operation is sufficiently great. In addition, more specialized and productive machinery can be employed in large scale operations. These economies may be internal or external to the firm.

   b. If two nations are identical in every respect (factor endowments, technologies and tastes) relative commodity prices will be the same in the two nations in autarky. According to the factor proportions theory, there will be no incentive for trade. However, if both commodities can be produced with increasing returns to scale, each nation could specialize in production of one of the commodities and, through trade, each could reach a higher level of satisfaction attributed to the increased supply of both goods.

ANSWERS TO CHAPTER 7 REVIEW QUESTIONS

1. a. The production function for food is upward sloping in labor supply. The slope is the marginal product of labor, which is increasing but at a decreasing rate.

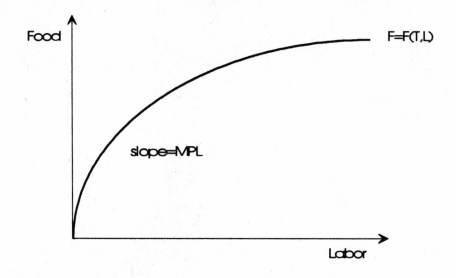

b. The production function has this shape because of the decreasing or diminishing returns to labor, given the fixed supply of land. In other words, as the ratio of labor to land increases, the marginal output of each additional worker declines.

c. In a perfectly competitive economy, the real wage earned by each unit of labor depends on the marginal product of labor. Since the marginal product of labor declines as the number of workers increases, so do the wages received by workers.

d. If the landlord employs 2 workers, he must pay them each $10, implying a total wage bill equal to $20. The rental fee earned by the landlord is the remaining area under the MPL curve and above the MPL=10 level.

e. If the landlord hires 4 more workers (total workers=6) the real wage will fall to $4 per worker. The total wage bill will equal $24. The rents received by the landlord increase substantially.

2. a. Since Foreign is labor abundant, workers earn less than workers in the Home country. Consequently, Foreign workers would prefer to move to Home where they can earn higher wages.

   b.

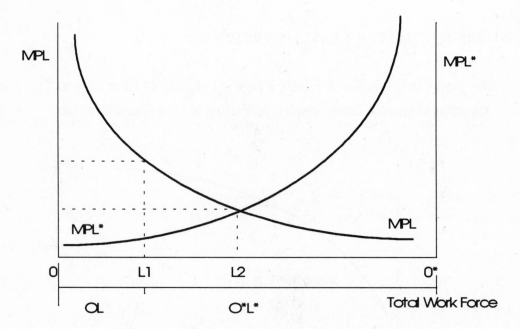

The initial labor allocation might have OL_1 workers in Home and $O*L_1$ in Foreign, where $OL_1 < O*L_1$. At this allocation, the MPL and wages are higher at Home than in Foreign.

c. Labor will shift from Foreign to Home until the real wage and MPL are equalized

288

across the two countries. This occurs at point E in the figure, where the labor allocation is now OL_2 and O^*L_2. Home gains labor at the expense of Foreign. The real wage and the MPL fall in Home and increase in Foreign.

d. While those who remain in Foreign gain from higher wages since labor becomes more scarce, those who remain at Home now receive lower wages. Likewise, landowners at Home benefit from the increased supply of labor while Foreign landowners become worse off.

3. a. If we denote present consumption by C_0 and future consumption by C_1, the intertemporal production frontier is

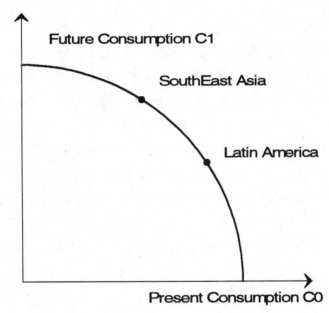

b.

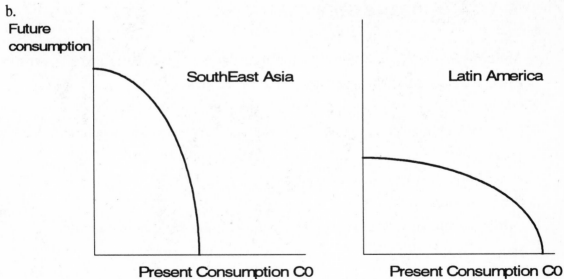

c. The relative price of future consumption (the real interest rate) facing Latin America is higher than the real interest rate in Southeast Asia.

d. The relative price of future consumption suggests that Latin America would export present consumption (textiles) while Southeast Asia imports future consumption (capital goods).

e. The high real interest rate facing Latin America is also partially attributable to the perceived riskiness of such loans. The risk arises from forces such as the threat of loan default and political instability.

4. a. direct investment; b. direct investment; c. direct investment; d. international lending; e. direct investment.

5. When resources are loaned internationally, the borrower's sole responsibility to the lender involves the eventual repayment of the loans. Under direct investment, control and influence are also transferred to the lender. Specifically, the borrower now shares some risk with the foreign investor who in return receives some say in the management of the operation which is intended to yield future revenues.

6. Direct foreign investment usually is undertaken by multinational corporations who may wish to establish a subsidiary in an LDC to take advantage of cheap labor costs, rich natural resources, a less restrictive regulatory environment, or beneficial tax, tariff and legal structures.

ANSWERS TO CHAPTER 8 REVIEW QUESTIONS

1. a. More dispersion because the need for specialized labor declines and the benefits of external economies from having labor in one place fall.
   b. More dispersion because of a decrease in transportation costs.
   c. More concentration because of the increase in the advantage associated with centralized production.
   d. More dispersion because these advances lower the cost of setting up facilities if different places.
   e. More concentration would occur in because of lower transportation costs.

2. Case I

Region	Automobile Workers	Brick Workers	Total Workers	Share of Workers in Production of	
				Autos	Bricks
North	8 million	4 million	12 million	2/3	1/3
South	2 million	1 million	3 million	2/3	1/3

Case I: Regional Divergence Index = 0

Case II

Region	Automobile Workers	Brick Workers	Total Workers	Share of Workers in Production of	
				Autos	Bricks
North	12 million	0	12 million	1	0
South	0	3 million	3 million	0	1

Case II: Regional Divergence Index = 2

Case III

Region	Automobile Workers	Brick Workers	Total Workers	Share of Workers in Production of	
				Autos	Bricks
North	8 million	4 million	12 million	2/3	1/3
South	1 million	2 million	3 million	1/3	2/3

Case III: Regional Divergence Index = 2/3

b. In the above example, the maximum value that the Regional Divergence Index can take is 2. The minimum value that the it can take is 0. These maximum and minimum values do not depend upon the number of industries used in the analysis. A larger value for the index implies that regions are more different in their industrial structure.

3. a. The two regions that are the most similar in 1947 are Northeast and Midwest. The two regions that are most dissimilar are South and Midwest

   b. As in 1947, the two regions that are the most similar in 1985 are Northeast and Midwest. The two regions that are most dissimilar are South and Midwest

   c. These indices shows decreasing regional divergence across time. A possible reasons for this is that economies of scale have fallen with the advent of new production techniques since World War II. Another possible reason is that the mix of industries in the United States has moved towards those with lower economies of scale.

   d. The pattern of divergence for the four European countries in 1985 and for the four regions of the United States in 1985 suggests that the regions of the United States are more diversified. A possible reason for this is that transport costs among European countries are higher than transport costs among regions of the United States (because of trade barriers and border restrictions in Europe). Therefore, it would be easier to sustain a wider range of industries in individual European countries than in separate regions of the United States.

4. a. i. All factories are located in Daisy:

	In Daisy	In Rose
Sales to Farmers	4.5	4.5
Sales to Factory Workers	3	0
Shipping cost if locate factory in:	4.5	7.5

   Location Decision: Locate one factory in Daisy.

   ii. Half of all factories are located in Daisy and half are in Rose :

	In Daisy	In Rose
Sales to Farmers	4.5	4.5
Sales to Factory Workers	1.5	1.5
Shipping cost if locate factory in:	6	6

   Location Decision: Locate one factory in each region.

b. i. All factories are located in Daisy:

	In Daisy	In Rose
Shipping cost if locate factory in:	2.25	3.75

Location Decision: Locate one factory Daisy.

ii. Half of all factories are located in Daisy and half in Rose:

	In Daisy	In Rose
Shipping cost if locate factory in:	3	3

Location Decision: Locate one factory in either region.

c. In either case (b.i) or (b.ii), the best strategy is now to build two plants.

ANSWERS TO CHAPTER 9 REVIEW QUESTIONS

1. Using the information provided in this problem the import demand schedule is

Price	Import Demand
$ 5	70
10	60
15	20
20	0

2. a. Ad valorem tariffs are measured as a fraction of the value of the imported good. If we levy a 30 percent tariff on Foreign televisions this increases their price to $5000+.30($5000)=$6500 which is equivalent to the Home price. Given such a tariff, domestic consumers will not "buy Foreign" because of lower prices. The Home infant television industry can be protected in the way, but, as you will see, such protection can be quite costly. Note that our framework does not fully capture the infant industry story since you would really need to analyze the potential for future reduced costs in the Home industry which arise because of their higher operations in the current, protected period.

b. Before the tariff, domestic assembly of televisions would take place only if it could be done for $2000 or less. With the tariff in place, domestic assembly will occur even if it costs $3500, which is the difference between $6500 and the cost of parts. Consequently, a 30 percent tariff rate provides domestic assemblers with an effective rate of protection of 75 percent.

c. By raising the Home price of televisions and lowering the Foreign price of television, consumers in the importing country (Home) lose while consumers are better off in the Foreign country. Foreign producers are make worse off while Home producers are made better off. In addition, the Home government receives tariff revenues.

3. a. Home production of vodka increases from 20 units to 30 units, while Home consumption falls from 60 to 50.

b. Producers gain by the area equal to "a" while Home consumers lose by an amount equal to the sum of areas a, b, c and d.

c. Tariff revenue is the product of the tariff rate and the volume of imports. Since the tariff is $6 and the volume of imports is 20 units, the government tariff revenue is $120. Graphically, this is the sum of areas c and e.

d. If the government wishes to help the consumers, it could begin by redistributing the tariff revenues back to consumers through tax rebates, consumer subsidies, increased social services and so on.

e. If Home were a small country, it would not be able to drive down the foreign export price to $9. Consequently, it would lose the terms of trade gain from the tariff represented by area e. Welfare in the small country clearly would be reduced under such a tariff.

4. a. While the price in the exporting country (Home) rises from $6000 to $6450, while the price in the Foreign country falls from $6000 to $5550. The price increase at Home is less than the subsidy.

b. As a result of the price increase, Home production of tractors expands from 70 to 80 units and exports expand by 20 units, from 50 to 70 tractors.

c. Tractor consumers at Home are hurt by the price rise. Producers of tractors gain. The government loses. Instead of receiving the revenue as it does in the tariff case, it must expend money on the export subsidy.

d. Graphically, the consumer loss is equal to the area a+b, the producer gain is the area a+b+c, the government loss is b+c+d+e+f+g+h+i.

e. The export subsidy worsens the Home terms of trade by lowering the export price in the foreign market. This is in direct contrast to the terms of trade effects of a tariff.

294

5. a. Under free trade, Home imports of cheese equal 60 (65-5) pounds. Under the quota, cheese imports are restricted to 40 pounds.

   b. The quota increases the domestic price of cheese and leads to a reduction of consumer surplus equal to the area (a+b+c+d). Home cheese producers gain from the higher price: this amount is equal to area a.

   c. The quota rents are equivalent to area c.

ANSWERS TO CHAPTER 10 REVIEW QUESTIONS

1. a. When a tariff of 25 percent is imposed, the new small country price is $(1+t)p_w=\$10,000$.

   b. In the large country case, the imposition of a tariff increases the domestic price of the protected good and lowers the foreign price of the good. However, in the small country case neither the price on world markets of the terms of trade are affected.

   c. The tariff causes a net loss to the Foreign (small) country which is measured by the production and consumption distortion triangles.

   d. The United States is relatively less dependent on trade than are other large industrialized countries. There is also relatively less protectionism in United States markets.

2. a. Increases in any tariff rate t<t* will benefit national welfare; declines in any tariff rates greater than t* will also increase national welfare.

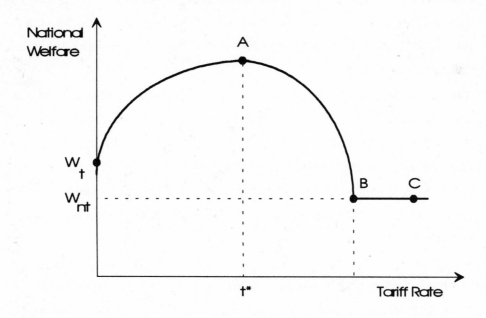

b. A large country that can influence the price facing foreign exporters can improve welfare by imposing a small tariff because it causes the relative price of imports to decline. At t*, the optimal tariff rate, the marginal gains from the improved terms of trade are precisely equal to the marginal efficiency losses associated with the imposition of the tariff.

c. At point B, the tariff rate is so prohibitively high that all trade ceases. The country is worse off than with free trade (t=0) or any lower tariff rates. Increasing the tariff further has no additional effect since trade is already wiped out.

d. A large country can potentially exploit its national monopoly power to extract rents from its trading partners. In doing so, it risks bad economic relations as well as retaliatory actions.

3. a. The theory of second best argues that if certain markets (for example, labor markets or capital markets) are not functioning properly, government intervention may actually lead to increased national welfare it some of the costs of market failures are offset. The gains from reducing the market failure costs could potentially exceed the negative distortionary effects of tariffs and other protectionist policies. Applied specifically to trade policy, it is argued that imperfections in the domestic internal economy may justify interference in the external economy. This requires that domestic policies aimed directly at the domestic market failure are infeasible.

b. The price facing the small country rises to $P_w + t$, causing textile production domestically to increase and production to fall.

c. Standard trade theory argues that such a tariff will produce consumption and production distortions. There are no terms of trade gains which could potentially offset these efficiency loses.

d. The extra social benefits yielded by textile production must also be included in the calculations of producer surplus. Therefore, the small country can gain from the imposition of the tariff if this additional societal gain (area c) exceeds the production and consumption deadweight losses (areas a+b).

e. The same increase in textile production caused by the tariff could have been achieved by directly targeting the industry with a production subsidy. This would have avoided the consumer surplus losses (area b) .

4. a. A small country that imposes a tariff can expect: unchanged prices on the world markets; domestic prices of the imported good to increase by the full amount of the

tariff; domestic production of the imported good to increase and be absorbed by world markets; domestic consumption of the imported good to decline; welfare of the small country to decline.

b.

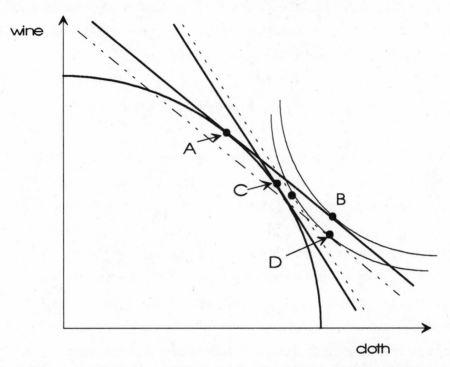

If the small country imposes a 100 percent ad-valorem tariff on cloth imports, P_C/P_W will remain at 1 on the world market, but will increase to 2 for domestic producers and consumers, thereby reflecting the full tariff without any terms of trade adjustment. At this new relative price, the small country will produce at point C and consume at point D, where the lower indifference curve reflects the decline in national welfare.

5. a. A 50 percent ad valorem tariff increases the home price from $2 to $3, by the full amount of the tariff without any effect on foreign prices. At the new price, Home consumption is 20 units less (from 100 to 80 units) and domestic production of cloth rises by 20 units (from 20 to 40). Consequently, the net effect on trade is a 40 unit reduction in imports of cloth. Since 40 units remain imported,, the government revenues are $1*40=$40.

b. Consumption and production effects, and the effects of the trade balance, would be increased the greater the elasticity of the demand and supply curves. However, when demand and supply curves are highly elastic, the tariff will lead to lower revenues. This implies that a government can collect higher levels of tariff revenues on more inelastic goods. However, it should be noted that the accumulation of such revenues is not the

297

primary objective of trade policies.

c. A prohibitive tariff is one which is high enough to stop all imports of a good. If the Home price of cloth increases to $4 then domestic production is sufficient to satisfy domestic demand, resulting in zero imports. This could be achieved by a 100 percent ad valorem tariff on the initial price. If there are transport costs this ad valorem tariff can be less than 100 percent and achieve the same goal.

ANSWERS TO CHAPTER 11 REVIEW QUESTIONS

1. Traditional trade theory is often criticized for being static, meaning that it is only useful for determining a nation's comparative advantage and trade patterns at a point in time without adequately considering the potential for economic growth. To properly consider economic growth arguments, a more dynamic framework is required. Traditional trade theory prescribes that LDCs should specialize in the areas in which they have comparative advantage. For many LDCs this implies the production and export of raw materials, textiles and agricultural products, and the import of manufactures and high technology goods from the developed nations. LDCs fear that these prescriptions relegate them to a subordinate and dependent position relative to developed nations.

b. Proponents of the traditional theory would argue that it is quite straight-forward to extend traditional arguments to take into account any changes in factor endowments, technologies and tastes of LDCs. As LDCs acquire new capital, skills and technologies, even traditional trade theory would modify the production orientation of the LDCs. Of course, it can be argued that by adopting the initial production and growth strategy, a country might develop skills and vested interests which delay the development of an alternative mix of industries.

2. The nineteenth century development and rapid economic growth of the Western Hemisphere was spurred by large inflows of capital and skilled labor from overpopulated Europe. The Industrial Revolution was also associated with increased demand for food, raw materials and other products from the developing countries.

Todays less developed countries, however, are generally overpopulated and resource poor (with the exception of those which export petroleum) and face declining terms of trade for their products, including foodstuffs and raw materials. This seriously damages their immediate prospects for export led growth. As you saw in Chapter 9, this leads to pressures to protect the agricultural and raw materials sectors, further aggravating the problems. The absence of demand driven growth, (in fact demand has slackened) accompanied by reluctance to transfer factors across sectors of the economy hinder the potential for a repeat of the phenomenon of the massive Western Hemisphere growth.

3.

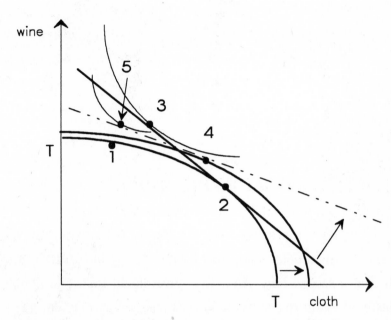

The LDC can be made worse off if the growth is immiserizing, resulting from an export-biased growth strategy which severely deteriorates the terms of trade of the LDC. Under export-biased growth, the production possibilities frontier shifts out in favor of cloth, to T'T'. Production in the economy shifts to point 4, and consumption occurs at point 5. Since the terms of trade have deteriorated to P_W', so that the price line which is tangent to the production possibilities frontier gets flatter, a lower indifference curve is attained. In such a scenario the LDC can be made worse off through this development strategy. However, for this to occur, the LDC must have a large enough position in the cloth market that it can actually affect world prices.

4. a. It is argued that the international investment activities of multinational corporations are favorable to LDCs because these investments:
   i) can fill gaps in technology, entrepreneurship, and skilled labor.
   ii) address the gap between the availability of domestically supplied savings and domestic investment opportunities.
   iii) supply needed foreign exchange.

iv) provide revenues to the government through such channels as taxes paid on land, plants, and profits.

v) provide employment opportunities.

b. There are also numerous arguments against the LDC activities of western multinationals. Among these is the concern over the appropriateness of the technologies transferred to LDCs by the multinationals. Such technologies are often suited for capital-abundant, labor-scarce developed economies, but not for the poorer labor-abundant developing economies. Such technologies can run counter to the development objectives of the LDCs. It is also argued that multinational corporations stifle domestic savings; worsen the internal distribution of income in the LDC; interfere with or even dominate domestic politics; and strip the host country of valuable natural resources without adequate environmental protection.

ANSWERS TO CHAPTER 12 REVIEW QUESTIONS

1. a. Just as market failures provide a justification for certain trade policies as a second best approach to a distortion, government intervention in industrial activity and economic growth is also second best. An active government industrial policy which encourages the transfer of resources across sectors is justified if, when left alone to market forces, the shift would occur too slowly or not at all. The government intervention in the success of an industry encourages a transfer of resources which the market would not directly support. The market failure may be in the inability of producers to capture societal externalities.

b. Rather than examining which sectors should be growing more rapidly than that dictated by pure market forces, governments often attempt to predict which industries will be associated with future industrial growth. The industries which are often targeted and excessively encouraged are high value added industries, linkage industries, industries with high growth potential, and industries targeted by foreign governments. These are the wrong selection criterion. Instead, the government should assess the extent of the market failures afflicting an industry and the costs of these market failures.

c. It is generally inappropriate to target a domestic industry for expanded growth simply because a foreign country has targeted the industry. This choice can be damaging because it is independent of market failure arguments, because it ignores the principles of comparative advantage, and because it draws additional resources into a sector which is already expanding supply and therefore lowering profit rates.

2. a. Two market failures which occur among industrialized nations include: i) the inability of firms in high technology industries to capture the full social returns associated with their investment in knowledge (this is in part due to spillovers into other domestic firms, and in part due to spillovers appropriated by foreign firms); and ii) the presence of monopoly profits in highly oligopolistic industries.

   b. The creation of knowledge vis-a-vis the high technology industry can span the initial innovation through the range of eventual applications. Many of the innovations are never developed into products and don't find practical application. Research and development fulfills the dual role of generating many innovations which will never see practical applications nor reap profits and generating innovations which will contribute to social welfare and profitability.

3. During the 1950s and the 1960s the Japanese MITI followed a strategy of promoting economic growth which channeled funds into heavy industries with high value added per worker. The resources were drawn away from more traditional labor intensive industries. Industries which were believed to reflect Japan's current and future comparative advantage were encouraged. It is still questionable, however, whether the economy would have grown just as rapidly without such industrial policy and under the laissez-faire system. Some economists strongly hold the belief that Japan would have arrived at the same economic outcome without government intervention. Since the 1970s, Japan's industrial policy has been aimed at encouraging the "knowledge intensive" or high technology industries. This has included modest expenditure on research and development and the encouragement of joint government and industry ventures. Recent industrial policy efforts have been undertaken on a much smaller scale than in the 1950s and the 1960s, and the industries which are targeted are a small part of the economy. Such evidence indicates that the role of industrial policy in shaping modern advances in Japanese industry is exaggerated.

ANSWERS TO CHAPTER 13 REVIEW PROBLEMS

1. i. For a Closed Economy;
   a. $Y = C + I + G$
   b. $Y = C + S^p + T$
   $S^p - I = G - T$

ii. For an Open Economy

    c. $Y = C + I + G + EX - IM$

    d. $Y = C + S^P + T$

    e. $CA = EX - IM$

       $S^P - I = G - T + CA$

2. a.

Country	S/GNP	I/GNP	(G-T)/GNP	CA/GNP
Oceania	0.22	0.20	0.02	0.00
Armansk	0.22	0.15	-0.01	0.08
Vantu	0.17	0.22	0.00	-0.05
Klingon	0.21	0.15	0.05	0.01

b. There is no consistent relationship since the difference between the fiscal budget and the current account just reflects differences in national savings or investment rates.

c. Again, there is no consistent relationship since there are differences in national savings or investment rates.

3.   The Freedonia Balance of Payments Account (millions of Freedonia Dollars)

Current Account

1. Exports	$48
of which;	
2. Merchandise	e+h+j+k+r
3. Investment Income Received	p
4. Imports	-$44
of which;	
5. Merchandise	c+d+i+n+q+t
6. Investment Income Paid	b
7. Net Unilateral Transfers	m-u
8. Balance on Current Account	$ 8

Capital Account

9. Freedonian assets held abroad	-$28
of which;	
10. Official Reserve Assets	l
11. Other assets	g
12. Foreign assets held in Freedonia	$32
of which;	
13. Official reserve assets	o

14. Other assets   a+f+s

15. Balance on Capital Account $ 4

16. Statistical Discrepancy $ 4

ANSWERS TO CHAPTER 14 REVIEW PROBLEMS

1. Suppose that it takes 0.25 U.S. dollars to purchase 1 DM, and 2.0 U.S. dollars to purchase 1 British pound. Then the number of DM per pound is calculated by dividing ($/£)/($/DM) = 2.0/0.25 = 8.0 DM/£.

2. a.

University	Price of T-shirt		Exchange Rate		Dollar Price
Sorbonne	60	Francs	6	Francs/$	$10.00
Delhi University	153	Rupees	17	Rupees/$	$ 9.00
Seoul Nat. Univ.	8050	Wons	700	Wons/$	$11.50
Hebrew Univ	21	Shekels	2	Shekels/$	$10.50
Trinity College	4.75	Punts	0.5	Punts/$	$ 9.50

b.

Currency	Franc	Rupee	Won	Shekel	Punt
Exchange Rate:	5 F/$	15 R/$	770 W/$	1.5 S/$	0.45 P/$
Appreciation or Depreciation?	Apprec.	Apprec.	Depr.	Apprec.	Apprec.
Dollar Price Rise or Fall?	Rise	Rise	Fall	Rise	Rise

3. Currently, a one-year bond denominated in dollars pays an interest rate of 8%. A bond that is denominated in lira, and has similar characteristics in terms of risk and liquidity, pays 9%. This means that the implicit forecast by the foreign exchange market is that the dollar will appreciate against the lira over the next year by 1%.

  This month, it takes 1500 Italian Lira to buy one dollar. TCIS forecasts that next year at this time it will take 1575 lira to purchase a dollar. This represents an appreciation of the dollar against the lira of 4.8%.

  Based upon our forecast, we advise against purchasing lira-denominated securities. The reason for this is that the interest rate differential does not adequately compensate you for the loss in value due to the depreciation of the lira against the dollar. For example, if you used $1000 to purchase a dollar-denominated bond, a year from now you would have $1080. If you took the same $1000 and purchased a lira-denominated bond, a year from now you would have $1038.

Some of you may be concerned that we have focused on nominal returns and thus have ignored real returns. We do this because as consumers of U.S. goods, you are interested in the U.S. inflation rate, regardless of how you hold your portfolio.

4.	U.S. Interest Rate	U.K. Interest Rate	Spot Exchange Rate	Forward Exchange Rate
	10%	5%	2 $/£	2.10 $/£
	8%	6%	2 $/£	2.04 $/£
	10%	10%	2.10 $/£	2.10 $/£
	8%	9%	2 $/£	1.98 $/£

5. i. This yields the downward-sloping curve that is depicted in the text. Some of the points on this curve include (9%, 180 ¥/$), (10%, 178¥/$), and (7%, 184¥/$). The spot rate is 181.8 ¥/$ when the Japanese interest rate is 8% The spot rate is 176.5 ¥/$ when the Japanese interest rate is 11%.

   ii. The interest parity curve shifts up and to the right. Some points on this curve are (11%, 180¥/$), (9%, 184¥/$), and (7%, 187.5¥/$).

   iii. The interest parity curve shifts up and to the right. Some points on the curve are (9%, 190¥/$), (10%, 188¥/$), and (7%, 194¥/$). The exchange rate is 191.9 ¥/$ when the Japanese interest rate is 8% and 186.3 ¥/$ when the Japanese interest rate is 11%.

   iv. a. A fall in the Japanese interest rate; the exchange rate depreciates (the ¥/$ rate rises).

      b. A rise in the U.S. interest rate; the exchange rate appreciates (the ¥/$ rate rises).

      c. A rise in the expected future value of the ¥/$ exchange rate; the exchange rate depreciates (the ¥/$ rate rises).

ANSWERS TO CHAPTER 15 REVIEW PROBLEMS

1. a. The downward-sloping money demand schedule must intersect the vertical money supply schedule (which is drawn for a level of real balances of 10) at 8%.

   b. The money supply schedule shifts out to 15. The money demand schedule shifts out due to the increase in GNP. They intersect at 6%.

    c. No: this is the same schedule as in 1985. Real balances are the same, as is real GNP.

    d. Both money demand and money supply schedules shift out between 1988 and 1989. The money supply schedule shifts from 7.5 to 10. The net effect is a fall in the interest rate.

2. i. A temporary increase in the money supply shifts out the money supply line, lowering interest rates and depreciating the currency.

    ii. An increase in the price level shifts the money supply line up, raising interest rates and appreciating the currency. If the change in the price level is temporary, there is no effect on the interest parity line.

    iii. A decrease (that is, an appreciation) in the expected future exchange rate shifts the interest parity curve in but has no effect on the money market. This causes the spot exchange rate to appreciate.

3.

	Short-run Effect	Long-run Effect
Prices	N	I
Output	I	N
Nominal E.R.	I (depreciates)	I (depreciates)
Real E.R.	D	N
Real M. Balances	I	N

4. Graph 4.1 demonstrates an equilibrium where the money supply is $400 million, the U.S. price level is equal to 100, the U.S. interest rate is 7% and the U.S. dollar/ U.K. pound exchange rate equals its long-run expected level of 2. Not shown in the graph is the U.K. price level, which is equal to 50.

    i. The temporary decrease in the money supply to $300 lowers real balances, raises the interest rate, and causes the nominal and real exchange rates to appreciate. This effect is depicted by an inward shift of the money supply schedule.

    ii. The interest parity line shifts down when the money supply schedule shifts in. This causes a larger initial appreciation of the currency than if the money supply change were temporary.

    iii. The long run value of the U.S. price level is 75. The U.S. interest rate is still 7% in the long run. The dollar/pound exchange rate 1.5 (in order to return to the same real exchange rate of 2*50/100 = 1 we need the exchange rate to appreciate to 1.5 since 1.5*50/75 = 1).

iv. Over time, as the price level falls the money supply line shifts out, eventually returning to its original position. The price level steadily falls towards its new level, real balances first fall and then return to their original level, and the exchange rate appreciates, at first overshooting its long-run level and then depreciating back to 1.5 dollars/pound.

ANSWERS TO CHAPTER 16 REVIEW PROBLEMS

1. a. Calculate this by the following formula:

$/£ real exchange rate = [(nominal rate * British CPI)]/ U.S. CPI

   b. Absolute purchasing power parity predicts that the real exchange rate is constant across time.

   c. The data does seem to support absolute PPP in the 1960s, but certainly not in the 1980s.

   d. The 1960s were a period of fixed nominal exchange rates while the 1980s were a period of floating exchange rates. A large part of the movement in real exchange rates is due to nominal exchange rate movements, which were much larger in the 1980s than in the 1960s.

Year	$/£ Real Exch. Rate	% change from previous year
1961	1.49	
1962	1.54	3.4%
1963	1.54	0.0%
1964	1.57	1.9%
1965	1.63	3.8%
1966	1.63	0.0%
1967	1.60	- 1.8%
1980	2.33	
1981	2.06	-11.6%
1982	1.81	-12.1%
1983	1.60	-11.6%
1984	1.42	-11.2%

1985	1.41	- 0.7%
1986	1.62	14.9%
1987	1.81	11.7%

2. Relative purchasing power parity predicts that the change in the real exchange rate is zero. Using the data in question 1 we find that relative purchasing power parity held in the 1960s, but was violated in the 1980s.

3. $q = \{b(P^*_n/P^*_t) + (1-b)\} / \{a(P_n/P_t) + (1-a)\}$

4. a. The increased spending raises the price of nontraded goods in Jamaica which causes its real exchange rate to appreciate.

   b. There is a depreciation of Chile's real exchange rate since the fall in the price of copper lowers income in Chile and the price of nontraded goods in that country falls.

   c. The real exchange rate appreciates as the price of nontraded goods in Colombia rises with an increase in income. If the good harvest lowers the world price of coffee, this effect is reinforced as the price of the traded good falls.

   d. Nigeria suffers a depreciation of its real exchange rate as the price of nontraded goods in Nigeria falls with its fall in income.

   e. There will be no effect, at least in the long run, of this purely monetary change.

5. a. A one-time decrease in U.S. productivity relative to that of another country will cause the real dollar exchange rate to appreciate. The real appreciation combined with the fall in relative U.S. output makes the effect on the long-run nominal exchange rate ambiguous.

   b. In this case, there is a continual expected appreciation of the real exchange rate of the dollar against the other currency. The depreciation of the nominal exchange rate is greater.

6. A rise in the expected future rate of real dollar/DM depreciation causes the long-run exchange rate to depreciate. An increase in the expected rate of depreciation of the real exchange rate increases the domestic nominal interest rates, all else equal, as shown by the relationship between interest rate differences, expected inflation differences and the expected change in the real exchange rate. An increase in the domestic nominal interest rate causes excess money supply. The money market is brought back into equilibrium through an erosion of real balances due to an increase in the price level. By PPP, an

increase in the price level causes a depreciation of the currency.

7.

Year	$/¥ Real Exch. Rate	U.S./Japan Real Interest Rate Differential
1977	.0041	
1978	.0048	17.1%
1979	.0044	- 8.3%
1980	.0044	0.0%
1981	.0043	- 2.3%
1982	.0037	-14.0%
1983	.0038	2.7%
1984	.0037	- 2.6%
1985	.0037	0.0%
1986	.0051	37.8%
1987	.0058	13.7%

ANSWERS TO CHAPTER 17 REVIEW PROBLEMS

1. a. A temporary increase in output in a foreign economy shifts the DD schedule down and to the right, raising domestic output and appreciating the domestic currency.

    b. A temporary rise in the foreign interest rate shifts the AA schedule out and to the right, depreciating the domestic currency and raising domestic output.

    c. Fiscal expansion raises output and the interest rate. A monetary expansion raises output and lowers the interest rate.

    d. A foreign fiscal expansion shifts both the DD and the AA schedules out which causes domestic output to rise and has an ambiguous effect on the exchange rate. A foreign monetary expansion also shifts the DD curve out, but the AA curve shifts back which causes the exchange rate to appreciate, but has an ambiguous effect on output.

2. a. This causes the expected exchange rate to appreciate which shifts the AA curve in and appreciates the exchange rate today while decreasing output today.

    b. The expected exchange rate depreciates, shifting out the AA curve, causing output to rise today and the exchange rate to appreciate today.

308

c. Since there is an ambiguous effect on the expected exchange rate, there is an ambiguous effect on the AA curve and we cannot say what the effect will be today on the exchange rate or output.

3.   This is incorrect. If there is a monetary contraction coupled with a tax cut, the current account will be more in deficit than if there were no change in monetary policy, or if monetary policy were expansionary. In terms of the diagram, when the DD curve shifts out and the AA curve shifts in, there is a bigger current account deficit than when there is no change in the AA curve. Current account balance can be restored with a monetary expansion, but this would put even more inflationary pressure on the economy.

4. a. The AA curve now shifts with a change in the tax on foreign assets. An increase in T shifts the AA curve down and to the left.

b. A temporary increase in T causes the exchange rate to appreciate and output to fall.

5. a. In this case, the AA schedule is vertical and the DD schedule retains its former positive slope.

b. A temporary increase in the money supply has a larger effect on the exchange rate and on output when we assume that the exchange rate always equals its long-run level.

c. A temporary increase in the government spending has no effect on output, and a larger effect on the exchange rate when we assume that the exchange rate always equals its long-run level.

6.   A depreciation of the exchange rate may be caused by a fiscal contraction or by a monetary expansion. If prices of imports are affected by the exchange rate, we expect to find an increase in import prices with a depreciation of the currency. If import prices are also affected by demand conditions, the rise in import prices will be larger with a monetary expansion than with a fiscal contraction, for a given depreciation, since the former is associated with an increase in demand while the latter is associated with a decline in demand.

ANSWERS TO CHAPTER 18 REVIEW PROBLEMS

1. a. Balance of Payments=Current Account Surplus + Capital Account Surplus

   H$ 0 million = H$ 1 million + (- H$ 1 million)

   b.Balance Sheet of the Central Bank Balance Sheet of the Central Bank
       on December 31, 1991   on December 31, 1992

	Assets	Liabilities		Assets	Liabilities
Domestic			Domestic		
	H$100 mil.			H$100 mil.	
		H$ 120 mil.			H$ 120 mil.
Foreign			Foreign		
	H$ 20 mil.			H$ 20 mil.	

   c. Balance of Payments=Current Account Surplus + Capital Account Surplus

   H$ 1 million = H$ 1 million   + H$ 0

   d.Balance Sheet of the Central Bank Balance Sheet of the Central Bank
       on December 31, 1991   on December 31, 1992

	Assets	Liabilities		Assets	Liabilities
Domestic			Domestic		
	H$100 mil.			H$100 mil.	
		H$ 120 mil.			H$ 121 mil.
Foreign			Foreign		
	H$ 20 mil.			H$ 21 mil.	

2. a. The DD curve shifts out, causing the exchange rate to appreciate. Fiscal authorities, to maintain the exchange rate, would need to raise taxes or cut government spending to keep the exchange rate at E_0.

   b. The AA curve shifts out with a fall in money demand. Fiscalian authorities would need to increase government spending or cut taxes to shift out the DD curve and keep the exchange rate at E_0.

   c. Fiscal policy cannot alter output in Fiscalia since any attempt to use it results in its reversal to maintain the fixed exchange rate. Monetary policy, however, elicits a fiscal response that magnifies its effect on output. The reason behind this is which authority is responsible for maintaining the fixed exchange rate.

3. a. For example, we may find the following (only the direction of change, not the actual amounts, can be inferred from the question).

Balance Sheet of the
Federal Reserve Before Intervention

Balance Sheet of the
Federal Reserve After Intervention

	Assets	Liabilities		Assets	Liabilities
Domestic			Domestic		
	$500 bil.			$400 bil.	
		$ 600 bil.			$ 600 bil.
Foreign			Foreign		
	$100 bil.			$200 bil.	

b. For example, we may find the following (again, only the direction of change, not the actual amounts, can be inferred from the question).

Balance Sheet of the Bank of Japan
Before Intervention

Balance Sheet of the Bank of Japan
After Intervention

	Assets	Liabilities		Assets	Liabilities
Domestic			Domestic		
	¥ 2000 bil.			¥ 2300 bil.	
		¥ 2800 bil..			¥ 2800 bil.
Foreign			Foreign		
	¥ 800 bil..			¥ 500 bil.	

c. The risk premium on U.S. bonds rises, and the risk premium on Japanese bonds falls with either policy. The outstanding public holdings of US bonds rises, reflected in an outward shift in the vertical schedule in the US risk premium diagram. The opposite occurs in the Japanese risk premium diagram.

d. The U.S. interest parity schedule shifts up and to the right. Interest rates have not changed, since there is no change in the U.S. money supply or in money demand conditions, so the dollar depreciates. A mirror image of this occurs in the Japanese interest parity diagram.

4. a. The slope of the shadow floating exchange rate falls when the rate of growth of the money supply decreases. This delays the time when the balance of payments crisis occurs.

   b. Since any positive rate of growth of the money supply eventually leads to a balance of payments crisis, no positive rate of money supply growth can avoid an eventual crisis.

   c. An increase in initial reserve holdings by the central bank shifts the shadow rate schedule down (without affecting its slope) which delays the time of the speculative attack.

   d. Only an infinite amount of reserves (which is not possible unless we consider unlimited borrowing opportunities) can avoid a balance of payments crisis if there is a positive rate of growth of the money supply.

5. a. An expansion of the money supply in Britain (not matched by a similar expansion in Germany) would lower interest rates in the U.K. and depreciate its currency relative to the DM. The implication of this is that, under a (mostly) fixed rate with the DM, Britain would have less latitude for conducting monetary policy.

   b. A contraction of the German money supply shifts the interest parity curve out. British monetary authorities would be forced to contract their money supply in response to maintain the fixed £/DM exchange rate.

6. a. An increase in output raises money demand which increases the foreign assets held by the central bank. The domestic money supply rises.

   b. An increase in the rate of growth of domestic-currency assets held by the central bank will just be offset by a decline in the central bank's foreign- currency assets since there is no change in money demand. There is no net effect on the money supply.

   c. When there is a fall in money demand, balance of payments equilibrium is maintained by decreasing money supply. A fall in investment, which causes output and thus money demand to fall, would also require a decrease in the money supply. In the first case, there will much less of a change in output than in the second case, where we would expect that the fall in investment demand coupled with a monetary contraction would cause a big decline in output.

1. a. The discovery of gold in Alaska represents an increase in the United States money supply. This raises U.S. prices, appreciating its real exchange rate and leading to a current account deficit. The current account deficit causes a balance of payments deficit that decreases the U.S. money supply.

   b. There will be no long-run effect of the discovery of gold on real balances in the U.S.

2. a. A country with a current account deficit that follows the rules of the game will see its money supply shrink.

   b. The decline in the money supply can be avoided if a country has an open market purchase of domestic assets. This, however, represents a violation of the "rules of the game."

   c. These findings imply that Germany and France were following the rules of the game while Great Britain was not.

   d. The gold standard may have represented an asymmetric system, with Great Britain at its center. This framework would give Great Britain control over its monetary policy while other countries would not have similar control over their respective monetary policies.

3. a. The XX curve shifts up and to the left to X'X'. If the exchange rate and fiscal policies do not change, Midas stays at point a where there is internal balance, but there will be an external imbalance: specifically a balance of payments deficit.

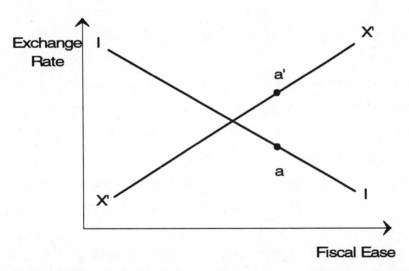

   b. A devaluation (to point a') can restore external balance, but Midas cannot have both internal and external balance with just this one policy. At a', there is internal imbalance in the form of overemployment and inflation.

c. The II curve shifts out to I'I'. While external balance is not affected, now there is unemployment and deflation.

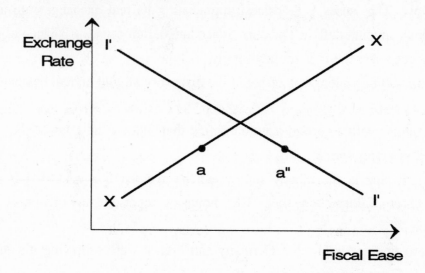

d. This would restore internal balance, but at the cost of a balance of payments deficit. Again, one policy tool by itself cannot restore internal and external balance.

4. a.

Real Money Demand	Income	Interest Rates
$100	$120	10%
$100	$122	11%
$100	$126	13%
$110	$130	10%
$115	$135	10%

b. i. Income will rise by 2% per year.

ii. The price level will rise by 2% per year.

iii. The interest rate is constant.

iv. The interest rate is constant.

c. Since the dollar was "as good as gold", world liquidity grew at the rate of the rate of growth of the world stock of gold plus the rate of growth of the world supply of dollars; that is, the rate of growth of the U.S. money supply.

d. The "confidence problem" occurred when the world stock of dollars grew faster than the world stock of gold. As the supply of dollars rose faster than gold, there was pressure for the dollar price of gold to rise.

e. As seen in part a, unless the liquidity of the world outpaced that of gold, there would be pressure on world economic growth not to exceed the rate of increase of the gold stock unless there was deflation. The problem was to maintain both liquidity (through an increase in dollars) and confidence in the dollar. Both of these goals could not be maintained, however, and this led to the collapse of the Bretton Woods system.

5. Below are stylized balance sheets for the central banks of the United States and of Canada during the Bretton Woods era. The assets of the United States central bank consist of U.S. dollar-denominated assets while the assets of the central bank of Canada consist of U.S. dollar-denominated assets and Canadian dollar-denominated assets.

Balance Sheet of U.S. Central Bank (changes in billions US $)

Balance Sheet of Canadian Central Bank (changes in billions Canadian $)

Assets	Liabilities	Assets	Liabilities
U.S. $ Assets	U.S. Money Supply	U.S. $ Assets	Can. Money Supply
		Can. Dollar Assets	

a. United States bonds would become less attractive than Canadian bonds with fixed exchange rates since the interest rates on these bonds would fall.

b. In response to the interest differential, there is pressure for the US dollar to depreciate against the Canadian dollar.

c. The Canadian central bank must purchase dollar assets to keep the dollar from depreciating. This would increase the Canadian money supply.

d. If the Canadian central bank attempted to increase its money supply, holders of Canadian dollar-denominated debt would want to trade their assets for those denominated in U.S. dollars. The Canadian central bank would have to oblige these demands to maintain the exchange rate. In the end, there would be no net effect on the money supply of the open market operation; instead it would only decrease the Canadian central bank's holdings of U.S. dollar assets.

ANSWERS TO CHAPTER 20 REVIEW PROBLEMS

1. a. A change in investment demand shifts the DD curve. Under a floating exchange rate system, a shift in DD changes output by less than the horizontal distance the DD curve

shifts since the AA curve does not move. Under fixed rates, the AA curve must shift to maintain the exchange rate parity, and this exacerbates the movement in output.

b. Changes in money demand shift the AA curve. Under a flexible exchange rate system, a shift in the AA curve affects output and the exchange rate. Under a fixed exchange rate system, the monetary authorities offset any shift in money demand with a change in money supply. In this case, there is no net effect on the AA curve, and thus no net effect on the exchange rate or output.

c. If most of the shocks in an economy are the type that affect the AA curve, a fixed exchange rate system works well in keeping both output and the real exchange rate stable (movements in the nominal exchange rate translate one-for-one to movements in the real exchange rate in this fixed-price model). If there are primarily shocks that affect the DD curve, flexible exchange rates work better in keeping output stable, but fixed exchange rates work better in keeping the real exchange rate stable.

2. a. A monetary expansion in Home shifts both the HH curve and the FF curve down and to the right. This causes output in Home to rise and output in Foreign to fall.

b. Neither the HH nor the FF curve shifts in this case since the equally-sized monetary expansions offset each other and have no effect on the real exchange rate.

c. A fiscal expansion in the Home country shifts the HH curve down and to the right and the FF curve up and to the left. This results in an expansion of output in both Home and Foreign.

d. As discussed above, a fiscal expansion in Home shifts the HH curve down and to the right and the FF curve up and to the left. A fiscal expansion in Foreign causes these schedules to shift further in the same direction. The net effect is a larger increase in output in each country than that which occurs when there is a fiscal expansion in only one country.

3. a. The communique affected the expected value of the dollar. The expected future value of the dollar after the Plaza meeting was more depreciated than before the meeting. On the day following the communique, the dollar depreciated, even before there was any money market effect of the planned coordination. In terms of the diagram, neither the money demand nor money supply curves are shifted between Friday, September 20, 1985 and Monday, September 23. The interest parity curve shifts up, however, with the increase in the expected future exchange rate. This shift in the interest parity curve causes the dollar to depreciate, even though interest rates have not changed.

b. The "hands-off" approach by the United States to exchange rate management before the

Plaza meeting meant that there was no intervention to slow the appreciation of the dollar in the first half of the 1980s. When monetary authorities' concern with the current account manifested itself in a willingness to intervene, news of a larger-than-expected current account deficit caused participants in the foreign exchange market to rationally believe that there would be a loosening of United States monetary policy and a depreciation of the dollar in the future. As shown in part a, this shift in expectations causes an immediate depreciation of the dollar.

4. a. At a one-to-one conversion rate, the West German Bundesbank will trade each Ost-mark for one Deutschemark. If conversion had taken place at a less favorable rate, say five-to-one, then the Bundesbank would have created fewer deutschemarks when monetary union occurred. The actual increase in the German money supply under the enacted play was about DM120 billion, which represented about a 10% increase over the West German money supply before unification. This increase represents a one-time rise in the money supply that would not contribute, by itself, to ongoing inflation. In fact, had money demand risen by more than 10% with the incorporation of the East German population into a greater Germany, prices could have fallen as a result of unification.

   b. East German labor becomes more expensive as the conversion rate becomes more favorable to the Ost-mark. By choosing a one-to- one conversion rate rather than a five-to-one conversion rate, it is likely that more East German firms will go bankrupt and that unemployment will be higher, at least initially, in East Germany. No matter what the initial starting point (which is determined by the conversion rate), however, East German wages will eventually have to change to reflect market conditions and productivity.

   c. Wage differentials encourage labor movement from low-wage areas to high-wage areas. The relatively high wages in West Germany encourage East German workers to migrate there. This would have the effect of making wages throughout Germany more comparable, to the benefit of East Germans and, perhaps, to the detriment of West Germans. For more information on labor mobility you may want to re-read the material in Chapter 7.

   A good article on the effects of German unification is "The Ost-mark's last laugh," *The Economist*, 28 April - 4 May, 1990, p. 71.

ANSWERS TO CHAPTER 21 REVIEW PROBLEMS

1. a. Inflation rates in each country decline over the 1980s, moving towards the inflation rate in Germany.

   b. In a quasi-fixed exchange rate system like the EMS, monetary policy cannot be set independently in each country. Instead, members of the EMS must either follow one central country's policy or some fixed rule, as in the gold standard. The evidence in the graph suggests that Germany did not change its monetary policy as much as other EMS countries (as reflected in its relatively stable inflation rate over the period). This provides evidence that the EMS is an asymmetric system, with Germany at its center (other studies focusing on different types of data reach the same conclusion).

   c. These data show a declining inflation rate in the United States and the United Kingdom during the 1980s.

   d. An alternative to the hypothesis that inflation convergence in a number of European countries was due to their membership in the EMS is the hypothesis that declining inflation rates in industrial countries was a worldwide phenomenon in the 1980s. The data for the United States and the United Kingdom suggest, at a minimum, that some countries that were not members of the EMS had similar inflation experiences to member countries in the 1980s. Empirical work by Professor Susan Collins of Harvard University fails to find a significant difference in inflation experience between members of the EMS and other industrial countries in the 1980s, thus suggesting that membership in the EMS was not a significant factor in declining European inflation rates.

2. a. Nominal Exchange Rates:

	1979	1985
DM/ lira	0.0022	0.0016
DM/ franc	0.43	0.33
franc/ lira	0.0051	0.0048

b.   Bilateral Real Exchange Rates:

	1979	Actual 1985	If No Realignment
DM/ lira	100	132	182
DM/ franc	100	107	140
franc/ lira	100	122	130

c. Inflation differentials and fixed exchange rates led to currency misalignments. Had there been no realignments, the lira would have appreciated by 82 percent against the DM and by 30 percent against the franc while the franc would have appreciated by 40 percent against the DM. The realignments partially offset the appreciations due to inflation differentials, as shown in the above chart: for example, the actual appreciation of the franc against the DM was only 7 percent.

3. a. $(0.25*2.6) + (0.75*2.8) = 2.75$

    b. Expected depreciation of the DM/Pound exchange rate was

       $(2.75 - 2.8)/2.8 = -0.0179$. Thus, pound-denominated securities paid 1.79 percent higher rates than comparable DM-denominated securities.

    c. $(0.5*2.6) + (0.5*2.8) = 2.7$

    d. $-0.02 = \{[(0.5*2.6)+(0.5*E)] - E\}/E$

           $E = 2.71$ DM/Pound

4. a. This makes the establishment of the Quebec franc less desirable. The differences in language and customs would tend to reduce the economic integration (especially as regards labor mobility) between Quebec and the rest of Canada. This reduces the desirability of a fixed exchange rate area. In terms of the GG-LL diagram, the actual level of integration would be smaller (closer to the origin) than if the cultures and languages were more similar. Therefore it is more likely that, all else equal, the intersection of the GG and LL schedules is at a level of integration higher than the actual level of integration.

    b. This makes the establishment of the Quebec franc more desirable. There is a high level of integration between Quebec and Ontario. This makes it more likely, all else equal, that the intersection of the GG and LL schedules is to the left of the actual level of integration. If this were the case, a single currency would be desirable.

c. This makes the establishment of the Quebec franc less desirable. Sector-specific shocks will have different effects in Quebec as compared to the rest of Canada. This reduces the desirability of a common currency. Shocks that shift the DD curve for Quebec are likely to have different effects on the DD curve for the rest of Canada.

d. This makes the establishment of the Quebec franc less desirable. The small amount of fiscal federalism means that region-specific shocks, which can be exacerbated by a single Canadian currency, are less likely to be mitigated by transfers from the central government. This question was posed using the benchmark case of the United States; your answer might have differed had the question been stated by making the comparison between relatively high transfers within Canada and relatively low international transfers within Europe.

5. a. This implies that Scandia would benefit more than Cyrillica from E.M.S. membership; the LL curve for Scandia is below and to the left of the LL curve for Cyrillica.

b. This implies that Scandia would benefit more than Cyrillica from E.M.S. membership; the exchange rate uncertainty in Cyrillica means that its GG curve is below and to the right of the GG curve of Scandia.

c. This implies that Scandia would benefit more than Cyrillica from E.M.S. membership; there is greater actual integration between Scandia and the E.M.S. than between Cyrillica and the E.M.S..

d. This implies that Scandia would benefit less than Cyrillica from E.M.S. membership; the potential for greater trade means that Cyrillica's GG curve is above and to the left of Scandia's GG curve.

1. a. Balance Sheet of Baybank   Balance Sheet of 1st NJ   Balance Sheet of Barclays

Assets	Liabilities	Assets	Liabilities	Assets	Liabilities
-$5,000	-$5,000	+$5,000	+$5,000	+5,000	+5,000

   The monetary base of the United States is unaffected because the decline in the assets of Baybanks are matched by an increase in the assets of the First New Jersey Bank. The amount of Eurocurrency deposits created by this process are $5,000.

   b. Balance Sheet of Barclays

Assets	Liabilities
-$4,000 in dollar reserves	no change
+$4,000 in loans	

   The amount of Eurocurrency deposits rises by $4,000.

   c. Balance Sheet of Baybank   Balance Sheet of 1st NJ Bank

Assets	Liabilities	Assets	Liabilities
+$4,000	+$4,000	-$4,000	-$4,000

   The U.S. monetary base does not change because the loss of assets by one bank is matched by the gain in assets by the other bank.

2. a. U.S. Onshore Bank: Revenues = 10% x $ 90 = $ 9

                         Costs = $1 + 8% x $100 = $ 9

     Offshore Eurobank: Revenues = 10% x $ 100 = $ 10

                         Costs = $1 + 9% x $ 100 = $ 10

     Spread   =   9% - 8% = 1%

   b. U.S. Onshore Bank: Revenues = 10% x $ 80 = $ 8

                         Costs = $1 + 7% x $100 = $ 8

     Offshore Eurobank: Revenues = 10% x $ 100 = $ 10

                         Costs = $1 + 9% x $ 100 = $ 10

     Spread   =   9% - 7% = 2%

c. U.S. Onshore Bank: Revenues = 20% x $ 90 = $ 18

                             Costs = $1 + 17% x $100 = $ 18

   Offshore Eurobank: Revenues = 20% x $ 100 = $ 20

                             Costs = $1 + 19% x $ 100 = $ 20

   Spread   =   19% - 17% = 2%

d. The onshore bank faces a reserve requirement of 10% and each bank has an annual operating cost of $2 per $100 of deposits. Each bank receives 10% interest on loans it makes.

   U.S. Onshore Bank: Revenues = 10% x $ 90 = $ 9

                             Costs = $2 + 7% x $100 = $ 9

   Offshore Eurobank: Revenues = 10% x $ 100 = $ 10

                             Costs = $2 + 8% x $ 100 = $ 10

      Spread   =   8% - 7% = 1%

3. a.

Asset	Expected Return	Volatility of Return	Risk-Neutral Utility (B = 0)	Risk-Averse Utility (B = 1)
A. Share in an Umbrella Store	6	4	6	2
B. Share in a Sunglasses Store	5	1	5	4
C. Share in a Steel Mill	5	0	5	5

b. The highest utility for a risk-neutral investor is from the umbrella store. The highest utility for a risk-averse investor is from the steel mill.

c.

Asset Combination	Expected Return	Volatility of Return	Risk-Neutral Utility (B = 0)	Risk-Averse Utility (B = 1)
I	5.5	1.25	5.5	4.25
II	5.0	1.00	5.0	4.00
III	5.5	0.25	5.5	5.25

d. Combination I and III provide the highest utility to risk-neutral investors. Combination III provides the highest combination to risk-averse investors.

4. a. If the foreign exchange market is efficient, a=0 and b=1.

b. A constant risk premium would result in b=1 still, but a would no longer equal 0.

c. The risk premium is not zero, and it varies over time if b does not equal zero and if the forward rate accurately measures people's expectations.

d. The market is excessively volatile since the actual change in the exchange rate is less than the change predicted by the forward rate.

ANSWERS TO REVIEW QUESTIONS FOR CHAPTER 23

1. There is not a one-for-one increase in seigniorage revenues with inflation. Seigniorage is the product of real balances and the inflation rate. An increase in the inflation rate, which raises seigniorage revenues, also tends to lower money demand since, by the Fisher equation, nominal interest rates rise with an increase in expected inflation. Thus, a rise in inflation raises one component of the determinant of seigniorage while reducing the other component. This is clearly seen by comparing Nigeria with Peru where the inflation rate in the latter is more than ten times that in the former, but the seigniorage revenues, as a percent of GNP, are only five times as high in Peru. Also, seigniorage in Peru is higher than that in Argentina even though Argentina has an inflation rate half-again as high as that in Peru.

2. a. The black market rate is more depreciated than the official rate. Otherwise, there is no incentive for a black market since foreign exchange could be purchased more cheaply directly from the central bank.

b. A depreciation of the official rate to a level equal to the black market rate increases the price of imports and reduces the standard of living of residents (at least those who do not benefit from being able to export more due to an increase in competitiveness that comes with a depreciation).

c. Exporters receive less domestic currency for each unit of foreign currency they earn at the official exchange rate than at the black market rate. This serves as a tax on export earnings. The "tax rate" is the difference between the market exchange rate, that is the black market rate, and the official exchange rate.

3. If inflation remains high while the crawling peg reduces the rate of depreciation of the exchange rate the real exchange rate appreciates. This makes foreign assets cheaper. These assets are especially attractive if people think there may be a large devaluation

which would give holders of foreign assets large capital gains. Thus, capital flight increased in the face of a crawling peg policy which lacked long-term credibility.

4. a. The likelihood of default rises since the costs of default falls (the country has less assets that can be seized).

    b. The likelihood of default rises since the benefit of default is higher when the cost of servicing loans rises.

    c. The barter arrangements allow countries to by-pass commercial banks and trade credits. The costs of default fall, and the likelihood of default rises.

    d. The benefit of continuing to service debt falls and the likelihood of default rises.

ANSWERS TO REVIEW QUESTIONS FOR CHAPTER 24

1. a. For a given amount of production, the negative terms-of-trade shock will mean that less income is received for exportables and imports become more expensive. Income contracts and the trade balance worsens.

    b. The costs include retooling of production facilities, retraining of workers, relocation of workers, renegotiation of labor and benefits contracts, and establishing new ties with suppliers and outside marketing channels. New environmental and safety standards also may be very costly.

    c. It can take three to five years for industrialized market-based economies to recover from shocks and up to ten years for developing countries. The delays may be even longer for countries that also need to simultaneously establish governing institutions, property rights, and market mechanisms.

2. a. The raw materials producer would receive a higher price for exports and therefore experience an improvement in its terms-of-trade. The producer of manufactured goods would have a worsened terms-of-trade since export prices fall while import costs rise.

    b. In the absence of bilateral trade agreements, Country A might seek to charge higher relative prices for its raw materials if it is unsatisfied with the value of its manufactured imports. Alternatively, or additionally, trade between Country A and Country B would decline with Country A increasingly relying on world markets for sales of its raw material exports. Country B would need to reevaluate the feasibility of its production mix.

    c. The relative price distortions may be viewed as a mechanism for income transfers (subsidies) between countries, and from Country A to Country B in our context. These transfers are a vehicle for exerting influence and creating a pattern of dependency (economic and political) of Country B on Country A markets.

3. a. Western countries could be faced with increased competition from those goods in which the former communist countries (with relative cheap wages) have a short-run comparative advantage due to specialization. This may lead to welfare improving trade or may invoke a protectionist backlash from special interests in the industrialized countries. The opening of these markets also creates many opportunities for Western exporters.

  b. The migrant workers generally are willing to accept lower pay for tasks previously performed by Western workers. This creates pressures for wage declines in the Western industrialized countries and some substitution away from Western workers. Labor unions may call for stricter border controls and attempt to limit the threat caused by labor migration from the East.

4. For the non-oil producing former republics, the shift toward world-market pricing on trade will imply large negative terms-of-trade shocks and therefore cause deep income declines. While these countries will be able to capture a greater share of seignorage rents, these seignorage revenues will not compensate for the financial losses from the terms-of-trade and output shocks. These contractions also will spillover to Russia, since there will be reduced demand for some Russian products. Restructuring is required in all countries. Departures from the ruble zone will also free the former republics to pursue independent reform strategies, somewhat smoothing but not eliminating the sharp contractions and restructuring requirements. Beggar they neighbor policies may arise.